The
Temporary City

PETER BISHOP trained in town planning at Manchester University and has spent his entire career working in London. Over the past 25 years he has been a Planning Director in four different central London boroughs and has worked on major projects including Canary Wharf, the development of the BBC's campus at White City and the King's Cross development.

In 2006 he was appointed as the first Director of Design for London, the Mayor's architecture and design studio. He is an advisor to the Mayor of London and a Director at the architectural firm Allies and Morrison – Urban Practitioners. Peter lectures and teaches extensively, and is a Visiting Professor at the Faculty of Architecture and the Built Environment at Nottingham Trent University, an Honorary Fellow of University College London and an Honorary Fellow of the RIBA.

LESLEY WILLIAMS trained in environmental sciences in Bradford and in town planning at the Bartlett School of Architecture, and is a writer and sculptor. She has worked for the Civic Trust, CAG Consultants and the Environment Trust. For the last 15 years she has worked as a freelance consultant specialising in the design and facilitation of stakeholder involvement processes, consensus building and partnership development.

The Temporary City

Peter Bishop
and Lesley Williams

Routledge
Taylor & Francis Group

LONDON AND NEW YORK

First published 2012
by Routledge
2 Park Square, Milton Park, Abingdon, Oxon OX14 4RN

Simultaneously published in the USA and Canada
by Routledge
711 Third Avenue, New York, NY 10017

Routledge is an imprint of the Taylor & Francis Group, an informa *business*

British Library Cataloguing in Publication Data
A catalogue record for this book is available from the British Library

Library of Congress Cataloging in Publication Data
Bishop, Peter, 1953–
The temporary city / Peter Bishop and Lesley Williams.
    p. cm.
Includes bibliographical references and index.
1. City planning. 2. Buildings, Temporary. 3. Temporary housing.
I. Williams, Lesley, 1957– II. Title.
HT165.5.B57 2012
307.1'216–dc23
2011020635

ISBN: 978-0-415-67055-5 (hbk)
ISBN: 978-0-415-67056-2 (pbk)

Designed and typeset in Franklin Gothic by Alex Lazarou

Printed and bound in India by Replika Press Pvt. Ltd.

Contents

Case studies

Acknowledgements

The authors wish to acknowledge a huge debt of gratitude to all those who have given their time, ideas and experiences so freely during the preparation of this book. We are particularly grateful for their enthusiastic response and encouragement at a time when the book was more aspiration than reality.

Our particular thanks go to Pat Brown of Central, who generously offered to read the final draft and provided invaluable insights on the structure and coherence of the arguments at a time when our closeness to the trees was obscuring the view of the woods. Clive Williams too, one of the greatest unpublished writers of our acquaintance, contributed some of the more eloquent turns of phrase. Liz Fidlon was enormously helpful in turning the original idea into a proposal. Special thanks go to professional architectural photographer John Sturrock, who was extremely generous in allowing us to use so many of his images. We are particularly grateful to Urban Catalyst in Berlin, whose groundbreaking work opened up the world of the temporary to us. We would also like to acknowledge Design for London for their ideas and inspiration on how to shape cities and make them better places to live in.

Many of the case studies have evolved from our interviews and discussions with practitioners who are out there 'doing it' and we greatly appreciate the help and generosity of the following people: David West, Studio Egret West; Eric Reynolds, Urban Space Management; Giles Barrie, *Property Week*; Bill Dunster, Zed Factory; Ken Dytor; Rebecca Molina, Studio Raw; David Barrie; Isabelle Allen; Lisa Fior, *muf* architecture/art; Stephen Witherford, Witherford Watson Mann Architects; Cany Ash, Ash Sakuler Architects; Peter Murray, New London Architecture; Pieter Klomp, City of Amsterdam; Chris Shaw, Shaw Corporation; Sarah Ichioka, The Architecture Foundation; Robert Evans, Argent; Alex de Rijke and Sadie Morgan, dRMM Architects; Steve McAdam, Fluid Architects; Libby Sellers, Libby Sellers Gallery; Paul Murphy, Shopjacket; Roland Smith, Theatre Delicatessen; Dan Simon, The Oubliette Arthouse; Roger Wade, Boxpark; John Gallagher, *Detroit Free Press*; Tim Tonkins, Times Square Business Improvement District; Blaine Merker, Rebar; Victoria Lee; Teodor Frolu; Andy von Bradsky, PRP Architects; and Kerry, GINGERLINE.

Finally we are profoundly grateful to each other for the humour, generosity and willingness to debate and change views that make the partnership so enjoyable.

The
Temporary City

POP UP BAR

POP UP SHOP

POP UP

THIS

THAT

POP UP

g2

Step, kick, bounce
How to do the
North Korean march,
page 2

Gareth Peirce
Why al-Megrahi
is innocent, page 10

Don't look!
Streakers are back,
page 13

Is there no end to
the pop up revolution?

G2 pop-up cover by Owen Gildersleeve
12 OCTOBER 2010

1: Introduction: the temporary city

MANY CITY AUTHORITIES in Europe and North America that are charged with the task of encouraging the revitalisation and redevelopment of urban areas are now finding that, for the most part, they lack the resources, power and control to implement formal masterplans. Instead some are beginning to experiment with looser planning visions and design frameworks, linked to phased packages of smaller, often temporary initiatives, designed to unlock the potential of sites now, rather than in 10 years' time. Such approaches are finding resonance and support in the emerging practices of some new multi-disciplinary architectural studios in the UK and elsewhere. They are also eliciting an increasingly sympathetic response from landowners and developers. Some are now recognising that their plans need to be more flexible, and that there may be a role for temporary activities or interim phases of development, in the face of economic uncertainty and rapidly changing possibilities. At the same time, there has been an upsurge of 'pop-up' shops, restaurants and theatres. Some are clearly making use of the glut of vacant property, particularly on the high street, and the reduced risks that short-term leases offer to new businesses. But there is also a cachet associated with time-limited exclusivity that has consumer appeal. In parallel there appear to be many more temporary 'claims' on the city, such as art installations, urban agriculture, sports and recreation activities, from individuals or communities with alternative concepts about its use. Many of these 'bottom-up' interventions or fleeting reconfigurations of space are seemingly spontaneous or arise without consent.

These emerging signs of temporary urbanism are novel. Hitherto, both theory and practice in urban planning and design have been overwhelmingly concerned with permanence. This raises some interesting questions. Given the overwhelming evidence that cities are a complex overlay of buildings and activities that are, in one way or another, temporary, why have urbanists been so focused on permanence? What changes in society, culture, technology and the economy are driving temporary urbanism, and its many intriguing manifestations? Do different types of temporary activity have different drivers? Are these drivers themselves transient or might they represent a more enduring influence on the form of cities? Could temporary uses be a manifestation of the emergence of a more dynamic, flexible or adaptive urbanism, where the city is becoming more responsive to new needs,

3

demands and preferences of its users? And if so, do the systems of regulation and planning need to adjust to the requirements and implications of this new fluidity? Can temporary activities be enabled, planned or designed in order to harness their positive characteristics without stifling their creativity? These are some of the questions that we have attempted to address in this book.

This book does not seek to expound a new theory of urbanism or to provide the ultimate academic treatise on urban impermanence. Neither is it a manual. While we do suggest some ways in which temporary uses can be enabled, the book does not seek to provide guidance for the would-be practitioner. This task is best left to those with direct experience of the process. Rather, it is an enquiry, a reflection on the obsession with 'permanent' urban outcomes, and an exploration of the different manifestations of, and undercurrents behind more transient urban phenomena. Temporary uses might be part of a solution to the challenges that are facing cities as they struggle to adapt to the conditions of the twenty-first century. They may become a permanent feature of professional thinking, or be a passing fad. Our purpose is not to draw any hasty conclusions. Instead we hope that by exploring the characteristics of temporary urban activities we open the topic further to debate that may in turn broaden our thinking about the future of cities.

Research on temporary urbanism is in its infancy, but we are particularly indebted to a small, but solid body of published work. Much of the recent thinking about the potential role of temporary activities in urban areas comes from Germany, in particular Berlin, where temporary uses have found a natural breeding ground. The cutting-edge research of Berlin's Urban Catalyst has provided an invaluable record of interim solutions to urban problems.[1] The results of this research and a follow on study, the Raumpioniere Project,[2] that documented almost 100 temporary-use projects in disused sites or buildings across Berlin, were published in the work *Urban Pioneers*.[3] Another publication, *Temporary Urban Spaces* edited by Florian Haydn and Robert Temel,[4] provided a series of essays around the topic, and a further 35 case studies of temporary uses in European and North American cities. This work has been picked up by those seeking a solution to the vast areas of dereliction and under-use caused by dramatic population loss in the world's 'shrinking cities', particularly in areas such as Detroit and Cleveland. Here, the work of the Cleveland Urban Design Collaborative (CUDC), based at Kent State University, Ohio, and others has similarly informed our work.

The intensification and diversification in the use of urban spaces is another aspect of the temporary city. In this respect we are indebted to a number of studies on the unintended or unsolicited uses of marginal areas of urban space as explored in *Loose Space* edited by Karen Franck and Quentin Stevens,[5] *Everyday Urbanism* edited by John Chase, Margaret Crawford and John Kaliski,[6] the *Post-It City* of Giovanni la Varra,[7] and Jeffrey Hou's *Insurgent Public Space*.[8] In relation to the emerging practice of temporary use and 'alternative masterplanning' a number of small multi-disciplinary urban practices such as *muf* architecture/art, Studio Egret West and David Barrie in the UK; Raumlabor, Studio Urban Catalyst, atelier d'architecture autogérée (aaa), STEALTH[9] and EXYZT in Europe, and Rebar in North America have been a source of great inspiration. We also acknowledge the contribution, in exploring and recording novel forms of urbanism, made by a growing number of websites in this field.[10]

4

Temporary uses are flourishing both in the in-between spaces where there is flexibility in the rigours of the property market, and in areas where multi-use is feasible. Some uses are planned and formal; some are informal, accidental, spontaneous or even illegal. Some occur when a city is shrinking, some when it is growing. Some uses last for a night or weekend, some are seasonal, while others may last five years or more. Some are acts of political defiance, while some are government interventions. Given this wide range of characteristics, temporary activities need to be defined with care.

'Temporary' is a difficult concept to pin down. The term denotes a finite period of time with a defined beginning and end. However, if we take a long enough time period or, for example, adopt the perspective of subatomic physics or Buddhism, everything is temporary, although it is certainly true that some things last longer than others. A fundamental problem with temporary activity is that it can only be accurately identified in hindsight. There are difficulties in trying to assess contemporaneously a phenomenon whose true context is historic. A use is not temporary until it has proved to be so, by disappearing. And by the time an interesting temporary phenomenon reaches our attention it may well no longer be there to be studied.

Some researchers have adopted working definitions that take into account the characteristics of temporary uses. However, this approach is difficult to apply to activities that are so diverse.[11] Therefore, for the sake of simplicity our definition is not based on the nature of the use, or whether rent is paid, or whether a use is formal or informal, or even on the scale, endurance or longevity of a temporary use, but rather the *intention* of the user, developer or planner that the use should be temporary. A temporary land use is an *intentional* phase. The phase itself may be short- or long-lasting, but the time element is merely a unit of measurement. When most buildings are planned or constructed, there may be an implicit understanding that their life will be finite, but there is little or no discussion of their longevity or of any subsequent uses at the time. With temporary land uses the time-limited nature of the use is generally explicit. We cannot always know the intention of the initiator of a temporary activity with any certainty. Even activities that sign a short lease or seek a temporary permission, may intend from the outset that they will endure. And there are many examples of 'temporary' activities such as squats or community gardens that have achieved this. There will inevitably be some ambiguity when discussing temporary activities.

We distinguish the definition of temporary used in this book from those that view 'meanwhile use' as an 'interim' or a 'stop-gap' solution in conditions where commercial letting is not presently viable.[12] Such definitions risk assuming that temporary activities are inevitably secondary. As Temel notes, temporary uses may be provisional, 'that is, conceived as a mere substitute for the "real thing"', but 'the temporary also has its own qualities and should not be viewed as merely a substitute for the fully adequate. This special quality can, for example, be that the temporal limitation permits many things that would still be inconceivable if considered for the long term'.[13]

In exploring the rise of interest in temporary urbanism, we are inevitably focusing on the UK, and in particular London, where our experience and practice are rooted. We have therefore written in the

5

context of the economic, legislative and social conditions that pertain to the UK, at the end of the first decade of the twenty-first century. We have, however, endeavoured to include case studies from elsewhere in the world, where relevant and appropriate. The conditions that are encouraging temporary activities are not, however, global. The interest in temporariness is arguably a luxury afforded only to those cities that are part of the post-industrial economy. In large parts of Africa, Asia and Latin America, many structures and activities are more tenuous or temporary and this reflects a hand-to-mouth existence where permanent structures, institutions, even hopes, are an impossible luxury.

In defining the scope of this book, the issue of how to cover temporary buildings has been challenging. Temporary housing has obviously been around for as long as humanity, as in the shelters of early hunter-gatherers and nomads. Even in the modern era more than 150,000 prefabricated homes with a structural lifetime of 10 to 15 years were built in the UK in response to the post-Second World War housing shortage, and some remain to this day. More recently the challenges of building 'temporary' camps and settlements for refugees have stimulated numerous books in their own right. So too have contemporary experiments in building with, for example, shipping containers, that offer quick, inexpensive and experimental solutions to a range of urban issues. We have chosen to focus on the planning rather than architectural responses to the temporary and for this reason temporary building per se is not covered in this book. It is, however, interesting that the debate on temporary uses and practical engagement has tended to be architecturally, rather than planning-led, with some of the most striking and interesting interventions in the field coming from a new generation of young architects. Many of the temporary uses that we do cover involve some kind of building, and in this

Housing in Bendhi Bazaar
MUMBAI

context, they are included in the book. So too are certain examples that illustrate the 'discovery' of temporary use as a profitable arena by the development industry itself. On balance we felt that the inclusion of such exceptions could be justified without the need for extensive context on temporary building itself.

Another challenge was whether to include the 'grand' temporary events, such as the Olympic Games, World Cup and Expos, and initiatives such as Cities of Culture, and Garden Festivals. Some have led to the long-term regeneration or 'rebranding' of sites or cities, or have left behind important permanent buildings and a place in the collective memory of the nation, but in other cases the legacy has been sterilised sites and debt. Such grand temporary projects have stimulated major research studies in their own right and have been explored extensively elsewhere. Again, on balance we felt that their inclusion in this book would have altered its focus substantially, away from the more everyday aspects of temporary urbanism.

Structuring this book has also presented challenges, not just because there are so many different ways of organising the information, but because interestingly, the boundaries between so many of the themes that could help to organise the material are becoming blurred. In fact the blurring of traditional distinctions between land use types and activities, and the interaction and overlap between the factors that are driving temporary activities are themes that run throughout the book, and are perhaps a key characteristic of temporary urbanism. Many of the themes that are covered could have found a natural and logical home in more than one chapter. The same, of course, goes for many of the case studies that illustrate the themes. Ultimately the material has been organised around the topics most likely to be of use to the reader.

7

The book falls loosely into three parts. The first chapters provide the context. Chapter 2 examines the essentially temporary nature of cities and explores the reasons why urbanists have become accustomed to viewing them as permanent. Chapter 3 provides an overview of the changes which are shaping our cities in the twenty-first century and their role as drivers for temporary urbanism. The themes raised in this chapter are picked up in the second part of the book, which explores temporary urbanism as it is manifested in consumerism, culture, urban space, community and private sector initiatives and in relation to 'creative milieus'. The third part of the book explores some of the emerging responses to the phenomenon, such as 'alternative masterplanning' and the scope to free up urban areas for the temporary through bringing greater flexibility to the planning system.

Until recently temporary activities have attracted little professional interest from architects or planners. Yet, from the travelling fairground to the designer pop-up restaurant such activities have always been a vital part of urban culture. They fill the gaps and enliven the urban experience, and they can bring considerable benefit when sensitively incorporated into urban planning. We hope that this book will offer a different way of interpreting cities. In the 'temporary city' strategies that recognise the essential transience of urban life can be more effective in an uncertain age.

8

The Dutch Pavilion
2010 SHANGHAI EXPO

Ruins of Barāqa'n
YEMEN

2: The dream of permanence

I met a traveller from an antique land
Who said: 'Two vast and trunkless legs of stone
Stand in the desert. Near them on the sand,
Half sunk, a shattered visage lies, whose frown
And wrinkled lip and sneer of cold command
Tell that its sculptor well those passions read
Which yet survive, stamped on these lifeless things,
The hand that mocked them and the heart that fed.
And on the pedestal these words appear:
"My name is Ozymandias, King of Kings:
Look on my works, ye mighty, and despair!"
Nothing beside remains. Round the decay
Of that colossal wreck, boundless and bare,
The lone and level sands stretch far away'.

PERCY BYSSHE SHELLEY, 'Ozymandias' (1818)

THE CENTRAL THEME of 'Ozymandias' is the inevitable decline of all people, and of the empires they build, however mighty in their own time, and the impossible dream of permanence.[1] Popes and emperors dream of an illusory legacy, yet everywhere their works are dust. Cities, towns and neighbourhoods have always been dynamic entities that rise and fall reflecting the great social, economic and political movements of the time.

The quest for permanence, however, guides many of our choices. We want to achieve 'lasting results', or find 'permanent solutions' or 'enduring love', to make 'continuing commitments', to invest our savings with 'permanent' investment funds and to achieve 'sustainable' regeneration. For most people, the notion of permanence brings a sense of security and a hedge against risk and the winds of change. Meanwhile there is implicit criticism in 'short-termism', while solutions that are labelled 'temporary' are deemed to be secondary to more permanent visions. However, we deceive ourselves in believing that the world is permanent. In reality, the only certainty is that everything changes. All of life has a cycle of birth, growth, death and decay. Even the human species shows few signs that it will remain a permanent feature of the planet.

For many people who live in the East, the concept of impermanence is culturally deeply embedded. In both Buddhism and Hinduism the impermanent nature of life and change are the undeniable and inescapable truths of existence. Because conditioned phenomena are impermanent, attachment to them can become the cause of future suffering. Acceptance of the shifting nature of the sands is a necessary step on the path to stability and peace of mind. Philosophers such as Heraclitus and Aristotle dabbled with the notion of impermanence and endless time, but such teachings did not take root in Western culture. The West may mark the changing nature of life, but still cherishes the belief that it is possible to find a centre of security in this circle of impermanence, and imagines that although the world is uncertain it can be controlled and given a material basis.

For large sections of the world's population, however, 'permanence' is an unattainable dream. Urban poverty is often characterised by living in a temporary physical environment and in a state of extreme and challenging uncertainty. The urban experience in most of the developing world, outside the established city cores or new residential and business districts, is largely one of temporary structures, temporary activities and impromptu and often inadequate infrastructure. Paradoxically, while experimentation with temporary uses is at the creative edge of urban planning in many developed nations, some of the most innovative work taking place in cities in developing countries is exploring mechanisms to imbue the temporary with permanence. In the favelas of Rio de Janiero, for example, the objective of the Morar Carioca initiative is to urbanise or integrate temporary districts into the city through the provision of a new infrastructure.[2] In the developing economies of Asia, by contrast, city growth often remains driven by government-sponsored masterplans utilising state or private sector capital. The exponential growth of Mumbai or Shanghai, for example, has led to the wholesale clearance of districts that might have been considered temporary in nature, to be replaced by a hard-wired city of streets, plazas, malls and tower blocks. Such development changes have clear parallels with the growth of European and North American cities in the nineteenth and early twentieth centuries.

History abounds with examples of mighty cities that turned out to be temporary – Troy, Pompeii, Carthage and Babylon. Yet we tend to assume that cities today are different and that contemporary works, built as they are on rational plans and the belief in a stable world order, will endure and generate a permanent legacy. However, natural and man-made disasters continue to empty towns and cities. Beichuan in Sichuan, China, is likely to be abandoned following the earthquake of May 2008, while Pripyat in the Ukraine was emptied by the Chernobyl nuclear disaster. Towns have been abandoned when the natural resources that sustained them were depleted, when railways or roads bypassed them or new infrastructure, such as dams, required their expropriation.

The Polish journalist Ryszard Kapuściński provides a vivid illustration of the impermanence of our cities in war in his description of the final days of Portuguese rule in Angola in 1975.[3] Back in Lisbon the government has washed its hands of the colony. The MPLA and Unita are closing in on the capital Luanda and the Portuguese colonists, realising that there is no future, prepare to leave en masse. The only economic activity is the construction of wooden packing cases, thousands of them. A wooden city slowly emerges under cover of darkness. The settlers pack their belongings. They

12

The shape of the Roman amphitheatre outlined in Piazza dell'Anfiteatro
LUCCA
SOURCE: © Google Earth 2011, Tele Atlas, Data SO, NOAA, US Navy NGA, GEBCO

13

pack their furniture. They take out their kitchens, bathrooms and appliances. They strip their homes right down to the brickwork. The city is slowly dismantled, crated, and stacked in neat rows on the dockside. Eventually the packing cases are loaded onto ships that sail off over the horizon never to return. Whole districts of Luanda have been removed; a vanished city awaits its conquerors. Later, we are told, the wooden packing cases find new life in wretched shanty towns around Lisbon.

In most cases, however, cities are not completely abandoned, but new layers are superimposed and everywhere older cities protrude into the modern fabric. The surviving structures are generally the grand buildings (arenas, stadia and great religious buildings), or infrastructure (defensive city walls, roads and water supply), or the vestiges of landownerships or field boundaries. The names of streets and neighbourhoods, too, often become permanent. These elements often remain as an imprint that continues to shape urban areas today, either because they have seen such extensive investment that it remains 'locked in', or because they have been so deeply engraved into the earth that their shape remains embedded. In Lucca, the imprint of the old Roman arena dating from the first century AD is still clearly discernible in the quiet Piazza dell'Anfiteatro, home to a few cafés and an occasional market. The City of London, the city's financial centre, is still largely defined by the outline of the Roman town, and within this the medieval street pattern still exists. These small land plots still define the footprint of new high-rise commercial buildings, forcing them into a different architectural form from, for example, the offices at Canary Wharf where the *tabula rasa* allows optimum floor plates.

At one time, many European cities were, like the African or Latin American city of today, largely a complex overlay of temporary structures and uses. Civic leaders and patrons established, or facilitated the construction of the essential infrastructure – the religious and administrative buildings, grand avenues and squares. This framework was then filled by everyday uses that developed in natural confusion and diversity at a liveable scale. The great buildings of church or state were valued as permanent, but the fabric of day-to-day life was essentially temporary. Street markets, workshops, shops and housing (especially for the poor), existed in a largely unregulated environment. They arose without permission, and after a while were replaced. Ultimately, most of the urban fabric was expendable. However, successive layers of legislation in the fields of planning, building, fire prevention and public health have acted to 'solidify' such transient structures. We tend to forget that this regulation is a largely twentieth-century phenomenon and may not necessarily represent an enduring paradigm.

The UK, like many countries in Europe, has a long history of legal controls on building construction, all of which have tended to produce higher levels of invested capital and ever more permanence. As early as the twelfth century, controls were introduced on the thickness of party walls, the siting of privies and the use of thatched roofs.[4] Later, the Great Fire of London led to controls on the construction of timber buildings and the width of streets to act as fire breaks. The first national Building Regulations in their modern form were introduced in 1965, and since then various amendments and revisions have extended their scope to cover all aspects of building design. Their general effect is to ensure that buildings are robust and safe, but they also make it harder to erect more temporary structures.

UK planning legislation has similarly had the effect of solidifying urban areas. A raft of legislation in the Victorian era had already sought to tackle the health problems of the industrial revolution – over-crowded housing, smogs from coal fires, the lack of a sewage system, contaminated drinking water and disease. At the turn of the century, new legislation introduced controls over housing design and enabled slum clearance.[5] The end of the Second World War brought consensus over the need for comprehensive planning. Land uses were effectively fixed as those existing in 1948.[6] Henceforth the change of use of land would be controlled, and planning permission would be required for most development. Planning thus acts as the gatekeeper of land value by allowing development. It also inevitably acts as a brake on change and experimentation.

While the planning system can be said to have replaced temporary land uses with semi-permanent designations for every parcel of land in the UK, building conservation legislation takes this process one stage further, seeking to conserve or protect, apparently for all time, historic areas, building façades and even interior details. Legislation has made it illegal to demolish or alter a building 'listed' for its 'special architectural or historic interest' without consent, and has extended such protection to buildings within Conservation Areas.[7] The areas covered by such powers have expanded rapidly. There were 373,892 listed buildings in England in 2010.[8] The number of Conservation Areas expanded from 3,500 in 1977 to more than 9,600 in 2010, and over 1.5 million buildings are now under the control of heritage law. In the UK we are not just preserving buildings, but also artefacts. Many urban features that were probably viewed as temporary when they were built, such as capstans, phone boxes, post boxes, bollards, horse troughs, shop fronts and even kerb stones, are now preserved.

As writer Dan Cruickshank has noted, in the West it is the materiality of buildings that is paramount.[9] The very stones are perceived to bear witness to our history. However, such a perception is not universal. In Asia and the East, the focus is not so much on the material aspect of a building, but the spiritual aspect and the site on which it stands. In China, traditional buildings are constantly rebuilt in the original manner. In Japan, Shinto shrines may be rebuilt every 20 years, yet they are still venerated as traditional structures. In the Buddhist nation of Bhutan it is often hard to tell the new structures from the old. In the UK though, we venerate the stones, the materiality rather than the spiritual nature of place.

There is no doubt that the value of the built heritage is extremely high and makes a significant contribution to quality of life, economic vitality, civic pride and even the tourist industry.[10] Yet conservation has become a British 'sacred cow' that has developed with little criticism or review. Its position today is largely unchallenged. While a Google search of terms such as 'UK building conservation' produces half a million references, it is extremely difficult to locate any references that offer an 'appraisal' 'evaluation' or 'critique'. This is in effect an artificially imposed permanence. The longer-term impact on the ability to renew large swathes of cities that are now locked into a time vault, or on the rate of turnover in the built fabric outside historic areas, or indeed on temporary uses, is largely unknown.

Architect Rem Koolhaas' exhibition for the Venice Architectural Biennale 2010, *Cronocaos*, was one of the few explicit challenges to the seemingly unlimited growth of conservation in recent years.[11] The exhibition noted that 'preservation's ever-increasing ambitions mean that the time lag between new construction and the imperative to preserve has collapsed'. When the legislation was first introduced in 1882, it sought to preserve prehistoric structures; by 1983 it had changed to structures only older than 30 years: 'There is in effect an ever-accelerating rate at which architecture is being declared as an item of permanence'. From this Koolhaas extrapolates that the next step, prospective preservation, would presumably predefine a building's status as monument, even before it is physically manifested. In response, Koolhaas presented a theory of its opposite, not what to keep, but what to give up, erase and abandon: 'properties which represent a lack of human creative genius; are (an) average example of a type of building, architectural or technological ensemble or landscape which illustrate (an) insignificant stage(s) in human history; contain appalling synthetic phenomena or areas of overdeveloped saturation and aesthetic insignificance'.

A parallel process of legislative restraint has meant that the temporary forms of housing favoured by squatters, travellers and 'New Age' communities have come under increasing pressure. Squatting has a long tradition in England and squatting itself is still a civil rather than a criminal offence, governed by legislation dating back to 1381. However, successive governments have sought to change the situation, and the UK Ministry of Justice announced in 2010 that it intends to make squatting a

Funfair
ISLINGTON, LONDON

16

criminal offence.[12] Travelling people have played an important role throughout European history providing music, shows, fairs, circuses, stories, goods, services and a seasonal workforce. However, existing on the fringes of established society, they trigger suspicion and a desire by 'permanent' communities and governments for control. While in the UK, local councils are required to provide sites for gypsies, compliance has been patchy. The Criminal Justice Act (1994) has since made it a criminal offence to park a caravan or similar vehicle on any land without the landowner's consent. The intention apparently, was that travelling people would acquire their own land for sites, apply for planning consent and 'settle down', but in practice such planning consents have been difficult to gain. This has also curtailed the activities of many would-be 'New Age' communities such as Tinker's Bubble wishing to live the good life on the fringes of established society.[13]

It is not just the regulatory systems that tend to favour more permanent structures or activities. Some temporary activities have an internal dynamic that leads them to become permanent. Some of the squatters who occupied vacant homes in the 1960s and 1970s were ultimately granted tenure, in this case due to the length of their residency, and have become respected members of the local community. Some of the prefabricated housing, erected as a stop-gap solution to the post-war housing shortage, has endured to this day. The reasons here are inertia, a lack of resources or, ironically, because 'pre-fabs' became popular with those living in them. Some of the few remaining have now been 'listed' by English Heritage.[14] Other structures, such as the London Eye or indeed the Eiffel

The Eiffel Tower, originally a temporary structure
PARIS

Tower, which were intended to be temporary, have endured due to their popularity and have become iconic landmarks. Numerous community gardens around the world, which were permitted temporarily following intense public campaigning, have become permanent too. Often it is public support that has ensured that it will never be expedient politically to remove them. The fear that it may be difficult to remove temporary activities is one of the reasons why some landowners resist them today.

Temporary activities are not new; there have always been gaps and niches in the urban landscape that have been used for the time being for car parking, storage, scrap yards or charity shops. These may be seen as fringe activities, but they are a vital part of the urban economy. The UK and many

Allotments
HIGHGATE, LONDON

18 other places have an honourable tradition of temporary experiments in land use. However, in recent years temporary activities have flourished, attracting growing interest as a developing 'phenomenon' from academics as well as the media. The suggestion is that temporary activities have an important role to play even in the modern city. In the UK, the national press has featured regular articles on the new wave of 'pop-ups' and 'meanwhile' activities in the last two or three years.[15] For instance, Andy Beckett, writing in the *Guardian* notes:

> in the crevices the developers have left behind, there is a counter-trend at work. You can see it in the guerrilla gardening movement and the boom in music festivals; in the vogue for temporary 'pop-up' shops, restaurants and cinemas in empty urban spaces; in the artists occupying disused high-street stores from Durham to Margate; in the sudden appearance and popularity in London of outdoor ping-pong tables; and in the Edinburgh crowds last summer queuing to see spooky late-night art installations in the city's usually staid Royal Botanic Garden.[16]

In London, magazines such as *Time Out* now have frequent references to the 'pop-up' shop, theatre or restaurant.[17] Temporary urbanism is no longer consigned to the fringes of professional thinking. In March 2010 the Architecture Foundation (with support from Design for London), hosted a three-day symposium that explored the role that temporary and interim land uses could play in the future of east London after the 2012 Olympics.[18] Similarly New London Architecture held an exhibition in London in 2010, on the *Pop-Up City: Ideas for Re-using Vacant Urban Sites.*[19] The journal *Property Week* has also launched the Site Life campaign for the temporary re-use of vacant sites and, in partnership with the owners of major unused sites, has held several competitions seeking ideas for their temporary animation.[20] In 2011 the Royal Institute of British Architects, again with Design for London, held a three-day exhibition and conference on temporary uses and how to plan for them. The internet too now hosts a growing number of websites that record or support temporary, ephemeral and experimental land uses.

We know that the city is never an end state, but is perpetually evolving. The evidence lies all around us. The historic layers of cities co-exist in a rich mosaic of contrasting architectural styles. Sometimes these historic structures are embedded successfully within the life and function of the modern city; sometimes their outline is written in its present street patterns; and sometimes they seem stranded incongruously in its fabric. This four-dimensional city is the reality, yet much urban thinking and many strategies are still strictly three-dimensional. City authorities continue to seek permanent and final solutions and to plan for an end state. Strategic planning processes are increasingly unsuited to the pace of modern urban change and leave areas in a curious limbo while they are being prepared. Plans are often outdated before they are even published, while on a day-to-day basis the control of development perpetuates categories of use that are inflexible and unsuited to times of continuous change.

In the planning and design of cities temporary activities are generally considered to signify a time of crisis or a failure to develop. There has been little analysis of their role, their importance or their key attributes. Transience is rarely viewed as an explicit and vital characteristic of cities, or a key component of growth and regeneration. Despite this, in the cracks in the mortar, temporary activities are flourishing.

Many apparently new thoughts and ideas appear to emerge from a variety of seemingly different sources with strange concurrence. The idea that there is a need to pay more attention to temporary activities and phases of development has similarly arisen from several directions at once. It is, of course, possible that the new wave of temporary activities may just be a passing fashion that will fade away once the novelty value has diminished. But there is also a possibility that it represents a more fundamental shift in the use of land and buildings with deeper implications for urban policy and practice. For this reason, one of the key questions that is addressed in the next chapter is why there is such growing interest at present in the potential of temporary uses.

19

Credit Crunch: installation by students of St Martin's School of Architecture / Victoria Lee
ISTANBUL

3: Temporary urbanism: drivers and conditions

THE POLISH SOCIOLOGIST Zygmunt Bauman argues that in the last 40 or 50 years we have moved from a phase of what he terms 'solid' modernity to a 'liquid' phase.[1] 'Solid' modernity was based on a belief that it was possible to make a 'fully rational perfect world'. Change was seen as temporary and it was only a matter of acquiring enough information, knowledge and technical skills to construct a world that did not require further change. Solid modernity involved removing unknowns and uncertainties through control over nature, and by creating hierarchical bureaucracy, rules and regulations. All of these control mechanisms sought to remove personal insecurities, making the chaotic aspects of human life appear well-ordered and familiar. Strategies such as following precedent and accumulating experience made sense in a world of relatively slow change.

Bauman maintains that we have now moved to a phase of 'liquid' modernity – a phase that, like a liquid, 'cannot keep its shape for long'. We no longer believe that a state of perfection will ever be achieved: change is here to stay, as 'a permanent condition of human life'. This brings increasing ambivalence and feelings of uncertainty. The global passage from solid to liquid modernity has confronted individuals with a series of new challenges. Social forms and institutions no longer have enough time to solidify and cannot serve as frames of reference for long-term life plans, so individuals have to find other ways to organise their lives. They have to splice together an unending series of short-term projects that may not add up to the kind of sequence to which concepts like 'career' and 'progress' can be meaningfully applied. It is a form of 'nomadism' where the individual flows through life like a tourist, changing places, jobs, spouses and values. Liquid modernity is characterised by uncertainty, continuous risk and shifting trust. What is trustworthy today may not be tomorrow. Such fragmented lives require individuals to be flexible and adaptable – to be constantly ready and willing to change tactics at short notice, to abandon commitments and loyalties and to pursue opportunities according to their current availability. We might speculate therefore, that in such a world temporary activities of all kinds could be expected to flourish.

22

Dismantling the permanent: protestors at the Berlin Wall
BERLIN, NOVEMBER 1989

Uncertainty

Without doubt, there is growing uncertainty about political, economic and environmental conditions that we had once assumed were inviolate. On the big screen, the last 20 years or so, particularly since the fall of the Berlin Wall and the end of Communism, have seen a fundamental shift in the way we see the world. It has become more fluid; no longer are the great power blocks locked in overt conflict as they were through most of the twentieth century. The removal of such barriers has seen the end of many of the political certainties of our era, even the idea that there can be consensus. Global warming, the occurrence of natural disasters like the tsunami that hit the shores around the Indian Ocean in 2004, the hurricane that devastated New Orleans in 2005, the earthquakes that hit Haiti and Chile in 2010, or Japan in 2011, have contributed to a dawning sense that man-made structures, even mankind itself, are more fragile and temporary than we may have assumed.

In parallel, the financial crisis of 2007–8 has significantly undermined our faith in perpetual growth. Caused by speculation and the over-valuation of assets in a global economic boom that was itself seen as permanent, the crisis was triggered by a liquidity shortfall in the US banking system, and it came close to causing global financial meltdown. Its effects are still unfolding today. It has resulted in the collapse of large financial institutions, the bail-out of banks by national governments and huge losses on stock markets around the world. In Europe and North America major businesses have failed, consumer wealth has declined and the housing market has collapsed in many areas, resulting in widespread evictions, foreclosures and vacancy. Governments and central banks have responded with unprecedented fiscal stimulus, monetary policy expansion and institutional bail-outs, but significant risks still remain for the world economy. As a result faith in the ability of global laissez-faire capitalism to provide continued growth and prosperity has been significantly undermined.

The fallout from the financial crisis is now being exacerbated by its effects on the very credit worthiness of governments. Iceland, Greece, Portugal and Ireland required financial bail-outs despite the introduction of severe austerity measures that decimated public expenditure. Britain, Spain and other countries have responded by slashing government budgets, including many of those that fuelled urban development, regeneration, infrastructure and public works. City authorities now have to adapt to these conditions of uncertainty with massive cuts to their budgets. In practice, however, the adaptive tactics of city dwellers and businesses are generally far more responsive. And it is here that temporary urbanism is providing an outlet for innovation and experimentation.

23

Vacancy

Since the 1960s enormous areas in Western Europe and North America have become redundant due to industrial restructuring. The collapse of the Soviet Union in the 1990s had a similar, even more dramatic impact on Eastern Europe. The loss of traditional industries such as mining, textiles and engineering has created vast areas of vacant land in some urban areas. New technologies mean that goods can be provided when they are needed and obviate the need for large inner-city storage units. Most traditional ports now have large areas of land lying unused, often close to the city centre, as the increasing use of containers and larger shipping has shifted such operations downstream. Elsewhere, suburbanisation and out of town shopping have created a centrifugal force that has eroded the uses and economic rationale that once held many city centres together.

Economic restructuring is affecting cities in different ways, some of which are quite extreme. According to a European Commission study of 220 large and medium-sized European cities, 57 per cent of the cities and 54 per cent of larger urban areas lost population between 1996 and 2001. Included in the list are 22 German cities, 19 Italian cities, 11 British cities and five Spanish cities.[2]

24

The reasons for shrinkage include satellite suburbanisation, economic decline in structurally weak industrialised cities and profound demographic change. In some areas all these factors overlap. In the US, industrial decline and suburban development in cities such as Buffalo, Detroit, Cleveland and Pittsburgh have 'hollowed out' the inner-city areas, leaving vast areas of vacant land. Herron, writing about the demographic rollercoaster in Detroit and the consequent massive rise in the amount of vacant land, argues that it represents a throw-away attitude to cities that is a particular characteristic of American urbanism.[3] He suggests that due to a combination of individualistic democracy and the rapid spread of urban culture, there has never been a sense of the city as a precious repository of civilisation in America. As a result the history of America is 'a centuries-long exposition of mapping and remapping, as if the land the newcomers confronted were a blank state, endlessly renewable, for the purposes of drafting whatever propositions seemed best at the time. And whatever got in the way was reduced to bunk'.[4] In a similar vein Villagomez argues that '(t)he creation of meaningless, residual spaces has reached an extreme in North America where early illusions of limitless material resources have translated into a value system that encourages – and legally mandates – low-intensity land use'.[5]

Some commentators now consider that shrinkage might be an enduring structural component of urban development.[6] There is consequently a significant body of research underway into the options for dealing with dereliction on a city-wide scale. Some of the most interesting programmes are experimenting with the role and potential of temporary land uses.[7]

Vacancy may persist for longer than landowners or the public authorities would like for a range of reasons. The sheer size of the area may be daunting and require a long development process. The vacancy may coincide with a slump in the property market in which demand is low for the anticipated end use. Even where demand exists, land contamination or the requirements of building conservation may make development complex or uneconomic, or the costs of providing infrastructure may be prohibitive. Some researchers have postulated that the continuing rise in vacant space around the world may be the result of a greater turnover of land uses today, an 'accelerated functionalism'[8] and 'ever shorter utilisation cycles'.[9] Although there is little statistical evidence to back this up, buildings do seem to be intended, more than ever before, to fulfil a market requirement and be abandoned as circumstances change. Sites are seen increasingly as a cost factor in their own right; those that do not have the requisite 'yield' may be closed. Capital is highly flexible in relation to changing locations. As Temel notes, 'the requirements of an accelerated capitalist economy … conflict with the immobility of real estate'.[10] He maintains that temporary use liberates 'land as a means of production from the fetters of the permanent', either as 'interim uses that make it possible to utilise unproductive idle times', or through 'making every use temporary on principle, since the market requires that every use gives way to the next, more productive one'.

Whatever the cause of vacant property, the ready availability of vacant spaces or voids appears to be significant in allowing temporary activities to take hold, and in the right circumstances, flourish. Vacancy represents both a temporal and spatial vacuum between old and new uses, and temporary users tend to select those sites that are of little interest to property investors at a given time. One of the immediate effects of the financial crisis of 2007–8 was the withdrawal of finance from the property market. Across America and most of Europe, development projects were halted and projects rephased, replanned or simply abandoned. A significant outcome of the current slump in the UK property market, that has not occurred in previous property crises, is that some property owners have overcome their traditional resistance to temporary activities and are actually *initiating* temporary-use schemes. These are explored further in Chapter 4.

Another driver to temporary use in the UK has been the continuing rise in the amount of vacant retail floorspace in town centres. A recent study of 700 towns and cities in the UK, by market research firm Local Data Company, found that 13 per cent of shops were vacant at the end of June 2010.[11] Many property researchers predict that a high proportion of vacant units will never be a traditional shop again. The government has responded by encouraging greater flexibility in the use of such retail units particularly for temporary activities. A recent report by think-tank the Policy Exchange argued that, with annual household formation at 250,000 running well ahead of the 160,000 new homes built on average between 2000 and 2009, there are strong grounds for allowing the conversion of vacant retail properties into residential use.[12]

The explosion in 'pop-up' shops and restaurants cannot be explained simply by the glut of surplus retail units on our high streets, massive though it is. It also reflects new trends in marketing, selling and even market research that are both legitimising and encouraging temporary uses. In the perpetual quest for new consumer experiences, there is a significant cachet associated with time-limited exclusivity.

25

The revolution in work

The revolution in work is changing the way organisations function, the way people live and the way in which we use space. A study by the Chartered Management Institute predicts that in the next 10 years the world of work will see further rises in flexible working, self-employment, virtual organisations, virtual meetings, work-life integration, greater diversity in the workforce, and more creativity and playfulness.[13] Flexible office working covers a wide range of options outside the traditional nine to five full-time job – flexibility in location (home working, mobile working, 'teleworking'), flexibility in time (flexi-time, part-time working, job share, compressed working weeks and annualised hours) and flexibility in terms of workplace.[14] It has enabled many businesses to reduce their floorspace requirements. Business consultants *Flexibility* maintain that most desks in most offices are actually used just 45 to 50 per cent of the time through the combined effects of staff vacancies, holidays, sickness, part-time working, meetings away from the office, training courses and fieldwork.[15] Employees too are demanding greater flexibility, and enlightened employers are recognising that they need to change their organisational models in order to attract and maintain a quality workforce. Flexible working favours those who find it difficult to be at a fixed workplace all week – parents, carers or people with disabilities. For others it is becoming a lifestyle choice that enables them to merge the need to earn a living with other activities that interest them. Researchers have found a correlation across the globe, between commuting times and staff who are considering leaving their jobs.[16] Flexible working generally entails less commuting, less pollution and more use of local resources, and can bring considerable health and social benefits.[17]

The number of people working from home continues to rise. At the end of 2009, 12.8 per cent of the UK workforce (3.7 million people) worked mainly at or from home: an increase of 21 per cent since 2001.[18] The spread of flexible working is changing the nature of entrepreneurship. Around two-thirds of these homeworkers are self-employed. A recent UK study found that the number of freelancers[19] grew 20 per cent between 1998 and 2008 to around four million people.[20] In the USA, the number of homeworkers rose from 19.8 million to 20.7 million from 2001 to 2004, a five per cent increase.[21]

Home-based businesses now make a significant contribution to the UK economy, having a combined turnover of over £364 billion in 2009.[22] Over 60 per cent of new businesses are started at home, that is 1,400 new businesses each week. As Anderson reports, 'involuntary entrepreneurship' is booming as a result of the current recession.[23] Most new businesses intend to stay small, preferring to outsource new work rather than employ staff. The ethos of running a home business and lifestyle benefits from blending home and work life are therefore paramount. Anderson also argues that small organisations are at an advantage in situations of rapid change and uncertainty. They are nimbler and better able to take risks, and the internet allows them to collaborate on projects, or order supplies globally, just like the giants. The result is that the emerging economy increasingly favours the small. New developments in technology can only accelerate this process. For example, 3D printing technology could potentially turn every garage into a micro-factory and every citizen into a micro-

The flexible office: multi-tasking in St James' Park

entrepreneur.[24] It will enable one-person or collaborative enterprises, operating on low overheads, to become increasingly competitive. With flexible working and self-employment becoming increasingly common, work itself is evolving into a sequence of temporary projects that are diverse in range and may operate from different bases within the city.

27

Intensity in the use of space

Significantly, the downside of homeworking, its isolation, is being alleviated by social networking and the creation of new places to meet and work such as coffee shops and business hubs, increasingly in residential areas. Such places cater for the needs of the mobile workforce and have resulted in greater multi-use of space – both internal and external. All of this has been enabled by the revolution in information and communications technologies that has removed the need to work in one place and made the old workplace routines less relevant. The impact of a more flexible workforce is being felt physically, with more places or facilities to allow workers to 'touch down', or meet up. By having control over one's hours, the individual (at least within the privileged urban elite) can also *play* during the extended and flexible working day. Other enterprises catering for this new user demand must also operate flexibly outside the weekend and evening hours where entertainment was traditionally concentrated. The impact of WiFi technology has further blurred the boundaries of the working day, both spatially and temporally. We can now work or play anytime and anywhere.

Spitalfields Community Festival
LONDON

28

The trends towards multi-use are affecting many types of property. As both a cost-cutting exercise and a drive to create community hubs, schools are being opened up to the wider community either outside, or sometimes during, the short school day. Such community schools frequently host adult education and literacy classes, provide community meeting rooms and may even provide a base for services such as community policing, health and social services. While the quest for greater sustainability is generating pressures for denser development in urban areas, such policies relate more to the intensification of the built form. In future, however, they may also embrace the intensification of *activity* and contribute further to the opportunities for temporary activities.

The perpetual drive to cut operating costs and achieve greater efficiency is also opening up opportunities for more temporary use. Despite growing population densities, many buildings have rooms or even floors that are under-used. Industrialists have long recognised that they must organise their production schedules around 24-hour working, seven days a week to be competitive. Similarly, the trading floors of finance houses now operate around the clock, although in this case the motive is to capture potential profits across different time zones. In contrast, it is cuts in public sector funding that are now encouraging public authorities to use the resources available within their property portfolios more productively to generate revenue. Many schools, for example, now hire out their playgrounds for weekend car parking, car boot sales and farmers' markets, while their assembly halls may be rented to choirs, dance and theatre clubs.

In theory, new technology could allow the transient use of empty rooms scattered throughout the city. Hitoshi and Masahige's lifestyle proposal Megahouse envisages 'inhabiting the entire city as if it was one enormous house' through using a digital interface to activate such dispersed empty spaces. A management agency would rent empty rooms and equip them with a centralised management system. Members could then 'find, reserve, and use a particular room that fits their objectives', for several hours or several months. In this way, the project 'furnishes rooms everywhere in the city, (which) ... collectively constitute a "house" for the users'.[25] The 'house' would enable the city to evolve into an intensive overlay of temporary activities within a semi-permanent physical framework.

Changes in working practices, new technologies and increasingly transient and mobile urban lifestyles mean that more activities are simply spilling onto the streets. In parallel, public spaces now host an ever wider range of entertainment – pavement art, busking and performance art, street parties, parades, markets, races, demonstrations, concerts, festivals, fairgrounds, circuses, sports events, exhibitions and ice rinks. This reflects growing urban population densities, new consumer demands and generally higher levels of disposable income. Alongside these trends, the ever more diverse ethnic composition of cities has expanded the range and number of what John Chase, Margaret Crawford and John Kaliski term 'everyday uses'.[26] Immigrant communities with different cultural attitudes to public and private space bring new ways of colonising the street. Meanwhile, foreign travel and the impact of the media have created a new generation of 'consumers of cities' who travel, compare and import new ideas, such as the café culture of southern Europe.

The result is that public space has both a greater diversity and intensity of uses, the majority of which are fleeting. In response to this demand public authorities are starting to recognise the value of public space and its many benefits. We have seen a greater spirit of experimentation in the remodelling, for example, of the banks of the Seine in Paris as summertime beaches (Case Study 6.14), or the reclamation of roads as pedestrian space as in Times Square in New York (Case Study 6.11). Cities are responding with public space and cultural strategies and these are becoming essential parts of their strategic planning.

29

The Oubliette Arthouse
LONDON

Counterculture and activism

Temporary use can also be seen as a response to the inherent inability of the property market to meet certain needs. Kohoutek and Kamleithner note that 'there are numerous activities within the whole spectrum of urban uses, for which the private real estate market has only inadequate supply'.[27] Similarly, Merker argues that 'it is only by the tacit *undervaluing* of certain activities (such as, say play or eating or socialising) that other activities (such as parking and driving) can thrive'.[28] There is, for instance, always latent demand from those who wish to establish projects without commercial returns, such as community projects, and youth and sports initiatives. Such activities tend to operate outside, or on the fringes of the mainstream property market. The fringes also provide a base for those without access to start-up capital and the wherewithal for lease guarantees, which excludes them from the commercial lettings market. Business start-ups and creative industries often require spaces that the normal market only offers to a limited degree or at a prohibitive price.

The radical American poet/philosopher Hakim Bey's essay on 'Temporary Autonomous Zones' (TAZs)[29] was widely seen as one of the countercultural bibles of the 1990s. Bey seeks to provoke thought and his ideas have been picked up by several writers on temporary urbanism. While many of his concepts share an affinity with anarchist doctrines, he departs from the rhetoric of overthrowing governments. Instead, he explores various ways in which the individual can experience freedom in a world that increasingly encourages conformity and regimentation. For Bey, the TAZ is a short-lived environment that eludes formal structures of control and which is full of alternative social possibilities.[30] It is an experience where participants temporarily free themselves from the restraints imposed by social conditioning and regulation, and experiment in creative events with new codes of behaviour. He sees TAZs as 'moments of intensity' that can give shape and meaning to life, or as pockets of freedom that enable the individual to escape the norms of established society and to establish a realm where he or she can briefly experience total freedom. Ultimately Bey seems to suggest that instead of waiting for the revolution, with a little ingenuity one can experience the fruits of freedom right now and uncover one's true, rather than conditioned, needs and desires.[31]

The TAZ may acquire a location or locations, somewhere at some time, but is primarily a fleeting network of like-minded people. Bey cites examples of countercultural movements in America, the communes of Paris, Lyons and Marseilles, and even spontaneous urban happenings such as break-dancing and graffiti art.[32] For Bey, the beauty of such 'uprisings' is in their spirit rather than their permanence. Such zones have to be temporary because the state inevitably reacts, imposing a new order and restricting freedom. It is the opportunity for creativity that is real empowerment. In the formation of a TAZ, information is the key tool that sneaks through the cracks of formal procedures. Thus the internet could provide potential opportunities to undermine the control of information, through piracy and hacking, and, freed from all political control, could act as a support system that could enable an entire world of virtual autonomous zones.[33]

Bey's ideas have been taken up by a number of writers on temporary urbanism. Urban Unlimited, for example, describe the historical importance of what they call 'freezones' which they liken to modern-day 'creative milieus' and to TAZs.[34] They argue that throughout history such 'freezones' have acted as places in which dissenters and free-thinkers have found protection and living space. They cite examples such as the mercantile cities of Western Europe, those founded by settlers far from the control of their mother countries in America, South Africa and the Far East, and urban havens for refugees (Jews, non-conformists and runaway slaves). Modern examples include the lively squatters' scene in Amsterdam and other cities in the 1970s where 'artists, musicians, foreign dissidents and refugees formed a mixed, activist and dynamic culture'.[35] Another example: Christiania in Copenhagen, a former military area covering 34 hectares, has been squatted since 1971 as a self-proclaimed autonomous neighbourhood of about 850 residents.

For Urban Unlimited, such freezones 'have been of particular importance for the origins of urban culture, the expansion of states, the protection of minorities and the renewal of the city. In short, they have been essential during all phases in the development of urban society'.[36] They are not just an historical phenomenon, but remain firmly on the agenda as the creative milieus of today. Urban Unlimited conclude that the 'formal, regulatory, ossifying, territorially-based aspect of urban policy needs to be complemented with far greater attention to the informal, pioneering, elusive, network-based' freezone issues.[37] In a similar reference to Bey's work, Bieber, in discussing the proliferation in recent years of informal, unsolicited, often anti-authoritarian artworks that have hit the streets, declares that such '(u)rban interventions, then, are de facto temporary autonomous zones'.[38] The role of temporary activities in culture and counterculture is considered further in Chapter 7.

In their study of temporary uses in Berlin, Urban Catalyst suggest that temporary colonisers of space, or 'space pioneers', are 'evidence of a trend to greater social commitment, to more participation, to active networks and the desire to try out something new'.[39] Thus we must also consider the possibility that there are now more people who are prepared to act out their demands for new uses of urban space. A number of underlying policies and trends may be contributing to this. Government policies to devolve power, reduce public expenditure, strengthen the legitimacy and accountability of democracy, and build social capital, may be encouraging more activism, particularly among the young for whom the prospect of long-term unemployment is very real. Stakeholder involvement is enhancing the ability of communities and activists to stop development plans and put forward alternative proposals. The current economic hiatus has created not just some of the physical conditions for temporary uses, but a generation facing exclusion from the economic certainties of traditional careers, or the entry requirements into business. In other words, there is now a pool of both potential entrepreneurs and activists who see the 'temporary economy' as their natural constituency. This driver to temporary urbanism is considered further in Chapter 8.

New technology

New technology is playing an absolutely central role in enabling and spreading the word about temporary uses with a speed and penetration that would not have been possible even 20 years ago. The mobile phone releases us from the need for a fixed place of contact, and the latest smart-phones enable each individual to carry more of the gadgets that facilitate a transient lifestyle: maps, GPS, compass, camera, video recorder, music, books and games, address book, email and internet. The number of people with access to email from a mobile device was nearly 150 million worldwide in 2009, and is expected to reach one billion by 2013.[40]

Many temporary activities do not have the luxury of time in which they can build up a client base. If they are located in the fringes of the city where rentals and controls are lower, they may lack visibility and footfall. Internet access and mobile networks overcome these problems by providing the ability to advertise their existence quickly, cheaply and widely. For temporary uses such as festivals, parties, flash events and 'happenings', communication via email, text or social networking has the added advantage of being able to target very specific social groups, and in a way that is less visible to the controlling hand of the state.

Broadband comes to Bucharest
ROMANIA, 2010

33

New technology also facilitates networking among communities of interest which can then spontaneously organise activities: the park becomes a studio for the yoga club or a venue for a roller-blading party, a car park becomes a drive-in cinema, or an empty office hosts a rave.[41] Indeed it is difficult to envisage many of these activities existing in a world without cheap, accessible mobile communications technology. Abhinav and Shetty postulate that as people are starting to carry 'more of their lives into the outdoors', they want to 'configure outdoors to their taste and preference'.[42] They argue that this will be greatly enabled by user-generated content or open-content or 'Creative Commons' license. This has already created vibrant platforms of user-created content such as Flickr and Wikipedia. The increasing use of 'permanent beta' (an infinitely iterative software development model in which user feedback, requests and analysis is the major feature) allows developers to be continuously open to user demands, and can facilitate active user configuration of the urban realm. The authors propose a web-based project called CitySpinning that would help communities of interest to reconfigure the city for their needs through providing information on available sites for projects from gardening plots to star-gazing.

We can only begin to speculate about the impact of the 'smart city' on the use of space. Cities across the world are starting to use ultra-fast broadband and remote monitoring to splice together new sources of information to tackle the realities of urbanisation. These are changing all aspects of cities, from the way we access information on our neighbourhoods, to the ability to monitor and control energy consumption and production through micro-generation schemes. Virtual rather than face-to-face meetings with service providers, virtual schooling and tutoring, smart reporting of street maintenance problems, online public consultations, greater targeting of police and other resources, real-time monitoring of flood dangers and traffic congestion, are all set to become the new infrastructure of the city, as basic a prerequisite for prosperity as the railways were in the nineteenth century.

Creative milieus

The growth of temporary uses has to be seen within the context of myriad economic, social and technological changes that come together spectacularly in relation to the creative or cultural industries sector. It has long been observed that creative entrepreneurs, artists and others are often early entrants to marginal areas, squatting or occupying vacant buildings on temporary leases, adapting them, testing the market and helping to change the image of an area. In fact the role and impact of temporary uses has received most attention in relation to such 'creative milieus'. This is not a new phenomenon or driver, but in recent years there has been growing interest in culture and creativity as essential components of the vibrant, competitive post-industrial city. The creative industries are an important economic sector and many cities are now using cultural policies to project a new image in an increasingly global market.

As we explore in Chapter 9, the creative industries sector, which in its broadest sense is driving many temporary uses, is increasingly based around collaborative projects among individuals, often with diverse professional backgrounds. This reflects broader social changes and the emergence of a more individualistic, entrepreneurial generation, who have no prospect of the linear career enjoyed by their parents. The impact of such changes on the use of buildings could be significant, leading to increased demand for temporary, flexible spaces for design, prototyping, production and storage. Some city governments are beginning to grasp the fact that assisting this new creative sector through the provision of cheap floorspace will enable them to retain their competitive edge in a global economy that is tilting rapidly Eastwards.

34

In conclusion

It would be misleading to isolate any single factor as explaining the growth in temporary urbanism. Temporary activity is an outward manifestation of uncertainty and of many other complex forces present in European and North American cities today. It is not new in itself; what is significant is the range and intensity of such uses today, and the way in which the boundaries between different types of transient use appear to be merging. It is also significant that much of this activity is greeted with evident public delight. Urban planners need to recognise that this enthusiasm is not incidental but represents an appreciation of experimentation and a willingness to 'see what happens' that is perhaps the spirit of our time. When planners and policy makers start to experiment as well, this could represent a powerful mechanism to retune our cities for whatever lies ahead.

Temporary activities also resonate with political agendas. They can be made to happen quickly and can therefore animate spaces that are lying idle and may be attracting public criticism. They can house 'crowd pleasers' for a relatively low capital outlay and most importantly, no perpetually recurring revenue costs. And politicians like nothing better than a 'quick win'.

Scott King's *Temporary Eyesore*: installation commissioned by the Architecture Foundation
BANKSIDE, LONDON, 2008

4: The private sector response

ONE OF THE IMMEDIATE effects of the economic crisis of 2007–8 was the withdrawal of finance from the property market. Across North America and most of Europe development projects were halted and projects rephased, replanned or simply abandoned. In January 2008, property analysts at the investment bank Morgan Stanley warned that the world's largest banks could have about $212bn (£110bn) of assets at risk of default as a result of the global contraction in the commercial property market and the slump in prices. In the UK the commercial property sector had been on a long-term roll, with prices rising by almost half from the end of 2002 to the end of 2006 on the back of cheap credit. However, in the first few months of 2008 the pipeline of commercial transactions dried up and the volume of office developments fell for the first time in four years. Property values were over-inflated and there was a sharp reduction in capital values driven by uncertainty and a lack of confidence caused by the debt markets.[1] While the market did subsequently recover, widespread concerns over the impact of public spending cuts in 2009–10 sent confidence among UK developers plunging to an 18-month low. In the UK the recovery of the market has been slow, and where developers do have access to funds, the tendency has been to invest in land rather than develop it.

As a peripheral outcome of the slump in the market, some property owners in the UK and elsewhere have overcome their traditional resistance to the temporary use of vacant sites and are actually *initiating* temporary schemes. Property slumps have always created both the impetus and the space for new ideas and activities to evolve. In part this is due simply to void spaces becoming available, but it also reflects the response of individuals and companies in having to rethink established practices that no longer work.

The UK property industry had in any case been slowly changing its practices. In the 1980s the standard institutional lease was generally 25 years, on full repairing and insuring terms, and required clear covenants. This has only broken down in the last 15 years. According to the British Property Federation/Investment Property Databank (IPD), the average length of all lettings in 2009–10 was

5.0 years.[2] This is a continuation of the trend for a contraction in lease lengths since 1999, when the average lease length was 9.6 years.[3] Apart from the strict economic drivers, various factors have influenced this. The property recession of the early 1990s allowed new developers to enter into the property market who were prepared to challenge established practices. Occupiers still fresh from the 1990s recession were no longer prepared to accept 25-year commitments.

Institutions are still fighting a rearguard action on the length of leases, but the negotiating power is moving in favour of the tenants. Long-term commitments are seen as not just difficult but risky. Property agents are recognising that shorter leases, especially in a period of fast change and innovation, result in occupiers who 'work' their premises better, creating a 'buzz' that affects the wider area. Although more difficult to manage, it is recognised that value can be created. The mould has been broken and the way opened for far more daring experiments around temporary uses.

The major impediment to wider encouragement of temporary use has been the fear on the part of the property owner that once a site has a temporary use it will be difficult to get repossession, or that the user may demand relocation or even compensation. However, while there have been well-publicised cases of this in several countries,[4] there are relatively few instances of such problems arising in the UK. A more significant issue is likely to arise where the temporary use gains political support in a campaign to make it permanent.

Concerns about the owners' ability to ensure vacant possession of the building, when required, can be overcome by the use of simple tenancies at will, 'meanwhile leases'[5] or through intermediaries such as local authorities taking on the lease and subletting to temporary users. The reliability of temporary occupiers as partners is an important criterion for success. Temporary uses generally flourish where there is a good working relationship between landlord and tenant. Central for this is a clear and mutual understanding that a temporary use is just that, and that it will grow and move on, or fail and disappear. One of the key success factors is certainty around repossession dates. This allows fledgling businesses to plan their next move before the temporary period comes to an end. With exit strategies agreed in advance, temporary occupiers can plan rationally regarding the write-off time for their up-front investments.

The example of Theatre Delicatessen (Case Study 7.3), that to date has successfully negotiated two peppercorn leases with the owners of vacant properties for temporary theatre venues, illustrates that where there is a relationship based on trust, the arrangement can be mutually beneficial. Forming temporary-use associations or alliances can help create the necessary foundation of trust. In Berlin, for example, the Club Commission acts as a reliable contact for the city council.[6] Temporary use also appears to have little real impact on management costs (which can largely be absorbed through the windfall income in contrast to a vacant building providing no return at all). Longer-term portfolio valuation does not appear to present a problem either. Most landlords who are working with temporary occupiers fit them into strategies where the property is untenanted or awaiting redevelopment. In either case the alternative is one of zero return.

Temporary art installation
KING'S CROSS, LONDON

39

The property industry still remains ambivalent about temporary uses. This is illustrated by the attitude of Argent, developers of the 57-acre King's Cross site in central London. They are cautious about temporary uses on their sites, seeing them as symptomatic of a failure to develop. While they acknowledge that lease and license arrangements offer adequate protection, they are more concerned with the less tangible political risks. These, they argue are factors which they cannot control, and a developer can change from local hero to public enemy very quickly when it is time to gain repossession of a site for development. Argent does, however, actively promote arts and cultural events as a stage in the establishment of 'place'. Organised art events are becoming a far more common feature of development than would have been the case 20 years ago. Like any temporary use they serve to create activity and profile for a development. In this case Argent have worked with Sadler's Wells Theatre to put on a temporary production, the Electric Hotel (Case Study 7.2), and have encouraged installations in some of the existing warehouse buildings. They have also sponsored an artist in residence, and invested in art work on temporary site hoardings. Argent has, however, sponsored one truly temporary venture and that is a small market garden run by a local community group. This is housed within building skips that can, and will, be moved as development progresses (Case Study 8.8). There are no formal lease or license agreements beyond a simple exchange of letters.

The fact that a small but growing number of owners are accepting and even initiating temporary activities on their sites suggests that there are no insuperable barriers to managing it from a property owner's perspective. Indeed there can be commercial advantages which justify the extra work and risk. First, occupation improves security and removes the costs of protecting an empty building from damage or illegal use by *uncontrolled* temporary users, such as squatters. This can have a knock-on effect by reducing building insurance. In fact much of the bad press around temporary use centres on the occupation of vacant premises by squatters. However, even within the squatting movement there are responsible occupants. The Oubliette Arthouse, for example (Case Study 7.6), which, squats vacant properties for arts venues, sees itself as 'a group of serious grown-ups running a proper organisation, not a bunch of anarchic chancers daubing graffiti on the walls'.[7] The Arthouse is committed to minimal interference with the property and maintains that it always returns property in a better condition than it found it. It also maintains that its presence can save the owner £200–300 a week in security and maintenance costs, and can prevent fly tipping and damage from break-ins.

Second, temporary use can save money on empty property rates. Businesses with empty properties faced higher business rates from April 2011 when the rateable value thresholds were lowered. The 50 per cent Small Business Rate Relief on empty property has also been cut. This may act as an incentive for landlords to seek temporary occupiers. If a property is let on a casual basis for at least six weeks, then it can be empty again for three months (for retail premises), or six months (for industrial premises), before the owner is once again liable for business rates.[8]

Third, temporary non-commercial uses can attract commercial uses. For example, if part of an empty building is rented cheaply to an independent theatre company, the other part can be leased to a commercial café or restaurant at a higher rent, to service the needs of the audience. Temporary uses often develop a mix of functions, thus supporting planning policies aimed at heterogeneity. Finally, and most importantly, the right kinds of temporary use help to create a 'sense of place' and therefore hasten long-term or permanent development, and make this more profitable as well (Case Studies 4.1 and 4.2). An example of this is Gabriel's Wharf on the South Bank of the Thames, owned by the Development Trust, Coin Street Community Builders (CSCB), established as a time-limited project in 1988. The blank wall of the adjacent London Studios was painted to resemble a typical London high street, shop fronts were added to what were once old garages, and the area was given a simple landscaping treatment. It allowed CSCB to demonstrate to funders and prospective tenants that uses proposed for the more ambitious Oxo Tower Wharf development were viable. It also brought commercial and public life to a part of the river that had long been derelict.[9] The scheme provides jewellery and craft shops operated by designer-makers, as well as cafés and restaurants, and it has remained a highly popular part of the South Bank scene ever since.

40

Gabriel's Wharf
SOUTH BANK, LONDON

A new generation of UK developers such as Chris Brown of Igloo and Ken Dytor of Urban Catalyst, have been experimenting in this environment and are changing the way in which land is developed and used. Ken Dytor speaks of 'creative colonisation' whereby sites are considered for a mixture of uses and activities.[10] Some parts of a site can have high value from the outset, whereas other areas which are less valuable can be used temporarily to allow for eventual colonisation as development rolls out. By opening up land and buildings to itinerant entrepreneurs, options become more fluid. The mantra is moving away from 'planning it' towards 'getting on with it'. Often there are secondary benefits from this approach, that are not planned or even anticipated, but are capable of adding real energy to the process of urban regeneration.

Ken Dytor was behind an early temporary initiative to use a vacant office building as a hostel for rough sleepers. In the 1990s the office market was stagnant, and mirroring the sluggishness of the economy, London had a considerable population of rough sleepers. First Avenue House on High Holborn in central London, owned by British Land, was in need of comprehensive refurbishment in order to be relet. While applying for planning consent for its long-term re-use, British Land entered into a license with a charity to provide temporary hostel accommodation. Although legally covered by a property agreement, there was a high degree of trust between the parties. The use was extended into a second winter, consent was obtained for the refurbishment, a vital need was met in the local area, and temporary rates relief was obtained for the developer. This was a virtuous circle, and an interesting precursor to more recent trends in corporate social responsibility which now forms a key area of reporting to shareholders. The 'political credit' gained by British Land also stood them in good stead for other developments in the area.

Another motivation for the development sector to consider temporary uses is that they can provide a vehicle for experimentation and local consultation as well as an important bridge between developer and community. Temporary events and activities, or community facilities (Case Study 4.3), can build trust, develop long-term partnerships and can spin-off other short-term projects in the wider community. At the Bermondsey Square development in south-east London, for example, the local community wanted a cinema. While this was not financially viable, the developer, Urban Catalyst, responded by licensing premises to a community film maker, an 'unacceptable' institutional tenant who nevertheless was able to create a different kind of value through a series of local projects. Through engaging with local people, the film maker enabled the community to better articulate its ideas for, and needs from, the site, which were then fed back into the development process.

Social entrepreneurs such as Eric Reynolds of Urban Space Management (USM) argue that the temporary use of 'fallow space' should be the norm: 'Set-aside may be acceptable in the countryside, but is surely not in the middle of cities. The default position should be to allow any legally and socially acceptable use on vacant space.'[11] It is clearly upsetting for communities in need of housing or open space to see useful land going to waste due to projects that have been stalled through 'overloading a site with hope value'.[12] Reynolds argues that while this might be acceptable to the shareholders, where the land is in private ownership, when it is in the hands of a public agency it 'surely should not be acceptable to the taxpayer'.[13]

Reynolds has a long pedigree as a promoter of temporary uses. He set up Camden Lock Market in 1974, on a site once blighted by the now abandoned London Motorway Box scheme. The market started in vacant warehousing around a canal-side square, on a seven-year lease and was expected to be replaced by offices. Ultimately, the balance of demand and profitability changed in favour of preserving the market uses. It has now grown into one of the largest tourist draws in the UK and the centre of one of London's most dynamic creative and cultural hubs. A similar venture has transformed the once redundant Spitalfields Market into a crafts, food and arts market which also hosts a range

42

of temporary uses, activities and small start-up enterprises on short-term licenses. Both initiatives started for a temporary period, were developed incrementally and are now established as permanent destinations that have regenerated their hinterlands and, in turn, spawned a new generation of temporary uses and activities (Case Studies 4.4 and 4.5).

Eric Reynolds confirms the supposition that existing financial, legal and even planning frameworks are not necessarily a hindrance to the development of temporary uses. The biggest issue is the conservatism and capacity of professional advisers and city governments to take them up. The decision to allow temporary uses is often made far too late, and the length of time (and expense) in obtaining a temporary consent can similarly make the whole process costly and difficult to pursue. For this reason Reynolds argues that landowners should be required to register land that is out of use (just as car owners are required to register vehicles that are kept off the road), and that large, complex development schemes should have in place an interim- or transitional-use plan that should be triggered if the fallow time is excessive. It is not that the interim use should take precedence over the long-term plans, but that a 'twin-track of activity should be followed, with the meanwhile activity taking place alongside the sometimes protracted planning process'.[14]

That said, an increasing number of larger landowners and developers are now engaged in promoting temporary uses in a drive to gain at least some value from their property (Case Studies 4.6, 4.9 and 4.10). They see the fallow time as an opportunity to market a site or to start to change the image of the area, or even as a chance to gain some political capital with the local planning authorities. Such developer-led temporary initiatives have the advantage of keeping the developer in charge of the process. This should mean that issues around the repossession of sites are less likely to occur. Apart from being a necessary response to a dormant property market, they also represent a good training ground for younger staff to cut their teeth on deals. This is leading some companies to develop an in-house capacity for direct hands-on management. Temporary activities are beginning to acquire a permanent role in the thinking of the once staid property industry. Put crudely, they are good for business and good for the corporate soul.

Reflecting this new interest in temporary uses, the UK magazine *Property Week* launched a national campaign, Site Life, in March 2010, to find lively interim uses for vacant sites and buildings affected by the downturn in the development cycle (Case Studies 4.7, 4.8 and 4.11). The campaign was backed by some of the country's biggest developers, including Land Securities and Westfield, and has the support of the British Property Federation. It has also been endorsed by Prime Minister David Cameron who said that Site Life 'chimes perfectly with what this government is trying to achieve', in terms of building a bigger, stronger society. 'It says to people that when you pass a run-down wasteland or a derelict plot, don't just complain about it as an eyesore; see it as an opportunity. Bring it back to life.'[15] The campaign shows that some developers do care about the local environment and can come up with innovative solutions to the challenges of the economic crisis. With the coalition government proposing a greater localisation of planning powers, landowners are also keen to have more engagement with councils and communities. And since

43

commercial developers are focused on long-term engagement with communities, they can see the potential gain from comparatively minor investment.

The press is taking a lead elsewhere in the world. The *Boston Globe* has put out a call for projects to spruce up prominent eyesores, while the *Los Angeles Times* and *San Francisco Chronicle* have also drawn attention to the scope for interim projects (Case Study 4.13).[16] In another initiative, the Seattle Design Commission launched a competition, Holding Patterns, to solicit interim uses for stalled projects. The competition received over 80 entries from which a shortlist of 13 was selected. These included proposals for street hockey, bike polo and a dodge ball rink, a soccer court, a light installation, canvases for graffiti, a travelling cinema and transient urban farm. The next step will be to turn the ideas into reality on sites throughout the city.[17]

US-based *Architect Magazine* has observed that interest in temporary uses is only beginning to gain traction in the US. It notes that today's stalled developments are unlike those seen in previous slumps in both scale and prevalence: they are 'jumbo-sized', and 'resemble lunar craters, spreading over entire city blocks'.[18] The slow interest in temporary use may in part be due to memories of the confrontations that earlier, well-publicised temporary uses have etched into the minds of landowners.

44

Hawke suggests that there are few documented instances of interim use of brownfield sites in the US, and investigates the institutional barriers that have inhibited this.[19] In the US interim use has no precise definition as a planning term, and as most cities have no official policy on interim uses, schemes must therefore be initiated by private owners. While in Germany and other European countries, local governments have the power to invoke eminent domain (compulsory purchase) to spur interim development, in the US property laws generally require property owner willingness to sanction interim use. Hawke suggests that there is a need to establish and publicise precedents and models for temporary use; permit acquisition needs to be speeded up and made more affordable; rigid zoning needs to be loosened; and the land review process made cheaper. The issue of liability could also be addressed through the city acting as an intermediary.

In Portland, Oregon, No Vacancy!, a partnership between students from Portland State University and Central Eastside Industrial Council (CEIC), undertook a study of the potential for temporary uses in Central Eastside.[20] The study looked at the spaces available for temporary use and tried to match these to potential short-term activities. In the process it identified a number of barriers to temporary use, including a need for more openness between potential users and owners and more matchmaking. Some of the emerging regulatory initiatives to facilitate temporary use in US cities are considered further in Chapter 11.

The situation in the US is starting to change (Case Study 4.12), with more city authorities taking the lead and demonstrating the potential of temporary activities to the development industry. In Miami it is reported that the city is offering to rent empty sites at $1 a year to create temporary parks.

Developers would help to fund the landscaping, but their entitlements would remain for the length of the lease.[21] The concept of interim use already has some precedents in Washington DC. For instance, the old convention centre site doubles as a summer stadium for the Washington Kastles professional tennis team, a depot for discount bus companies, a rain garden for excess stormwater and a training site for the Trapeze School of New York. Vacant retail bays have also been filled with the work of local artists through collaboration with the Commission on the Arts and Humanities. Elsewhere in the city, the annual independent art show *Artomatic* uses empty office buildings in the MoMa neighbourhood. In response, the District of Columbia's Office of Planning (DCOP) has recently launched a Temporary Urbanism initiative to revive dead construction zones and storefronts. It has set up Temporiums (temporary retail projects) to transform vacant shops into places where local entrepreneurs can exhibit and sell their work.[22] Such initiatives are starting to attract attention and discussion from major property owners throughout the city.[23]

As further evidence that the property sector is starting to wake up to the potential of temporary use, a number of private sector intermediary agencies have recently been established to facilitate the process. Space-2 Consulting, a creative property consultancy specialising in short-term use, believes that the cost of short-term uses is 'laughably small' compared with long-term development value, and should be built into the initial development cost.[24] The consultancy has a portfolio of available spaces which can be used for all kinds of short-term business uses, film shoots, photographic projects, exhibitions, launches, theatre rehearsals, art fairs, graduate shows and car parking. Similarly, Brandhub is a company which enables brands to 'pop-up' in units in shopping centres, on retail parks, in business districts and on high streets across the UK on a fixed-cost basis from a week to a year. The company covers all aspects of the process from property search, leasing and insurance, preparation and exit from the space. They can even help to market the business occupant. Similarly, ExtraVerte Ltd was established in Bristol to help implement temporary landscaping schemes on vacant sites as well as seating, shelter, paths and cycle routes, community art, farmers' markets, food concessions, cafés and tennis courts.[25]

Private companies such as Camelot Property Management have also developed a role through matching owners who want live-in 'guardians', with people looking to live in an interesting empty building. It offers vacant properties across Europe that are awaiting a new purpose. The properties range from unique buildings such as abandoned warehouses, cinemas, churches and convents to empty houses and office blocks. For the owners the benefit is that their building is maintained and protected from squatting and vandalism. Guardians need to be flexible since the period of residency can vary from a few months to several years, and the notice period can be as short as two weeks. They are also expected to keep their temporary living space clean and to perform small maintenance tasks. In return they pay a fraction of the going rent to live in an interesting space.

It is easy to see commercial interest in temporary uses as a recent phenomenon. It is, of course, part of a long tradition going back to times when the city was less regulated than it is today. Fringe sites of low commercial value have always been used for marginal activities, particularly associated

45

with waste, recycling and storage (Case Study 4.14). As such their rights of occupation have always been tenuous. There is also a tradition of sites, particularly those near to city centres, being used for temporary car parking, or for income generation via advertising hoardings. In the UK, National Car Parks (NCP) developed their business from the fortuitous coincidence of sites vacant from wartime bombing, and the growth of the motor car. These 'traditional' temporary uses fulfil an important role in supporting the urban economy and the pressure in many cities for their permanent development is likely to leave significant gaps in a range of necessary supportive services.

46

Temporary landscaping screen
GREENWICH PENINSULA, LONDON

The significant change today is that there are a far wider range of temporary activities seeking space, and that commercial interest in them increasingly forms part of deliberate estates management, development and marketing strategies. Temporary uses are beginning to move into the mainstream. It is also noteworthy that many of the case studies in this chapter share similar geographical features. Some of the most creative applications are on the margin, on sites where commercial development risk is higher, and where the scale or location of the site creates long-term development challenges. A considerable number also occupy the 'Goldilocks zone', on the edge of successful commercial districts with high economic energy (and pedestrian footfall), but where long-term economic development is not quite ready to take place.

Case Study
#4.1 | The Lido
SOUTHWARK, LONDON

Developer, entrepreneur and urbanist Roger Zogolovich has owned the site in Union Street, Southwark for over 10 years. Although he has consent to build offices and flats, this awkward site is simply on the wrong side of the tracks from London's South Bank. His championing of temporary uses aims to start to create the conditions whereby this backland site is seen as a place in its own right. Zogolovich sees intrinsic value in temporary uses as a means of allowing communities to redefine their boundaries or 'turf'. This can be a dynamic urban model. As with the idea of 'colonisation' proposed by Igloo, temporary uses have the ability to move out and pioneer changes in their wider neighborhoods. Here gentrification is seen as a positive element of urban renewal. The success of temporary interventions causes upward price adjustment, displacement and the emerging pioneers move on to other areas.

The first temporary intervention, a lido, created by the French collective EXYZT (architect-builders, graphic designers and photographers), Alex Roemer of constructLab and film maker Sara Muzio, appeared in the summer of 2008. The event was curated by the Architecture Foundation (AF) as part of the London Festival of Architecture. The Lido provided a sundeck, chairs, paddling pool, beach huts, bar and, in the tradition of Roman baths and Turkish hammams, a functioning sauna as a venue for social gathering. It was conceived as an expression of EXYZT's approach to urban renewal, which is based on the idea that a community of users actively creating and inhabiting their urban environment is the key to generating a vibrant city. EXYZT see architecture as a 'means of opening up a space for invention, creation, improvisation, encounter, meeting, exchange and enhancing human relationships'. It was not intended to be a static piece of architecture dropped into Southwark, but a dynamic installation changing constantly through the contributions of its users. In the run-up to the installation the organisers formed links with local community groups, providing them with a new place to hold events. The Lido was built over a four-week period and was open for a variety of social activities (lunchtime picnics, after school clubs, evening drinks and film club) over a five-day period. It demonstrated how, within the context of an architectural festival, a temporary physical installation can create encounters with the unexpected. The project subsequently inspired *muf* architecture/art to commission EXYZT to design the Dalston Mill (Case Study 10.3).

SOURCES: www.architecturefoundation.org.uk/about/overview.

http://architecturelab.net/07/bankside-urban-forest-by-witherford-watson-mann/.

'Changing the settings, changing politics', 8 July 2008, retrieved from
    http://southwarklido.wordpress.com/changing-the-settings-changing-politics/.

www.lfa2010.org/event.php?id=103&name=finland_the_nest_an_urban_timber_garden.

D. Messu and V. Patteeuw, *Southwark Lido: The Book*, 11 July 2008, retrieved from
    http://southwarklido.wordpress.com/.

www.waywardplants.org/ (all accessed 23 February 2011).

48

The Lido by EXYZT Architects
100 UNION STREET, SOUTHWARK, LONDON

Union Street Urban Orchard

SOUTHWARK, LONDON

The second temporary use on the Union Street site, an orchard, emerged from Witherford Watson Mann Architects' Bankside Urban Forest Strategy (Case Study 10.2). This was one of a patchwork of interventions in a complex urban design strategy for the area. The AF again curated and commissioned this temporary use to coincide again with the biennial London Festival of Architecture in 2010.

The orchard was designed by Heather Ring of the Wayward Plant Registry and included 85 fruit trees and other edible plants, a seed library, greenhouse, a living wall, a tyre garden and a railway arch turned into a cinema. Many of the timber structures were reclaimed from the Southwark Lido project, producing an interesting layering of temporary activity. Other elements included a ping-pong table in a builder's skip created by Oliver Bishop-Young, and the Nest, a pavilion designed and built by a group of students and architects from the Department of Architecture at Helsinki's Aalto University.

The project incorporated a series of events and activities such as jam-making, bee-keeping, willow sculpture and discussions about alternative urban development. After three months of activity, the garden was dismantled, the AF organised 'Make and Take' sessions for people to build useful items from the orchard materials, and all the trees were donated for permanent planting in local estates, schools and other community gardens.

The scheme also hosted the Pod, a temporary building designed by Bill Dunster of Zed Factory. This is part of a wider set of ideas around temporary buildings that Zed Factory are developing with a view to identifying a series of sites which could accommodate communities of 20 or more people. The Pod is modular and comes in a flat pack at a cost of £25,000 (or £15,000 with self-assembly). It is off-grid, using photovoltaics, and incorporates a composting toilet. Individual Pods can be joined together, and when the site is required for development, the Pod can be craned onto the back of a truck and moved. This is a modern permutation of the post-war prefab or the trailer park. Unlike these, however, it is zero-carbon and a permanent building form where the location instead, is temporary.

SOURCES: www.architecturefoundation.org.uk/about/overview.

http://architecturelab.net/07/bankside-urban-forest-by-witherford-watson-mann.

www.lfa2010.org/event.php?id=103&name=finland_the_nest_an_urban_timber_garden.

www.waywardplants.org/ (all accessed 23 February 2011).

Urban Orchard by Heather Ring
100 UNION STREET, SOUTHWARK, LONDON

Case Study
#4.3 The Deptford Project

DEPTFORD, LONDON

Rebecca Molina of Studio Raw set up her first enterprise, a coffee shop, in an unused space in Greenwich Station in south-east London, at the age of 16. She was then drawn into the local hub of creative enterprises and the fast-moving world of digital graphic design at the end of the 1990s. The Deptford Project emerged from her involvement in staging community-business networking events (RSVP LONDON.co.uk), and she is representative of the emerging breed of social entrepreneur working in the cross-over of different professional disciplines and influences.

Deptford itself is an impoverished community on the fringe of the wealthier districts of Greenwich to the east, and the City of London to the north. It has been the subject of numerous unsuccessful regeneration attempts over the last two decades. The Deptford Project originated through the work of the Cathedral Group, a developer which had been in discussions with Lewisham Council, with a view to redeveloping vacant sites in the area. Studio Raw worked with Cathedral Group to develop the idea of a community hub, with a café and a meeting place to act as a focus for debate about the redevelopment. For Cathedral it was an opportunity to develop the local dialogue and gain community support in an area where genuine community engagement is difficult to achieve.

The Project is based in an old railway carriage which houses the café and meeting place. Adjacent land provides workshops and event space (including a stage and an open-air cinema), where the highly diverse local communities can socialise and develop new ideas. Intrinsic to the whole concept is the fact that this is temporary, and seeks to seize both the opportunities of the space and of the moment. The carriage stands on a length of railway track which is symbolic of the fact that it can and will move around the area.

The Deptford Project has become a successful place for community dialogue and engagement. It provides a much-needed café, meeting place and events venue in an area where such facilities are scarce. On an average day the café will serve over 150 customers, and as a community enterprise it manages both to cover its costs and make a small return. The cinema sessions are extremely popular and can draw 300 people over a weekend. Both parties see it as a long-term relationship where temporary uses will move from site to site as part of the development process.

SOURCE: Interview with Rebecca Molina, Studio Raw.

53

Railway carriage in use as a community hub by Studio Raw/Rebecca Molina
THE DEPTFORD PROJECT, LONDON

Case Study
#4.4

Spitalfields Market
LONDON

Spitalfields Market, an old fruit and vegetable market in London's East End, came up for office redevelopment in the mid-1980s. The 1990s property crash stalled commercial proposals, and created a 4.5-acre vacant site. Urban Space Management (USM) won a competition to manage the space. They carried out very basic adaptations to the 240,000 square feet of market buildings to accommodate a mix of interim retail, culture, sport, food, stalls, small retail units, workshops and studios. They also created an opera stage for the Market Opera House, and put a swimming pool into a redundant basement. The project has created over 1,000 jobs and has helped to transform the surrounding areas of Spitalfields and Shoreditch into one of London's newest and most vibrant cultural centres. USM's Eric Reynolds states, 'This is a good example of a meanwhile use rolling on through transition to become part of the long-term use'.

SOURCES: Interview with Eric Reynolds.

E. Reynolds, 'Interwhile uses', article submitted for publication in *Journal of Urban Regeneration and Renewal* 4, 2011, provided by the author.

54

Spitalfields Market by Urban Space Management/Eric Reynolds
LONDON

Case Study
#4.5

Trinity Buoy Wharf
LONDON

In 1998 Eric Reynolds founded Trinity Buoy Wharf, an enterprise that exemplifies his 'start-small-but-start-now' approach to development. The evolutionary approach has involved a 'ladder of interim uses through transitional to longer-term uses'. The growth in activity and value across the 3.5-acre site has been achieved without either wholesale demolition or major capital investment. The land was transferred free from the London Docklands Development Corporation and the Wharf is a trust that ploughs profit back into the area. Many of the new structures are shipping containers, symbolising the area's transient nature. Tenants have five-year leases with three-month notice periods. While it is unlikely to move and in this sense is a permanent fixture, its business ethos is to evolve, change its shape, content and offer and to spin off temporary interventions, installations and open-space improvements on adjacent sites. There are now 90,000 square feet of inhabited space, a third of which is in new buildings, and 450 people are actively engaged on the site.

SOURCES: Interview with Eric Reynolds.

E. Reynolds, 'Interwhile uses', article submitted for publication in *Journal of Urban Regeneration and Renewal* 4, 2011, provided by the author.

55

Trinity Buoy Wharf by Urban Space Management/Eric Reynolds
LONDON

Case Study
#4.6

Oxford Street

LONDON

Park House, Oxford Street was a 4,000-square-metre levelled building site near Marble Arch, owned by Land Securities. Oxford Street, which averages over 2,400,000 visitors per week, is perhaps an unlikely location for a vacant site, but the development was delayed during the recent property slump. Rather than leave the site empty, Land Securities employed events specialist Think Tank Events to launch the site as a flexible and adaptable space for hire. The aim was partly to generate income, but also to maintain activity and footfall in this part of the West End.

The programme of events on the site included the Big Smile Festival that ran for six days over the August Bank Holiday in 2009 and attracted over 55,000 people. It also hosted the final leg of the Disney XD Beach Soccer Roadshow, which involved bringing 300 tonnes of sand onto the site. The last event, the *Dinosaurs Unleashed* exhibition in 2010, saw it transformed into a Jurassic forest complete with 24 life-size animatronic dinosaurs that attracted 3,000 visitors a day, creating a real destination for the west of Oxford Street.

The programme had to strike a difficult balance between the potential public demand for activities and the restrictions imposed by the planners from Westminster Council. Initially activities were arranged under the 28-day permitted development rights. Land Securities were careful to engage local residents through a series of consultation meetings, and subsequently were able to achieve a temporary planning consent for the activities (which came with restrictions on operating days, noise and servicing arrangements). Long-term development of the site commenced in 2011.

56

SOURCES: 'Westfield and Land Securities back campaign to let communities use mothballed development sites', press release, 15 March 2010, retrieved from www.bpf.propertymall.com/newsroom/pressreleases/document/23863/westfield-and-land-securities-back-campaign-to-let-communities-use-mothballed-development-sites (accessed 23 March 2011).

Dinosaurs Unleashed exhibition, site of Park House
OXFORD STREET, LONDON, 2010

Case Study | Wellington Place
#4.7 | LEEDS

Developer MEPC recognised that its 22-acre site at Wellington Place, Leeds, was perceived to be just off the prime city centre and that with adverse market conditions, the site was unlikely to be developed in the near future. This presented an opportunity to initiate a process of place-making in order to change market perceptions. The company has planted saplings and gardens and spearheaded the development of 16 allotments, a five-a-side football pitch, beekeeping, an office suite made of containers, and a programme of events such as lunchtime fitness classes and concerts. It has also started to install the basic infrastructure of streets as set out in the site masterplan. Around £750,000 has been spent on demolition and preparation for the long-term redevelopment of the site, around £300,000 on making the site safe, accessible and presentable, while the football pitches cost around £70,000 and the allotments just £1,000.

The costs are offset against savings in security and maintenance costs, but more importantly against the value of the positive public relations. MEPC believes that the long-term value of the works is 'immeasurable in terms of changing perception, getting buy-in for the scheme from local people and the council and attracting tenants'. MEPC will ultimately redevelop the site, but will do so gradually. The company has since applied this learning to other sites in its portfolio.

57

SOURCES: J. Rigby, 'How meanwhile can be worthwhile', *Property Week*, 7 May 2010.

Site Life Debate (in association with the Meanwhile Project and *Property Week*), 2010, retrieved from www.meanwhile.org.uk/useful-info/misc/PW_roundtable_Meanwhile_06aaproved.pdf (accessed 28 January 2011).

'Westfield and Land Securities back campaign to let communities use mothballed development sites', press release, 15 March 2010, retrieved from www.bpf.propertymall.com/newsroom/pressreleases/document/23863/westfield-and-land-securities-back-campaign-to-let-communities-use-mothballed-development-sites (accessed 23 March 2011).

Case Study
#4.8

Westfield
BRADFORD

The subversion, by an unknown graffiti artist, of developer Westfield's name on hoardings around the site of the stalled £320m Bradford shopping centre scheme, into a sign saying 'wastefield', led the company to team up with the council to open the site up for temporary uses.

In April 2010, landscaping work commenced to create the Bradford Urban Garden on the 10-acre site. Westfield made the site safe and installed walkways, green spaces and lighting. The interim use also opened up pathways across the city and provided opportunities for local engagement and skills training. The council, Westfield and Yorkshire Forward committed £100,000 for the works, and the Meanwhile Project (supported by the government) put up another £25,000. Umbrella arts organisation Fabric had a small grant to animate the space with arts and community projects.

SOURCE: 'Westfield and Land Securities back campaign to let communities use mothballed development sites', press release, 15 March 2010, retrieved from www.bpf.propertymall.com/newsroom/pressreleases/document/23863/westfield-and-land-securities-back-campaign-to-let-communities-use-mothballed-development-sites (accessed 23 March 2011).

58

Case Study
#4.9

Camden Town
LONDON

Camden Town Unlimited (CTU) is a Business Improvement District (BID) established in 2006. Camden Town has a long history of experimental and temporary uses. Although only a mile from some of the wealthiest areas of central London, historically it has been an area with a transient population, and a home for artists, artisans and small businesses. More recently Camden Lock Market has established the area as a centre of youth culture with a growing cluster of creative industries in fashion, design and television.

CTU has established the Collective at 37 Camden High Street. This old bakery was purchased by London and Argyll Properties with the intention of turning it into a private art gallery. Adapting to the economic downturn, they have worked with CTU to develop it into a shop, flexible workspace and gallery. The workspace accommodates 30 businesses. The desks are on wheels allowing different layouts, and the entire space can be cleared for exhibitions. At present business occupants just contribute towards expenses, and the aim is that they will pay a nominal rent of around £2 per square foot. But this is not seen as a revenue-generating enterprise. For the BID and the landowner, it is about bringing a vacant building back into use and supporting new business start-ups that can add to the economic vibrancy of the area.

SOURCE: Interview with Chris Shaw, Shaw Corporation.

The Collective
CAMDEN TOWN, LONDON

Case Study
#4.10

Boxpark
SHOREDITCH, LONDON

Boxpark, sited on a corner of the 10.5-acre Bishopsgate Goods Yard site, is marketed as the 'world's first pop-up mall'. With a labyrinth of vaulted brick spaces, the Goods Yard site has been vacant for over 40 years, during which time it has hosted various temporary uses from raves to travellers' communities. It has now been acquired by the development partnership of Hammersons and Ballymore.

The site lies on the border between the City of London and the more edgy communities of Shoreditch and Spitalfields. The area is characterised by up-and-coming designers many of which trade out of converted warehouse units, studios within the ex-Truman's Brewery on Brick Lane or market stalls such as those at Spitalfields Market and Brick Lane. The area is one of central London's 'creative milieus' with galleries, studios and workshops running in a belt from Clerkenwell and Old Street to Brick Lane and Spitalfields. The potential for temporary uses in this area attracted retailer and entrepreneur Roger Wade, former owner of clothing brand Boxfresh. His marketing consultant, Donna Lambert, ex-PR/Marketing Director of Shaftesbury, has extensive experience of temporary retailing going back to one of the first branded pop-up shops selling Adidas trainers in Carnaby Street in 2001. Wade's enthusiasm is based on the fact that pop-ups offer an opportunity to test the market and bring in emerging talent, especially from art and design schools. The marketing of the units will be targeted at new fashion and product designers in the locality wishing to make a first step into direct selling to their customers. Traders will be offered leases as short as one year and will only have to pay for the fitting-out costs of a small container.

The concept: Boxpark
SHOREDITCH, LONDON

Boxpark takes the tried-and-tested practices of pop-up retailing and turning old shipping containers into functioning spaces to an entirely new level. There are already established shipping container developments in London, with one example at Trinity Buoy Wharf providing incubator units for small businesses. Temporary incubator spaces are not new to Shoreditch either as the re-use of redundant tube carriages at nearby Village Underground demonstrates (see pp. 171–4). The flourishing creative re-use scene locally is an apt reflection of the creative spirit of Shoreditch.

Boxpark opened in the summer of 2011 and comprises 60 containers stripped and refitted in a minimalist style to create low-cost, low-risk shop units. They were assembled to create a complete pop-up high street but are moveable around the site. As permanent development of the site will not start for perhaps another five years, Boxpark represents a pop-up scheme, but one with a sense of permanence. It has a three- to five-year lease from the developers, and expects either to disappear or relocate. However, a project as ambitious and long-lived as this will leave an imprint on the consumer's perception of the area, benefiting the landowner and the locality alike.

SOURCES: K. Long, 'Shopping and shipping', the *Evening Standard*, London, 2 March 2011, retrieved from
http://goliath.ecnext.com/coms2/gi_0199-14468686/SHOPPING-AND-SHIPPING-Boxpark-is.html
(accessed 16 April 2011).

Interview with Roger Wade, Boxpark.

The marketing suite: Boxpark and Brick Lane Flea Market
SHOREDITCH, LONDON

Case Study
#4.11

New Islington
EAST MANCHESTER

As part of *Property Week*'s Site Life campaign, the magazine teamed up with developer Urban Splash to launch a competition for a site in east Manchester. The winner will design and deliver an interim use for a prominent site in Urban Splash's New Islington development. The temporary use will remain in place for at least a year while Urban Splash develops other parts of the 30-acre site.

New Islington is a 10-minute walk from the city centre and was known for cotton manufacturing in the nineteenth century. Mills, warehouses and associated back-to-back housing once covered the entire area. The site has already been cleared and remodelled with canals and green spaces, and new buildings are starting to appear. However, the scale of regeneration is vast and there are still years of construction ahead. The aim of the interim-use project on Old Mill Street is to make one of the most prominent cleared sites both visually attractive and interesting for residents and visitors, while it awaits development.

The competition closed in August 2010. The three finalists included a lighting scheme to create a 'vivid field of red', reflecting its status as a 'space in waiting'; a field of flax, *Sow-Sew*, reintroducing what was once a locally grown product and providing sheds for local weavers; and *Loom to Bloom*, a planting scheme with flowers in colour coordinated rows, producing a striped field when in full bloom.

SOURCE: R. Hattan, 'Competition: new land of opportunity', *Property Week*, 2 July 2010, retrieved from www.propertyweek.com/comment/competition-new-land-of-opportunity/5002071.article (accessed 16 October 2010).

Field by Jock McFadyen and Chris Dyson: winning scheme for the Site Life competition
NEW ISLINGTON, EAST MANCHESTER

63

Case Study
#4.12

LentSpace

NEW YORK

LentSpace in New York City is a temporary project that was realised through the cooperation of the site's owner, Trinity Real Estate, and the Lower Manhattan Cultural Council (LMCC). Designed by Brooklyn-based Interboro, a temporary art park and a tree nursery have been installed at LentSpace, a cleared 0.5-acre site at Canal Street in Manhattan. It opened in the autumn of 2009, and will remain for a three-year period. The shortage of open spaces in the area drove the decision to create a tree nursery with planters that will be moved to surrounding streets when the project is over. Responding to the developer's requirements that the site should be closable at night, the designers installed a wooden fence of eight-foot-wide panels that pivot open, inviting passersby to enter. The panels also have built-in benches facing the open space, which features a programme of changing sculpture exhibitions.

SOURCES: http://archpaper.com/news/articles.asp?id=5236.

www.interboropartners.net/2009/lent-space/.

www.lmcc.net/cultural_programs/lentspace/ (all accessed 2 November 2011).

64

LentSpace

CANAL STREET, NEW YORK

Case Study
#4.13

Temporary uses
SAN FRANCISCO

In 2009, the *San Francisco Chronicle* invited local design teams to produce conceptual schemes for specific vacant lots. This inspired action by two property owners: Turnberry Lansing, proprietor of 45 Lansing Street, and Fifield Echelon Investors LLC, owner of 399 Fremont Street, both located in the Rincon Hill Neighbourhood. Both owners enlisted the help of multi-disciplinary studio Rebar to enhance their sites in the short term. At 45 Lansing Street, Rebar installed a pollinator garden in the spring of 2010. This provides a habitat for pollinating species such as honey bees, butterflies and hummingbirds. At 399 Fremont Street, Rebar installed a nursery for the propagation of street trees, in partnership with the Friends of the Urban Forest. In return for a small initial investment, the nursery will provide around 1,500 trees within 18 months of inception, while greening an otherwise barren lot and providing work experience for the local youth.

Urban gardens and retail stores are also blooming along four vacant blocks on Octavia Boulevard that were created when a section of the 101 Freeway damaged in an earthquake was torn down. The city had intended to sell the sites for residential development but the plans were halted when the recession hit. One plot was lent to a community group for an urban garden, the Hayes Valley Farm. Following this success the city has leased adjoining sites for a temporary beer garden and small cafés and shops within adapted shipping containers. Vendors are funding the majority of building costs in exchange for a low monthly rent.

65

SOURCES: *Property Week*, 'How the West was won over by temporary uses', 4 June 2010.

www.rebargroup.org/projects/ (accessed 15 June 2011).

Case Study
#4.14

Trafalgar Dock
LIVERPOOL

Trafalgar Dock, a redundant dockyard and demolished warehouse site in Liverpool, was used for two years as a temporary site for recycling demolition aggregates from an inner-city development site two kilometres away. It was the result of collaboration between the landowner (Merseyside Docks and Harbour Company), developer (Grosvenor Estates), recycling contractor (PP O'Connor) and the planning authority (Liverpool City Council), who recognised the growing need to recycle demolition wastes efficiently and sustainably. Once the issues of traffic management, planning permission and a waste license were dealt with, the temporary mobile facility provided a means of sorting and processing wastes locally, reducing both transport costs and the amount of material that ultimately required disposal in landfill.

SOURCE: CABE Space, *Public Space Lessons: Land in Limbo: Making the Best Use of Vacant Urban Spaces*, London: CABE Space, May 2008, p. 4.

Mobile café
SOUTH BANK, LONDON

5: Temporary arenas for consumption

CONSUMERISM, THE SYSTEMATIC CREATION and nurturing of desires to purchase ever more goods and services, drives many aspects of life today. What we consume increasingly defines who we are. We 'buy' lifestyles, consume to feel better, and use consumer status symbols to judge the socio-economic status and social stratification of others. We feel superior to those who consume less, and feel anxious if we do not consume as much as our neighbours. We define our 'wealth', by Gross National Product (GNP), a measure of the success of our society to consume. Some even argue that consumerism is increasingly a substitute for healthy human relationships.

Mass consumerism, a twentieth- and twenty-first-century phenomenon, is driven through ever more sophisticated consumer research, and more inventive advertising, display and promotional techniques. Large areas of cities have been carefully designed as arenas for consumption. The idea of 'fashion' has expanded to pressure people to buy not out of need, but for style or conformity, through stirring anxieties over the possession of things that are not in vogue. Attitudes, intellectual arguments, even spiritual values have evolved to glorify continued consumption as personally fulfilling and economically desirable. Consumer credit has been expanded to create mass markets for the consumer goods that stimulate economic growth, and in the process has created a culture where high levels of personal debt are the norm. Given the central role of consumption in society it is not surprising that temporary venues for consumption have been one of the most common manifestations of the phenomenon in recent years.

One of the key characteristics of the modern consumer is increasing time stress. The pace of life is accelerating, and we are cramming more and more activities into ever-diminishing timeframes. People often point to work, chores, childcare and other such duties as the reasons for time pressure. However, there is also evidence that the perception of increased time pressure may come from the sheer abundance of choices available to consumers.[1] Loy provides a more spiritual perspective on this issue and argues that the current experience of 'space–time compression should be understood as part of a more general social crisis of meaning'.[2] We try to fill a deep sense of 'lack' infecting our empty core, by objectifying ourselves in some fashion, but no object is ever truly satisfying since this sense of lack is a spiritual longing. The collapse of our faith in the future causes a heightened sense of anxiety that results in a compulsion to do things quickly and an increasing sense of time pressure. Whatever its cause, the consumer response to time stress has spawned a whole new sector of the economy in time-saving products from ready meals to gadgets, and services such as internet shopping and home delivery. The justification is that it allows the individual to get on with other tasks, fuelled by high-energy drinks and cereal bars. Advertising constantly reinforces the message that this is a desirable lifestyle, where we can 'enjoy more' and 'come alive' or 'feel free'.

Technologies, such as mobile phones, the internet and social networking, that demand instant responses have also speeded up the pace of life in affluent societies, as has the growing obsession with 'real-time' information (on other people, products, events and news), through 'alerts' via Twitter, email and texts. Market observers Trendwatching.com term the growing desire for real-time products, services and experiences, and for instant gratification as 'NOWISM'.[3] This revolves around pop-ups, vending machines and alerts that link instant information to the possibility of instant buying. Products and services are becoming more fragmented so that the 'budget conscious and time-poor consumers can collect as many different experiences as possible'. Trendwatching.com predicts that 'live' experiences and those that have even a hint of 'performance', will 'rise in value in a NOWISM world'. The tendency to live more 'for the moment' can be linked to Bauman's arguments on liquid modernity described in Chapter 3. As a result, survival tactics such as flexibility, adaptability and opportunism become increasingly relevant and individuals' lives can become ever more fragmented into short-term projects. The general outcome of all this is that fleeting opportunities for immediate consumption of all kinds are growing.

Trendwatching.com has also identified the emergence of what it terms 'transumers', that is, consumers who are motivated by experiences rather than 'fixed' goods that require a high outlay and quickly become outdated, boring or onerous to maintain.[4] On an everyday level, there is a boom in leasing, rather than purchasing goods. One reason is that with 'ever shorter product development cycles, leasing ensures consumers can always enjoy the latest'. The trend has moved beyond rental cars, mobile phones or timeshare properties and there are now options to rent handbags, dresses, even jewellery. The trend to enjoy objects for a shorter period of time results in many more second hand goods, which is where eBay, flea markets and car boot sales come into their own. They have made used goods an acceptable alternative to buying new, and have enabled both temporary ownership and easy disposal for the masses. There are, of course, strong and compelling reasons why this is being encouraged. Ever shorter consumer cycles, while disastrous for the environment, are extremely good for business.

There is also a growing range of public and private spaces catering for the needs of the time starved consumer on the move. Starbucks is the classic global example, offering sofas and free Wi-Fi to its customers. But such spaces are also springing up in supermarkets, hospitals, hotel lobbies, gyms, libraries, bookshops and airports. In Japan, China and South Korea there are even spaces offering gaming, reading and DVD booths. Such spaces are now beginning to play an important role, amidst the world of virtual communication, by 'reintegrating us into city life'.[5] Major cities like London and New York have also seen a growth in business clubs where individuals, often from a related field, can meet, eat and do business. Within all of these venues traditional distinctions between spaces for work, play, culture, eating or socialising are blurring. These 'commercial living-room-like settings'[6] facilitate a range of out-of-home and out-of-office activities – things like watching a film, reading, meeting friends and business associates. Taking over from the public house and public library, these new places supplement cramped or shared living space, and allow a temporary escape from work and family responsibilities.

Popupcity.net, a website recording new or temporary urban phenomena, has observed a recent trend for coffee bars to spring up in all sorts of unusual urban settings, effectively bridging the traditional divides between shops and services, meeting places, and eating and drinking.[7] Many urban shops and services such as print shops, launderettes and bike repair shops have introduced the coffee bar. The site notes that the combination works particularly well for services or shops that have some lifestyle component, and where groups of people with a shared subculture such as cyclists or photographers might like to meet. Wash & Coffee in Munich combines a launderette, a coffee bar and community meeting place. In Copenhagen, Fotocaféen combines a print shop, meeting place for the photography scene and coffee bar and provides free Wi-Fi. In London, Drink, Shop & Do, which started as a Christmas pop-up, is a design shop and café bar that sells products from emerging designers and, as the name suggests, also hosts activity workshops in knitting, card and hat making and ... Scrabble.[8] And there are numerous cycle shop coffee bars in places like Seattle, Amsterdam and New York combining bicycle repair services with meeting places for cyclists.

69

Pop-up shops

The new consumer phenomenon, the 'pop-up shop' cannot be explained simply by the glut of surplus retail units on the high streets, significant though this is. The pop-up also reflects new trends in market research, marketing and selling that are both legitimising and encouraging temporary retailing. One of the first 'cool' pop-up shops in the UK, The Shop, was opened by the Young British Artists Tracey Emin and Sarah Lucas in 1993 as a means of selling their work. For six months Emin and Lucas rented a former doctor's surgery in east London, where they made and sold their work: T-shirts, baby vests, badges, ashtrays and key rings.[9] They were followed by a wave of similar pop-ups by artists, designers and crafts makers seeking to sell their own work.

Zoe Williams neatly sums up the essential attractions of pop-up shops as 'trying to replicate what's cool about the internet, compared to the old media. It's instant, it's temporary, but most of all, it doesn't need a huge amount of cash to set it up, so the door opens to people who are outside the wealthy elite, younger, cooler, more subversive and less conventional'.[10] The limited time span, in combination with unusual locations, creates a buzz, cachet and hip image. Due to the recession, the increased availability of affordable retail space has made it easier and more attractive to set up such pop-up stores. In London, artists and designers continue to seek a first foothold on the fringes of established retail areas. For example, the Dialogue Collective, a London-based group of artists with a background in jewellery and silversmithing, opened a pop-up in June 2010 in Columbia Road, timed to coincide with London Jewellery Week.[11]

More recently another wave of temporary retail projects has emerged, backed by established global brands, that can loosely be described as marketing initiatives. Such corporate pop-ups have recognised the cachet that has been associated with pop-up restaurants, bars, galleries and shops that were widely perceived as 'cool happenings' even 'underground' events.[12] Trendwatching.com explains the phenomenon as a response to abundance: 'with a reduced need for constant securing of the basics, and goods so plentiful that the status derived from them is sometimes close to nil, the only thing that remains is consumption of the thrill, the experience, the new'.[13] The allure of special edition products will often attract consumers obsessed with the chance of buying something unique, and the very impermanence of the showcase provides an added exclusivity. This in turn attracts media interest and free advertising. There are numerous examples: a branch of Central Perk, the coffee shop from the TV series *Friends*, opened in Soho, London for a fortnight in 2009 and (in addition to actually selling coffee) was used to promote a limited edition DVD box set of the series. Marmite opened a temporary 1,776 square foot pop-up store in London's Regent Street in November 2009. Marmite's owner, Unilever, maintained that although the store made only a marginal profit, the project was successful because it created 'a buzz around the brand', and enabled the company to communicate directly with customers.[14] While it is hard to quantify the scale of pop-up retailing, on average two or three new pop-ups were reviewed in the London media each week in 2010.

Pop-up retailing offers novel opportunities for targeting and customisation and is now so widespread, that it is fast becoming a mainstream branding strategy.[15] As pop-up shops become abundant, brands are focusing on ever more outrageous pop-up ideas (Case Study 5.1). They are also turning their attention from merely selling to using pop-ups for consumer research, either to gauge the suitability of a new location, to try out a new form of service or to conduct product research. In October 2010, for example, smoothie maker Innocent ran a pop-up café in London that provided five portions of fruit and vegetables for £5. The setting allowed informal market research, generated considerable goodwill among participants as well as media coverage, and offered Innocent better value for money than a traditional advertising campaign.[16]

Pop-ups have even moved beyond vacant retail shops into purpose-designed temporary showcases and mobile shops. Mobile shops have always provided a service where few facilities existed, or have served a fleeting demand such as for ice cream in fine weather or fast food in association with festivals. But *targeted* mobile selling is spreading. Trendwatching.com cites many examples: Venue VBOX in Singapore is a portable store in a shipping container that can be set up temporarily wherever there is an event with which a retailer wishes to align its brand. Similarly, Uniqlo has used 'designer' shipping containers as stores in New York City. The company Vacant turns the temporary approach into a long-term exclusive retail concept. Its stores open for one month only in empty spaces in major cities across the globe, showcasing a range of limited edition products from established brands and emerging designers. Locations are announced by email to Vacant Club members just before opening thus taking the 'exclusivity element' one stage further. In a further elaboration on the pop-up concept, Boxpark, which claims to be the 'world's first pop-up mall' was established in London's Shoreditch in 2011 in 60 shipping containers (Case Study 4.10).

Temporary shops as a response to vacancy

As we showed in Chapter 3, the economic downturn is having a visible impact on town centres around the world, and in the UK around 13 per cent of shops were vacant at the end of June 2010.[17] With significant structural changes occurring in retailing, the outlook for the reoccupation of shops is not promising, and some predict that many vacant shops will not find a traditional use again.

The temporary use of vacant shops for outlets such as charity shops has a long history. While charity shops are often seen as a sign of declining retail health and rental values, they are an important part of the recycling chain and provide access to cheap goods for people on low incomes.[18] Boarded-up shops can attract fly-posting, litter and vandalism, can fall into disrepair and create a sense of neglect that has serious consequences for the wider area (Case Study 5.4). One study lists the benefits of temporary use as: reducing blight, providing accessible community space, reanimating the high street, adding diversity and avoiding waste.[19] Others see the downturn as an opportunity to loosen the stranglehold of national and multi-national brands that has reduced the differentiation and variety of UK shopping areas to an extent that is rarely seen in cities elsewhere in Europe (Case Study 5.2).[20] A recent UK government publication states:

> it is vital that we do all we can to enable vacant properties to be used for temporary purposes until demand for retail premises starts to improve. Not only will this help to ensure that towns and high streets are attractive places where people want to go, it can also stimulate a wide range of other uses such as community hubs, arts and cultural venues, and informal learning centres, that can unlock people's talent and creativity.[21]

Vacant retail units can also provide low-cost space from which would-be entrepreneurs can develop their ideas and test the market. In times of recession, policy makers have repeatedly turned to the potential of small firms to provide the future economic impetus and create jobs and growth. The present UK government is similarly promoting the potential of former retail units as business incubators.

Both the property industry and central government are urging local authorities to promote flexibility and innovation in the use of such retail units.[22] The UK Department for Communities and Local

71

Government (CLG) has established a £5.6 million fund to bring empty shops back into use in the recession. The Meanwhile Project aims to boost community uses of empty properties in town centres.[23] It works with landlords, landowners, developers and local authorities to relieve them temporarily of the liabilities (such as insurance and rates) that come with vacant property. It also helps to find 'meanwhile' uses, provides step-by-step guidance to would-be users, cash grants, training, help and advice lines and has a network of over 450 members.[24] Its model Meanwhile Lease overcomes the difficulties of the Landlord and Tenant Act of 1954 that states that if a business occupies a building for more than six months, it is able to claim the right to stay on the premises.[25] The agency is also building alliances with other intermediary organisations such as Space Makers Agency and the Empty Shops Network that promote temporary use.[26]

The approach of local authorities in relation to the meanwhile use of their vacant property assets is ad hoc. A recent report on vacant shop premises in the UK found that more could be done to identify vacant assets and match them to potential users.[27] Some UK local authorities have provided financial support to encourage the re-use of empty shops.[28] Others have acted as intermediaries through taking leases on privately owned vacant shop units and granting interim licenses to local groups to enable them to use the empty premises for community uses.[29]

72

There are now many examples of the temporary use of vacant shops from around the UK (Case Study 5.3). For example, in Brixton, 20 empty shops in a run-down arcade have been filled with community driven businesses, design collectives and workshops. The scheme is a joint initiative between Lambeth Borough Council, Space Makers Agency and the building's owners, London & Associated Properties. Following an advertisement for tenants, the scheme let rapidly. Occupants just cover the cost of rates to the council, and the project is helping to raise their business profile. In return, some are running crafts workshops for local people.[30]

Pop-up art

The Arts Council, England, Art in Empty Spaces project was established to help artists and arts organisations carry out activities in vacant premises, and in the process animate high streets. The initiative formed part of the Arts Council's response to the effects of the recession on the arts. Individuals and organisations were invited to apply for grants to transform empty retail units into creative spaces – art galleries, recording studios or arts workshops. A wide range of projects was supported. Imperial Buildings in Rotherham provides spaces for photographers, fashion designers, textile artists and graphic designers, to sell work, network and create new products and events such as workshops, music and fashion shows. In Windows of Opportunity, Margate, empty shops were given a creative make-over by artists Total Pap, who were commissioned by Thanet District Council to create recycled and environmentally friendly artwork. In Oldham, Small Cinema, which had 30 seats, was established in a former tourist information shop for screenings of popular films for local audiences.[31] Such re-use is not without its critics, however. A recent blog about a temporary art gallery in Ludlow in Shropshire, for example, observed that 'the shops looked as if they'd been squatted by GCSE art students. On drugs', and made the point that 'the whole point of an art gallery is that the gallery bit is just as important as the art bit'.[32] However, for most people such activity and its contribution to urban vitality is preferable to a boarded-up shop.

Pop-up art has also been used as part of a wide programme of initiatives by the Chicago Loop Alliance (CLA) to strengthen the competitive position of the Loop area in central Chicago as a mixed-use destination. Under the leadership of CLA Executive Director Ty Tabing, the area has blossomed into a vibrant, mixed-use district, filled with retail stores, restaurants and entertainment, along with respected educational and cultural institutions. This success has enhanced the area as a residential neighbourhood with a growing sense of community. One of the CLAs projects, the PopUp Art Loop™ transforms empty storefronts into public art galleries, exhibits and studios. The PopUp Art Loop™ does not own or rent gallery space but acts as a broker between artists and property owners, creating temporary gallery space at no cost to the artist, in prime locations. The locations range from shop windows, to storefronts and interior spaces. Beginning with three locations in 2009, the programme has expanded to exhibitions of photography, sculpture, 2D art, video and new media installations on sites throughout Chicago's central business district. The programme is promoted through regular gallery walking tours featuring live music and art making.[33]

73

Pop-up restaurants

In a similar vein, a new wave of pop-up restaurants is emerging. Some have taken advantage of the glut in empty property; others are symbolic of the need for lateral thinking to make ends meet in the recession. Removing longevity changes the profit structure. The restaurant does not need to build a reputation or a loyal clientele, thus it can dispense with high-end interior design and highly trained waiters. At a pinch it can even get away with poor food, although most do strive for quality. Being 'different' is enough. For the diners, the chance to eat well, at low cost, in unusual surroundings is clearly appealing. But as with the pop-up shop phenomenon, the main attraction is the cachet of the one-off experience that is accessible only to the cognoscenti. Pop-up restaurants can be 'discovered' and 'claimed' as their own, by small cliques. Thus it is not just the 'celebs' who can cash in on the cachet; we can all be intrepid urban pioneers and share that moment of exclusivity.[34]

The pop-up dining concept is being developed in various ways, combining art and cabaret, treasure hunting and even offering co-creation of the experience to its customers (Case Studies 5.5, 5.6, 5.7 and 5.8). The attractions of the pop-up restaurant have even been recognised by icons of the establishment such as Selfridges, Harrods and the Royal Academy in London.[35] Selfridges opened its pop-up Restaurant on the Roof for just eight weeks in November 2009. With spectacular views and a Michelin-Star-winning chef, it was fully booked from the start.[36] In 2008 the Royal Academy (RA) opened Flash for just 80 days. An artistic installation as much as a restaurant, it featured Rococo-style paintings and Wedgwood china and was designed to coincide with the RA's *GSK Contemporary* exhibition.[37]

Underground restaurants

An underground restaurant is an eating establishment operated out of someone's home, in effect, a paying dinner party. The countercultural combination of buzzwords like 'underground', 'secret' and 'illegal' (since they bypass local planning and health regulations) adds to their appeal. Being instructed to sing 'Happy Birthday' if the police arrive may bring excitement to the experience, but their illegal nature makes it hard to advertise them in a conventional way. Instead they function by word of mouth, and via internet sites like Facebook. There are even social networks dedicated solely to underground dining.

The practice of serving food in one's home to paying guests is not new and is found in many parts of the world. In Cuba *paladares* have been part of the culture for decades, and originally started as a private response to expensive state restaurants, only becoming legal in 1995. In Argentina too there is a huge 'closed-door' restaurant scene, while in France homes displaying the 'Les Routiers' signs originally fed simple meals at kitchen tables to passing lorry drivers.

However, in recent years underground dining has reached phenomenal proportions, albeit with subtle regional variations. In Italy, the Home Food Project focuses on reviving and promoting traditional regional food prepared to family recipes. In America, the supper clubs, or 'anti-restaurants', often concentrate on fine dining. Underground restaurants now appear to be taking hold in the UK, with a particular concentration in London. Some underground restaurants are professionally run (as in the Moveable Restaurant and Loft Supper Club), while some raise money for charity and others offer a concessionary rate for the unemployed. Establishments such as Horton's Place in Dalston, MsMarmiteLovers in Kilburn, the Secret Salad Club in Brixton and the Secret Ingredient in Stoke Newington have even attracted reviews in the national press. For the host, they provide an opportunity to make some money and experiment with cooking without the high costs of setting up in a proper restaurant. From the diner's point of view, it is an opportunity to sample new food, often at low cost outside the traditional restaurant experience. The anarchistic aspect of the experience makes it exciting and 'cool'.[38]

74

Markets

It is easy to forget the fact that the original and remarkably enduring form of temporary retailing is the street market. This has achieved a new lease of life in many areas, with declining markets being revived and new variations introduced such as car boot sales, yard sales, night markets and farmers' markets. Again the driving forces are surplus material possessions and growing disposable income for some, and poverty for others. Car boot and yard sales allow the disposal and purchase of inexpensive or second hand goods, while farmers' markets often offer relatively expensive organic food and handmade produce to those able to afford it. They are testament to the enduring popularity of markets as places of bustle, surprise and bargains, and exemplify the way in which shopping has become a leisure pursuit. For many start-up businesses they also provide a relatively inexpensive way of launching a product or business idea and have provided a first foothold for numerous successful companies. Supermarket giant Tesco, for example, started life in 1919 from a stall in the East End of London, while Tom Bloxham, the driving force behind developer Urban Splash, started his first enterprise selling posters in London's Portobello Road.

Car boot sales have grown enormously in popularity since they were first established in the UK in the early 1970s. Listings on websites suggest that hundreds of sales happen weekly, with over 25 in London alone.[39] They generally take place on greenfield sites in the summer months, although many are now held in the grounds of schools and other community buildings. They are the European equivalent of the North American garage or yard sale. There the idea has moved beyond the individual front yard and now encompasses neighbourhood sales. For example, the Highway 127 Corridor Sale, promoted as 'The World's Longest Yard Sale', facilitates simultaneous yard sales along the 630-mile route.[40]

75

Spitalfields Market
LONDON

Autobahn farmers' market
NEAR KÖLN

Farmers' markets have existed ever since mankind generated a surplus from farming the land nearly 10,000 years ago. In many towns and villages across the world they remain central to the farming economy, and are popular traditional weekly events. However, urbanisation, intensive farming, the advent of the supermarket and the introduction of refrigerated transport led to a decline in such markets in many parts of the world. The recent revival of interest in food and healthy eating, as well as the promotion of organic farming and more sustainable lifestyles, has led to a resurgence of interest. The benefit to consumers is fresh food produced relatively locally. Advocates say that the markets help farmers stay in business and preserve natural resources such as soil, water and wildlife habitats. They also help to reestablish important social ties, linking rural and urban populations. Farmers' markets in the US grew from 1,755 in 1994 to 5,274 in 2009. In New York City, there are 107 farmers' markets in operation. Since the first farmers' market was established in the UK in 1997, the number has grown to over 550 nationwide.[41] They have been supported by many city authorities as they appeal to middle-class voters and are perceived as not just a wholesome element within the street environment, but critically are easier to manage than conventional markets. When farmers' markets are deployed thoughtfully they can revitalise pieces of the city. Unfortunately, they are also often 'plugged into' public spaces with very little real thought about design and function.

In conclusion

As part of a response to the decline of traditional town centre retailing, temporary pop-ups, street- and market-based retailing potentially offer policy makers a way of bringing life and vibrancy back into urban areas. There are, as we have seen, various successful public initiatives which can support this, such as taking or guaranteeing leases. However, while pop-ups are ephemeral, public authorities work, of necessity, on longer timescales and within a regulated framework. In these conditions, outside limited direct action, the most effective public policy response is likely to be one of permissive enabling rather than direct intervention.

The pop-up retailing phenomenon is interesting not just because it has captivated consumer interest, but for the sheer variety of its forms. From car boot sales to farmers' markets, underground restaurants and brand marketing, it is becoming a feature of urban life, and represents a consumer world where the boundaries between product and experience are no longer clear-cut. It has clearly touched a need for both variety, against the backdrop of increasingly bland high streets, and for enjoyment of the moment. In short, people enjoy the immediacy of the temporary.

Case Study
#5.1 | Nike pop-up shop

AMSTERDAM

Nike launched a marketing campaign in Amsterdam in 2010, Unleashed Run, Take Mokum, to inspire more people to take up running (and, of course, to sell more sportswear). A local advertising and design agency, …,staat, created a temporary shop near the Vondelpark, as both a retail outlet and a meeting place for runners during the campaign. The campaign connected to its target groups through social networking sites and organised runs around the city. At the same time, Nike launched a GPS-based phone 'app', to monitor and encourage runners to take their runs further. Such campaigns provide brands with a greater profile in urban space.

SOURCE: J. Beekmans, 'Run Mokum, Run!', popupcity.net, 9 September 2010, retrieved from
http://popupcity.net/2010/09/run-mokum-run/ (accessed 20 January 2011).

Pop-up shop
AMSTERDAM, 2010

The People's Supermarket

BLOOMSBURY, LONDON

The People's Supermarket, promoted by social entrepreneur David Barrie, is in many ways an extension of the Middlesbrough Community Food Project (Case Study 8.9). The concept is to bring good food to low-income communities, at affordable prices, by co-opting its customers into shareholders. Anyone can shop at the People's Supermarket, but for a fee of £25 and a commitment to volunteer for four hours each month, members are eligible for a 10 per cent discount on their grocery bills. The project also aims to offer an alternative food buying network, by connecting the urban community with the farming community, and seeks to reduce food waste throughout the supply chain.

The first supermarket was set up in 2010 in Lambs Conduit Street, in central London. The empty shop unit was taken on a 10-year lease with a break clause after five years from the landlord, the Rugby Estate. It is supported by the local council and was started up with a mixture of capital from individuals, interest-free loans and pro-bono time from local and corporate businesses. The fixtures and fittings are low cost, and are capable of being dismantled and moved on. The idea, as with most temporary uses, is that it should be easy to stop, and move to other premises, and be replicated by other communities in other locations.

SOURCES: Interview with David Barrie.

www.thepeoplessupermarket.org/ (accessed 16 March 2011).

79

The People's Supermarket

BLOOMSBURY, LONDON

Case Study | Pop-up shops
#5.3 | CAMDEN TOWN, LONDON

Camden Town Unlimited (CTU) is a Business Improvement District (BID) that was established in 2006. CTU has sponsored a programme of pop-up shops. It offers a secure covenant to landowners and can cover insurance and local property rates. The rents are set at very low levels, and the leases or licenses are for a maximum of six to twelve months. Often the shops move to other premises after as little as two months. The initiative has wide support from the local business community. The distinctively designed shop fronts contribute to the appeal of the High Street and remove the depressing appearance of vacancy and inactivity.

SOURCE: Interview with Chris Shaw, Shaw Corporation/Chair, Camden Town Unlimited.

Pop-up shop
CAMDEN TOWN BUSINESS IMPROVEMENT DISTRICT, LONDON

Case Study   Shopjacket
#5.4   UK

UK-based Shopjacket has built a very successful business through the temporary transformation of the windows and external fascias of vacant shops. The project uses colourful three-dimensional bespoke graphic designs (*trompe l'oeil*) featuring a range of different shop types such as a bakery, delicatessen, florist or chocolate shop. The panels are fixed inside the windows or screwed to the fascia so they can be removed and re-used as required. This simple and cost-effective approach keeps the retail unit available for potential new uses while dramatically improving the street scene, as well as inspiring potential new business ideas.

The success of the business, founded by designer Neil Wilson and commercial property consultant Paul Murphy, has surpassed all expectations. The company has worked with local authorities as far afield as Bridgwater, Shepton Mallet, Hemel Hempstead and Dumbarton. Its private clients include Eldon Square, Newcastle which uses Shopjacket to demonstrate innovative and cost-effective ways of using and presenting empty units to potential investors. The approach is not just limited to shops, but can transform any vacant building or eyesore.

SOURCE: www.shopjacket.co.uk (accessed 16 June 2011).

81

Window dressing for a shopfront by Shopjacket
GLASGOW

Case Study
#5.5

GINGERLINE
LONDON

GINGERLINE is one of the latest pop-up restaurants in London and its variation on the pop-up theme is a union of dining, theatre and art. The restaurant takes place in different locations along the (recently opened, ginger-coloured) East London Line. The venue is announced to subscribers by text messages just an hour before opening. It aims to offer spectacular meals in unusual venues, but also hopes to spread good food and culture out along the Overground Line from its present concentration in trendy Hoxton and Shoreditch.

The team behind GINGERLINE includes a keen amateur chef, a performer and project manager, a graphic designer, a set designer, a photographer and web designer and as with the pop-up restaurant What Happens When in New York, it provides an outlet for their creativity. Apart from the food, each event has an art element. Even the menu is designed as a take-away artwork. The first venue was a photographer's gallery in Crystal Palace; the second Rotherhithe's Brunel Museum. In its third venture, GINGERLINE chose Prangsta costumiers on New Cross Road which provided a theatrical backdrop, crammed with stage clothes and accessories. Staff dressed in costumes of feathers, jewels and corsets, while a trapeze artist, accordion player and cabaret music added to the carnivalesque atmosphere. So far, the group has had no problems securing the loan of spaces, finding support from owners who recognise that the pop-up can bring free publicity. And like other pop-up restaurants its events sell out fast.

82

SOURCES: R. Halliburton, 'Pop-up goes extreme', *Time Out*, 10–16 February 2011, pp. 26–7.

S. Ignatidou, 'Popping up along the East London Line: the new way to dine', 26 January 2011, retrieved from www.eastlondonlines.co.uk/2011/01/popping-up-along-the-east-london-line-the-new-way-to-dine/.

P. McGuigan, 'GINGERLINE', retrieved from www.spectator.co.uk/scoff/6657798/gingerline.thtml (both accessed 16 June 2011).

GINGERLINE pop-up restaurant
NEW CROSS, LONDON

Case Study
#5.6

Hel Yes
LONDON

In London in September 2010, Hel Yes, an established Finnish restaurant, opened a pop-up for just three weeks in an industrial space in Islington. The space was both a temporary restaurant and an exhibition that showcased the best in Finnish food and design (in anticipation of Helsinki as the World Design Capital 2012), with tables, chairs, lighting, tents, beds, shawls and textiles by established Finnish designers.

SOURCES: www.dailycandy.com/london/article/88685/Hel-Yes-Finnish-Pop-Up-Restaurant-in-Islington.
www.londondesignguide.com/2010/09/pop-up-restaurant-hel-yes/ (both accessed 16 June 2011).

Case Study
#5.7

What Happens When
SOHO, NEW YORK

84

What Happens When, one of the latest pop-up restaurants to hit New York, is promoted as a temporary restaurant *installation* that changes its culinary, visual and sound experience every month for the nine months that it is open. The result of a collaboration between a chef, two designers, a photographer and a composer, it aims to provide each of the partners with an outlet (or studio) for their creative talents in a way that is free from the constraints of long leases and big investors. In a novel experiment in both client involvement and fundraising, it uses Kickstarter.com (a funding platform for creative projects) to raise funds for the project while offering sponsors the chance to have a say in how the next 'menu' is put together. By February 2011 when it opened, it had reached its fundraising goal of $20,000.

The first space, menu, brand and 'soundscape' was put together in three weeks. The interior comprised a black room, on which the design drawings of the space – the elevations and floor plan – were mapped onto their respective walls like a giant blueprint of the 'concept'. Background music was provided by a new 120-minute composition with speakers placed throughout the space. And at the start of each month, there is a complete change of menu, theme and music.

SOURCES: www.kickstarter.com/projects/emibee/what-happens-when-a-temporary-restaurant-installat.
www.urbandaddy.com/nyc/food/12356/What_Happens_When_Dining_in_a_SoHo_Madhouse_New_
York_City_NYC_NoLita_Restaurant.
www.whathappenswhennyc.com/ (all accessed 9 February 2011).

Street Dinner

FERRARA, ITALY

Street Dinner, supported by the city council of Ferrara, takes the secrecy of the pop-up restaurant to an extreme and combines it with a treasure hunt and city tour aimed at the tourist market. Guests purchase a ticket for a package that includes aperitifs, a table, chair, menu choice, instructions and map of the city. They are notified by text first where the aperitif will take place, then where to pick up the table, chair and Street Dinner bag containing their selected menu. The third text reveals the location for dinner.

SOURCES: J. de Boer, 'Street Dinner: a secret pop-up restaurant', 10 December 2010, retrieved from
http://popupcity.net/2010/12/street-dinner-a-secret-pop-up-restaurant/.
www.streetdinner.it/home.html (both accessed 1 March 2011).

GINGERLINE pop-up restaurant signage
BRUNEL MUSEUM, ROTHERHITHE, LONDON

Girls in fountain
SOUTH BANK, LONDON

6: The city as a stage

CITIES CANNOT FUNCTION properly without public space. It provides the locus for exchange and informal transactions, and is where citizens meet, gossip, parade and rebel. It is in essence where civic life flourishes. The vast majority of the uses of public space are temporary. However, these transient uses of public spaces are both diversifying and intensifying in response to changes in lifestyle and culture, changes in the composition of city populations and ever greater urban population densities. The way in which 'public space' is viewed is also changing from a traditional focus on formal squares, parks and pavements to a broader conception that recognises the value of less formal 'left-over' spaces and the everyday uses that occur there.

Everyday temporary activities

A number of urban theorists are critical of the obsession of modern urban planning with formal public space and the interactions that occur there.[1] Instead they have focused attention on marginal urban spaces and the more informal 'everyday' uses which they accommodate. Such 'residual spaces' include those between, below and around buildings, roof-tops, awkward wedges between developed space, redundant or over-sized infrastructure and derelict land.[2] These are common in many European cities, especially those that are shrinking, and in many North American cities where low-intensity land use is the norm. These spaces provide voids where the unexpected can flourish, and the fallow space where intensification of the urban realm can occur.

Everyday Urbanism (which is discussed further in Chapter 10) has explored the value of such spaces as the setting for everyday behaviour such as casual meetings, games of chess, garage sales, skateboarding or barbeques.[3] Such activities are not an exceptional or new phenomenon, but they have only recently gained the attention they deserve. Giovanni la Varra coined the term 'Post-It City' to describe the informal alternatives to traditional official public space: 'Like a text made up of Post-its, the contemporary city is occupied temporarily by compartments that leave no trace – just like Post-its do in books'.[4] The Post-It City research project documented ephemeral, temporary and informal uses in over 80 cities around the world.[5] In these informal spaces the most varied activities take place, with people relating in non-conventional ways. According to la Varra these dynamics temporarily rewrite the spaces they fill and are a 'form of resistance' against the normalisation of 'public behaviour'.[6] He attributes three characteristics to Post-It phenomena: they have no predominant codification (any type of social exchange is possible), they are temporary (occupying a narrow interval of space and time in between hyper-codified environments) and they result in the 'intensification' of spaces and places. La Varra argues that Post-It City represents an implicit criticism of the formal, financed and sophisticated design of contemporary public spaces that are becoming less and less real. It is implicit because it does not give rise to any particular demand. Occupying a space temporarily and giving it another meaning, without modifying it, does not necessarily prefigure a demand for 'inhabitable space'. Instead it rediscovers the 'do-it-yourself' dimension.[7] And within this 'constellation of spaces, which continually "light up" and "go dark", the public life of the European city seems to find the energy of regeneration'.[8]

In their work *Loose Space*, Franck and Stevens provide a similar investigation of the informal use of everyday space.[9] They approach temporary activities from the point of view of the space that they occupy, rather than the uses themselves. 'Loose spaces' are those that provide a venue for activities that were not originally intended for those locations, as opposed to 'tight spaces' where 'rules, meanings and physical structure are explicit and relatively fixed'.[10] The activities in 'loose space' may occur alongside the intended uses on the pavement, street or town square, or they may appropriate places that no longer have a fixed use, such as abandoned buildings. In all these cases, spaces become 'loose' through people's activities.

88

> The activities that make a space loose may be impromptu or planned in advance.
> They may occur only once or they may take place on a regular schedule. They
> may be familiar, even strange, to passers-by or regular occurrences in the urban
> scene. They may be disruptive or unruly. But invariably, they are temporary,
> whether they last only a few minutes or months or years.[11]

Franck argues that it is such loose spaces that exhibit the 'key features of urbanity: access, freedom of choice, density and intermixing of different kinds of people and activities'.[12] These spaces give cities their life and vitality, providing opportunities to 'relax, observe, buy or sell, protest, mourn and celebrate', for spontaneity and discovering the unexpected.[13] The virtues of loose space arise from possibility, diversity and disorder and 'stand in direct opposition to the qualities of public space that many people value: certainty, homogeneity, and order'.[14]

A number of other researchers take the argument further. They praise the qualities of urban wastelands as a resource in their own right and question the inevitable tendency of urban planners to try to organise them or replace them with the predictable.[15] They argue that such spaces allow 'reflective

Seating installation

meditations' or 'playful drifting' and represent a 'different beauty in the city', and suggest that the very absence of use creates a sense of freedom and possibility.[16] Such perceptions are obviously highly subjective and one person's threatening unregulated wasteland is another's edgy alternative to the prepackaged, predictable realm that constitutes so much of the present urban experience. Stalker, a collective of architects and researchers connected to the Roma Tre University, have developed a particular interest in such spaces and argue that the most effective 'cure' for them is to leave them to be taken over by nature or the natural colonisation of experimental users with nowhere else to go.[17]

The unifying features of these approaches to public space are that they emphasise use value over exchange value, they broaden our conception of public space to embrace accidental left-over areas and they extend our understanding of the demands on public space. In so doing they question the way in which planners and architects shape the public realm,[18] and they suggest the need for a new approach in terms of both public space strategies and design. Crawford, for example, advocates the use of small packages of interventions that reinforce the heterogeneous qualities of small, temporary, undistinguished though well-used spaces,[19] with the aim of strengthening 'the connective tissue that binds daily lives together'.[20] This approach is illustrated by the work of *muf* architecture/art in Dalston, London, an area lacking a large open space, where the strategy was to create a discontinuous park of considerable size through making better use of existing space (Case Study 10.3). In a similar vein researchers from Tokyo University have demonstrated the value of small interventions in enhancing the public realm (Case Study 6.1).

The design of public spaces is also evolving. Emphasis is now moving towards simpler designs that maximise the flexibility of spaces. It is becoming accepted that formal, intricate and prescriptive designs are not suited to circumstances where the uses and activities that are likely to occur are varied and unpredictable. As de Boer notes on the popupcity website, 'the new generation of pop-up city makers continuously poses the question of whether current city practices are still up to date during the rapidly changing processes today's cities have to deal with'.[21] In parallel, a number of interesting experiments in pop-up street furniture have also emerged from industrial and product designers keen to tackle what has traditionally been seen as the preserve of city authorities. These allow the user to configure public space in ways that suit their immediate needs (Case Studies 6.2, 6.3 and 6.4).

Diversification of temporary uses

As the city becomes ever more complex (ethnically, culturally, economically and socially), and as it becomes increasingly densely developed and crowded, the range of uses of urban space is broadening. New generations of immigrants are exploring the city and are demonstrating alternative ways of using urban spaces. For example, Rojas describes how Latino migrants in Los Angeles bring different uses of urban space which they accommodate within the existing built environment: 'outdated gas stations become *taquerias*, defunct rail yards become parks, large abandoned manufacturing plants become *mercados*, and front yards become courtyards.'[22] Many of the examples quoted in *Everyday Urbanism* also represent new ways of colonising the streets by immigrant communities with different cultural attitudes to public and private space. Similarly, Wu describes the way in which the Filipino migrant community has gradually transformed the ChungShan neighbourhood of Taipei in Taiwan into informal and temporary meeting places, centres for support services and a focus for shopping and businesses.[23] In Hong Kong, the spontaneous weekly gathering by Filipino domestic workers at the HSBC building is simply an expression of a need for such community space. Post-It City, too, recorded the way in which Afghani immigrants passing through Paris safeguard the bags containing their personal possessions by hanging them in tall trees next to railway stations such as Gare de l'Est, a poignant reminder of how their lives, far from home, are suspended as they await a new life or the next stage in their journey.[24] This mirrors the large numbers of impoverished African merchants who set up temporary stalls on the pavements of many European capitals to sell handbags and sunglasses, a truly temporary activity whose lifespan is determined by the next police raid.

Multi-cultural cities like London have, to an extent, embraced these new activities as a positive trend. Formal events such as the Notting Hill Carnival or the St Patrick's Day Parade are well established within the city's cultural calendar. The importance of religious festivals has also been recognised by city authorities and practitioners, especially as a way of engaging with local communities. For

Traditional Bengali rice chalk painting

example, *muf* used traditional Bengali painting with soluble rice-based paints to engage the local 91
Bangladeshi community in the redesign of the Altab Ali Park during a festival to celebrate the
language martyrs of Dacca.

Changes in technology and lifestyles are also creating demands for space for an ever more diverse
range of activities. Wi-Fi and mobile internet access are helping to merge the indoors and outdoors.
In Chapter 3 we noted the emergence of a new wave of spaces in cafés, supermarkets, hotel lobbies,
gyms, libraries or bookshops that cater for out-of-home and out-of-office activities for the mobile
worker and consumer. The same trends are affecting the public realm. For example, 30 years ago it
would have been considered an unforgivable breach of etiquette to eat a sandwich or hamburger on a
tube train, but this is tolerated, even accepted today. Now, in contrast, the ban on smoking in bars,
offices or restaurants has created a whole new class of street itinerants, and has contributed to the
rise of the café society and al fresco dining on the pavements of northern Europe.

Sports and events

Public space has always provided a temporary venue for sports and pastimes. Some historical activities
such as bear-baiting are fortunately no longer with us, while others such as the annual Shrovetide football
match in Ashbourne, Derbyshire (almost as vicious) are survivals. Street football has a long tradition as
a spontaneous sporting event requiring only four pullovers as moveable goalposts. A new variation on

Table tennis skip by Oliver Bishop-Young for Young Creatives Network (YCN)
SPITALFIELDS, LONDON

92   this is Powerleague, which champions five-a-side football in the UK and operates two temporary sites in London. On one site owned by British Land at Regent's Place off Euston Road, the company has built six five-a-side pitches, one seven-a-side pitch and a modular building for changing and showering.[25]

Whereas some sports are informal, such as street cricket or ice skating, others, such as the Monaco Grand Prix are major events in the international sporting diary. More recently, the growth of the marathon or 'fun run' has changed the use of the streets in many cities for a day or two every year. Organised sporting events and festivals, temporary in themselves, attract a whole industry of other temporary activities. Street vendors, entertainers, buskers and touts appear, set up business and move on. Many churches along the route of the London marathon use the opportunity to spill out of doors, and hold services in their forecourts or on their steps. Temporary sports activities are also increasingly colonising under-used land. Ice rinks are now a regular feature of corporate or institutional spaces such as office plazas and museum forecourts. The fun fair and circus, popular survivals of a previous age, are now being joined by other activities from open-air concerts to temporary swimming pools (Case Study 6.7) and artificial urban ski slopes.

The new wave of urban culture (which is discussed further in Chapter 7) is also spawning activities such as pavement art, sand sculpture on the banks of rivers, busking in subways and performance art. Such temporary uses are often greeted with delight by those who discover them. They provide novelty, surprise and opportunities for fun and spontaneity. Such a response could be taken as evidence of latent demand for variety in public space, from a public bored with the predictable products of large-scale planned development.

Children's soft play equipment used to animate Gillette Square
DALSTON, LONDON

Folly for a Flyover, June, 2011. A temporary venue for film, performance and boat rides, and a café/bar. By Assemble CIC in conjunction with CREATE 2011 and the Barbican Art Gallery, with support from *muf* architecture/art
HACKNEY CUT, LONDON

Mourning and loss

The use of public space to express private mourning has grown into something of an urban phenomenon in the UK and elsewhere in recent years, with flowers marking the sites of road accidents becoming a common sight. It is difficult to trace the origins of this particular phenomenon, but the spontaneous laying of floral tributes following the death of Princess Diana in 1997 certainly planted the idea firmly in the public psyche. The recent appearance of ghostly white bicycles marking fatal accidents involving cyclists is another variation on the theme. The idea of painting bikes white apparently originated in Amsterdam in the 1960s as an anarchist project to provide free white bikes to anyone wishing to use them. In the US, they may have originated in a purely artistic project in San Francisco by artist Jo Slota, who was intrigued by the abandoned bicycles around the city, and began painting them white. From there the idea of ghost bike memorials spread throughout the world as a reminder of the fragility of cyclists in a world dominated by the car.[26] In New York, ghost bikes are set up and maintained by the New York City Street Memorial Project, and the memorials often serve as meeting places for members of bicycle-advocacy groups.[27] Memorials pose particular difficulties for public authorities. Most now accept that they will remain for a short period, often marked by the natural wilting of the floral tributes. Ghost bikes do not wilt and their lifespan is likely to be dictated by the time taken for their padlocks to rust.

94

Memorial to Steve Jobs, Apple
CENTRAL PARK SOUTH/5TH AVENUE, NEW YORK

Defence

Another recent diversification in the way public spaces are used and adapted reflects the fear of global terrorism. Streets and forecourts around government buildings, railway stations and airports, in London and other major cities, are being redesigned with a range of security bollards, barriers and chicanes to provide protection from car bombs and other threats. These are generally executed by engineers with little consideration for urban design. They often intrude upon and change the nature of surrounding spaces, excluding the public or limiting their access. Ironically, all of these structures have to be considered to be temporary, as politicians assure us that the 'war against terror' can and will be won within a reasonable timescale. Significantly though, some of these structures, such as the balustrades protecting government buildings in Whitehall, are beginning to look rather permanent. It is likely that many of these temporary barriers will remain in place, an implicit acknowledgement that we now expect terrorism to be a long-lasting rather than a temporary threat to our cities.

95

'Temporary' anti-terrorist barrier
WHITEHALL, LONDON

Protest

Some temporary projects represent an explicit protest against the way in which public space has become increasingly controlled and privatised (Case Studies 6.6, 6.8, 6.9, 6.10 and 6.12). It is becoming a common feature of cities in many parts of the world where malls, segregated from the rest of the city, have replaced traditional streetscapes and town squares, have 'disciplined their spontaneity'[28] and effectively become a 'one-dimensional venue for consumption'.[29] In the process, 'undesirables' are often excluded through surveillance by CCTV cameras or security staff, and the scope to use such spaces for spontaneous enjoyment and political protest may be reduced. Doron comments on the increasing segregation of public space that excludes, for example, unofficial economic transactions and protest.[30] In trying to reduce crime, many cities have adopted a zero-tolerance approach, closing underpasses to prevent rough sleeping and blocking roads to prevent cruising. 'Designing out crime' through, for example, introducing street furniture that is specifically designed to discourage street drinking, sleeping and even sitting is a particularly pernicious illustration of the way in which authorities attempt to regulate the city. But even this example pales in comparison with the recent attempts by Westminster City Council in London to pass by-laws that would outlaw soup kitchens for the homeless.

Since the Situationist International (a group of artists, film makers, writers and others mostly active in Paris from the 1950s), artists have sought to challenge the way in which contemporary city planning has ordered the possibilities for the public realm and made people blind to the manipulation of cities.[31] Many recent temporary interventions follow this tradition and seek to raise awareness of the increasingly controlled nature of public space. They invite strangers to suspend their conditioned habits and rethink the possibilities for the use of space. Hou argues that in cities around the world, temporary social and artistic interventions in public space by citizens and communities often 'represent small yet persistent challenges against the increasingly regulated, privatized and diminishing forms of public space'.[32] Merker, a member of San Francisco's Rebar group, considers the growth of temporary uses in the context of what he calls 'generous urbanism', a reaction against the trend in contemporary industrialised societies to banish 'unscripted, generous exchange in the public realm in favour of a hyper-commercial alternative'.[33] In the highly commercialised world of today, such generosity is itself subversive.

City-initiated temporary projects

The public areas of a city represent the stages upon which fleeting and transient activities can take place. As these activities grow in range, number and intensity, the design, management and maintenance of public spaces is attracting increasing interest across the globe. The importance of public space has gained a wider recognition following the success of public space improvements such as in Barcelona after the 1992 Olympics, and the Millennium Park in Chicago. London, New York,

Barcelona and Paris all have successful public space strategies. Many other cities from Vancouver to Bilbao and Hong Kong are investing in major projects to open up waterfronts for public use or landscape areas of derelict land. Design for London has initiated a Mayor's Great Spaces programme to improve over 100 spaces across the capital. In parallel the importance of the more informal city spaces is slowly gaining recognition, and this is prompting new strategies that seek to link the unremarkable but well-used everyday spaces into a 'connective tissue' of far wider significance.

A fast-growing body of good practice is now emerging as city authorities experiment with different ways to accommodate the more varied and intensive demands on public spaces. This spirit of experimentation is exemplified in New York's public space programme initiated by Janette Sadik-Kahn, New York Commissioner of Transport (Case Study 6.11). In a series of interventions, major streets such as Broadway and Times Square were closed overnight and new public spaces laid out. These employ very simple design concepts. Surfaces are often painted onto the highway, inexpensive tables and chairs are provided and landscaping arrives in a series of movable planters. The elements here are temporary, and the approach is one of experimentation. The instant popularity of the projects is apparent by the speed at which citizens colonise these areas. It is likely that many of these new public spaces will become permanent and will eventually be landscaped accordingly.

The New York City experiment is being echoed elsewhere in what is becoming a very significant reappraisal of how space is planned and utilised on the urban scale. In the last five years or so we have witnessed a growing number of projects in which roads are temporarily appropriated as pedestrian spaces (Case Studies 6.5, 6.13, 6.14, 6.15, 6.16 and 6.17). In some cases these are explicitly experimental. In other cases they are one-off or regular seasonal events. While the majority of public space continues to be designed to serve the motor vehicle rather than the pedestrian, the need to redress the balance is starting to gain acceptance. City authorities are also expanding from the more basic roles of cleaning and policing public space. They are recognising that by playing a more active role in promoting events, they can animate public areas and derive real economic benefits from them.

97

In conclusion

No city can evolve beyond a basic state without valuing its public realm. Inevitably this entails managing and imposing rules on public spaces, but the process of negotiation for the rights to use and control public space is at the heart of civic life. Increasingly, it would seem that the instigators of temporary activities are becoming active players in this continuously evolving debate. Through occupying and using urban spaces they are creating the conditions whereby experimentation can take place. Through this active intervention they are pushing the parameters of design and creating a public stage within the city not just for civic life, but for the arts and culture to flourish.

Kanda

TOKYO

As part of a study into the scope to renew and re-use existing urban areas without redeveloping them, a team from Tokyo Metropolitan University conducted a series of experimental interventions between 2003 and 2007 aimed at improving public access to the semi-public spaces of the Kanda area of Tokyo. The area has a diverse, high-density building stock that is largely in private ownership, but retains a network of under-used alleys and other spaces.

A series of small interventions turned areas with no identity into attractive community spaces. In the Re-Street project an alleyway was fitted with simple wooden boards and its walls were hung with canvas cloth, turning it into a neighbourhood cinema. Making the canvas cloth involved a large number of children who had not previously used the alley as a playground. The Kuuchi+ project focused on empty spaces around the existing building stock. One initiative turned a space into an exhibition of life-sized photographs of buildings illustrating the area's history. Another project, Batten School, turned an empty space into an evening school, providing lectures related to local history. In a third project an empty space in front of a building was transformed into a Footbath Café where people could remove their shoes and relax while enjoying food and drinks from neighbouring fast food stalls. The last project, Machi-oku, demonstrated the potential of roof-tops as public open spaces.

These projects illustrate the way in which small interventions can activate apparently insignificant public spaces for meetings and other social activities, thereby building community. They provided important opportunities for the local community to revisit the history of their neighbourhood and discuss and envision how it could be enriched through simple communal activities.

SOURCES: S. Aiba and O. Nishida, 'Re-City, Tokyo', in J. Hou (ed.), *Insurgent Public Space: Guerrilla Urbanism and the Remaking of Contemporary Cities*, London: Routledge, 2010, pp. 75–6.

Tokyo Metropolitan University Research project, '21st Century COE Program', retrieved from www.tmu-arch.sakura.ne.jp/pdf/35_recity_e.pdf (accessed 29 March 2011).

Re-Street: turning alleyways and streets into active social spaces
KANDA, TOKYO

Kuuchi+: bringing attention to old building façades and turning street corners into active public space
KANDA, TOKYO

Case Study
#6.2

Pop-up street furniture

UTRECHT, THE NETHERLANDS

Carmela Bogman and Rogier Martens have designed pop-up street furniture that has been installed in the city of Utrecht. The pop-up furniture is made from three retractable bollards, on which aluminum sheets are attached. They can be pumped manually out of the pavement by a hydraulic system that allows them to be fixed at any height up to a maximum of 75 centimetres, to create a bench, a stage or a lounge area. This means that city dwellers can decide for themselves when and how they use the pop-up. By placing the power to generate such urban forms in the hands of the individual user, the project invites new forms of interaction, collaboration and improvisation. Keys to the pumps are spread around the neighbourhood among the different potential users. After use the pop-up it is pumped back into the pavement, returning the street to unobstructed space.

SOURCES: www.carmelabogman.nl/?module=Basis%20Hoofdmenu&actie=&subactie=39.
www.rogiermartens.nl/producten/pop-up/ (both accessed 2 March 2011).

100

Pop-up street furniture
UTRECHT

Case Study
#6.3

Pop-Up Lunch
NEW YORK

Alexandra Pulver, a designer based in New York, has come up with an initiative, Pop-Up Lunch, that is designed to create instant lunch spots around the urban realm through the addition of simple pop-up furniture. Her designs are all portable, such as the pop-up hammock bag that can be attached to fences, transforming them instantly into a seat. The project was part of her Master's thesis in Industrial Design at the Pratt Institute in which she explored 'how non-traditional public spaces – like sidewalks – might be easily transformed into lively places to lunch'. Pulver aims to rethink the function of the sidewalk as more than just a pedestrian route.

SOURCES: J. de Boer, 'The pop-up lunch bag', popupcity.net, 16 August 2010, retrieved from
http://popupcity.net/2010/08/the-pop-up-lunch-bag/.
http://popuplunch.com/ (both accessed 1 March 2011).

101

Pop-Up Hammock Bag by Alexandra Pulver
NEW YORK

Case Study
#6.4

The Flying Grass Carpet

WORLDWIDE

The Flying Grass Carpet is one answer to the increasing need for loose, temporary and flexible structures in landscaping urban environments. Designed by HUNK-design and Studio ID Eddy, the Flying Grass Carpet looks like an immense Persian rug, and is an instant park that can be unfolded anywhere. The pattern is executed in different types of artificial grass, and the rug can be adjusted to fit any location. It is transportable by plane, train or truck, and the unique experience has already been enjoyed worldwide (in Matadero, Madrid, September 2009; Pécs, Hungary, May–June 2010; Essen, July 2010; Besiktas Barbaros Park, Istanbul, September 2010; and many other locations). Once it lands, the Flying Grass Carpet is ideal for casual recreation and all kinds of events, from frisbee tournaments, to picnics, contests and performances.

SOURCES: J. de Boer, 'Flying Grass Carpet: a landscaping fairytale', popupcity.net, 16 December 2008, retrieved from http://popupcity.net/2008/12/flying-grass-carpet-a-landscaping-fairytale/. http://flyinggrasscarpet.org/ (both accessed 1 March 2011).

102

Flying Grass Carpet, Willy Brandt Platz, Essen during EU Capital of Culture
RUHR, 2010

Case Study
#6.5

Champs Elysées

PARIS

In May 2010 the Champs Elysées was transformed into its namesake Elysian Fields by *Nature Capitale*, an event created by artist Gad Weil and the visual and landscape artist Laurence Medioni and organised by the French Young Farmers union and others. Eight thousand plots of earth, 150,000 plants, 650 mature trees, sheep, cattle, pigs, wheat, mustard and grape vines were imported overnight to transform three hectares of road between the Arc de Triomphe and Place de la Concorde into a scene resembling a vast farmers' market. The aim of the event was to celebrate French farming, encourage consumers to reflect on how food arrives on their plate and highlight the struggle of French farmers beset by soaring production costs and a fall in product prices. The event cost private investors €2m to stage and attracted an estimated 1.8 million visitors over two days.

SOURCES: L. Davies, 'Farmers bring rural reality to Champs Elysées', the *Guardian*, 24 May 2010, p. 15,
   retrieved from www.guardian.co.uk/world/2010/may/23/french-farmers-champs-elysees.
www.webinfrance.com/paris-avenue-becomes-farmland-for-a-day-562.html
   (both accessed 31 January 2011).

103

Case Study
#6.6

Space Hijackers

LONDON

Space Hijackers, a self-proclaimed group of 'anarchitects' set up in 1999, argue that public space is being eroded and made subservient to the profit motive, and local culture is being 'blanded out' or destroyed in the name of global economic progress. The group also oppose the way that users of space are increasingly scrutinised by CCTV, or controlled by rigid design features. They aim to raise awareness of such issues, claim back public ownership and encourage participation in how and where people use public space. Their first major event was the hijacking of a Circle Line carriage on the London Underground for the purpose of turning it into a moving disco. The point of the event was to completely disrupt the way in which the train works in terms of codes of conduct. They argue that such events not only change the history of the space, but also project a possible future: 'By setting up alternative realities and uses for space, we can spread confusion into the meaning and language of that space, reducing the authority of the people who own it'.

SOURCES: Space Hijackers, 'ANARCHITECTURE', retrieved from
   http://subsol.c3.hu/subsol_2/contributors0/spacehijackerstext.html (accessed 11 November 2010).
www.spacehijackers.co.uk/html/history.html (accessed 5 July 2010).

Dumpster swimming pools
NEW YORK

In the summer of 2009, David Belt, a real estate developer and president of Macro Sea, opened a pool made out of three dumpsters called the Lo-Fi Urban Country Club. Erected on a rented lot, hidden from the street on the banks of the Gowanus Canal in Brooklyn, the idea behind the pools was to experiment with under-used space and materials, repurposing them with urban renewal in mind. While there are few places to swim in Brooklyn, dumpsters are everywhere.

The dumpsters were donated by a construction company and the club was erected by volunteers in a week. The dumpsters were cleaned, the rough edges were filed down and the bottoms were covered in sand. They were then lined in plastic, and had a filtration system installed. The main costs were the wood for decking and the 18,000 gallons of water that were provided from a New Jersey aquifer. The three connected dumpster pools also housed a boules court, lounge chairs, grills and cabana hut. The idea was that a stand-alone dumpster, grill and chair could be rented by the public for under $1,000. The dumpsters show that without much expense urban detritus can be transformed into destinations that are cool and fun. The idea received huge and unexpected media attention and three mobile versions of the pool, with fold-up decks and filters included, capable of being transported on a standard truck were installed in the summer of 2010 in front of Grand Central Station and the Park Avenue Viaduct, as part of New York City's Third Annual Summer Streets programme.

Macro Sea view the project as a template for a range of other interim-use projects and a larger idea in which dingy strip malls could be turned into community destinations. By stripping the bland architectural features of such malls, adding community space and carefully curating vendors and the space itself, Macro Sea hopes to create places where people can shop, meet, learn and engage with one another.

SOURCES: C. Kuang, 'Macro Sea turns dumpster diving into family fun', 10 July 2009, retrieved from
www.fastcompany.com/blog/cliff-kuang/design-innovation/dumpster-diving-becomes-fun-family-outing.
http://pyramidbeach.com/tag/macro-sea/ (both accessed 16 June 2011).
M. Ryzik, 'Forget the trash bag, bring a towel', the *New York Times*, 19 July 2009, retrieved from
www.nytimes.com/2009/07/20/arts/design/20pool.html?_r=1 (accessed 2 March 2011).

Dumpster swimming pool arrives on site
GRAND CENTRAL STATION, NEW YORK, 2010

Dumpster swimming pool in situ
GRAND CENTRAL STATION, NEW YORK, 2010

Rebar: PARK(ing) Project

SAN FRANCISCO

Rebar, a San Francisco-based collective of artists, activists and designers, undertakes projects that aim to create non-commercial exchanges between people. The PARK(ing) Project started in November 2005, when Rebar fed parking meters in downtown San Francisco with the appropriate fee, and then built a temporary park within the white lines of the space, complete with lawn, shade tree and park bench. Since this initial act the idea has exploded into an international phenomenon. In 2006 Rebar organised a one-day global PARK(ing) event in which it was joined by 47 cities; the following year more than 200 parks were constructed in over 50 cities worldwide. 2010 was likely to be a record year with parks appearing as far away as Iran and China.

This intervention questions the domination of urban public space by the automobile, and the immense public subsidy that is given to parking cars, and demonstrates that even a piece of tarmac measuring 20 by 9 feet has other desirable potential uses. PARK(ing) Day has expanded to include a broad range of interventions well beyond the basic 'tree–bench–sod' park typology. Participants have built interventions ranging from free health clinics, urban farming demonstrations, political seminars, art installations, free bike repair shops and even a wedding venue. In other projects Rebar has found opportunities to temporarily fulfil unmet needs for rest, play or community within a variety of urban settings, and in the process, has influenced people's expectations of what is and is not acceptable in private and public space.

106

SOURCES: J.L. Chase, 'The space formerly known as parking', in J.L. Chase, M. Crawford and J. Kaliski (eds), *Everyday Urbanism*, New York: The Monacelli Press, 2nd edition, 2008, p. 196.

B. Merker, 'Taking place: Rebar's absurd tactics in generous urbanism', in J. Hou (ed.), *Insurgent Public Space: Guerrilla Urbanism and the Remaking of Contemporary Cities*, London: Routledge, 2010, pp. 45–58.

http://parkingday.org/about-parking-day/ (accessed 16 June 2011).

Rebar's first experiment in PARK(ing)
SAN FRANCISCO, 2005

Case Study
#6.9

Rebar: COMMONspace
SAN FRANCISCO

Although San Francisco's downtown office district now provides work and living space for more than a quarter of a million people, it has almost no publicly owned and managed open space. The district's large public parks are on the peripheries of the downtown office district. In an effort to provide more public space in the city centre, the city of San Francisco has created a number of privately owned public open spaces (POPOS) in partnership with private developers, in the form of plazas, atriums, terraces, roof gardens and small parks. Some of these spaces are open and inviting and are activated by public use. Others are difficult to find, appear to be private and are under heavy surveillance by CCTV or guards. Rebar's project COMMONspace (2006–7) aimed to evaluate, activate and reclaim such spaces as a critical part of the public realm and as a valuable part of the city's intellectual and artistic commons. It explored just how public these privately owned public spaces are through interventions such as 'napping' and kite-flying. Expanding on this project, the San Francisco Planning and Urban Research Association (SPUR) surveyed and evaluated existing POPOS in light of the requirements for their development laid out in the 1985 Downtown Plan and came up with a number of recommendations for their improvement.

SOURCES: www.rebargroup.org/projects/commonspace/.

107

SPUR, *Secrets of San Francisco: Our City's Privately Owned Public Open Spaces*, San Francisco Planning and Urban Research Association, 19 November 2008, retrieved from www.spur.org/publications/library/report/secretsofsanfrancisco_010109 (accessed 16 June 2011).

Case Study
#6.10

Guerrilla bicycle lanes
TORONTO

Toronto-based group the Urban Repair Squad makes urban interventions to 'encourage bicycling as an antidote to the poison that is car culture'. Their aim is to 'actively construct a positive future of what urban transportation could be by installing it NOW', rather than waiting for the bureaucrats to act. Instead they are making the city more cycle-friendly and creating bike lanes using stencils, spray paint and stickers.

SOURCES: J. Beekmans, 'Guerrilla bicycle lanes', popupcity.net, 11 February 2009, retrieved from http://popupcity.net/2009/02/guerrilla-bicycle-lanes/ (accessed 14 June 2011).

http://urbanrepairs.blogspot.com/ (accessed 1 March 2011).

Times Square
NEW YORK

Times Square provides a key destination in the heart of New York City, where the city is entertained and celebrates important events in its calendar. It has undergone many facelifts in its history but in 2001 was again felt to be on the cusp of potential decline. It had become sanitised, over-crowded and had lost its edge.

The Times Square Alliance Business Improvement District (BID) implemented a plan to create more space for pedestrians by widening the sidewalks, and on this 'captured space' ran public arts and other events. This was not necessarily a radical intervention, but its implementation was. Conventional pedestrianisation works would have taken more than a year (with associated congestion and disruption to business). Instead the BID closed the road overnight and created a pedestrian zone using traffic cones, mobile street furniture and planters. The recaptured space allowed an extended programme of events as well as a place to rest. The results were dramatic and the instant colonisation of this space by pedestrians proved the popularity of the project.

The success of the pilot scheme encouraged the NYC Department of Transportation to announce the permanent closure of Broadway at Times Square (scheduled to begin in 2012) and to launch a competition for a temporary installation to replace the red epoxy adorning the square. Over 150 design submissions were received; the winning entry by artist Molly Dilworth, *Cool Water, Hot Island*, is an interpretation of NASA's infrared satellite data of Manhattan as a cool, refreshing river of water flowing down Broadway and was installed in July 2010.

Temporary landscaping
TIMES SQUARE, NEW YORK

The project resonated with the wider focus in New York on public spaces, including the work of Danish architect Jan Gehl commissioned by Mayor Bloomberg in 2006 to study its public spaces. The importance of public space is now embedded in the PlaNYC 2030 Strategy. It is intended that no person will live more than a 10-minute walk from a green space. Where there is a deficiency, land is being acquired. Where land is not readily available, as in Lower Manhattan, the temporary spaces programme is being rolled out, under the leadership of Janette Sadik-Kahn, New York Commissioner of Transport. Overnight closures, painting of the road surfaces, and mobile planters and street furniture reinforce the changes from vehicle to pedestrian space. Spaces have been created on Broadway including Duffy Square, and these areas are now incorporated into civic life. It is likely that these will become permanent public spaces, but ones that would not have come into being without the experimentation provided by the temporary.

SOURCES: B. Meinhold, '*Cool Water, Hot Island* winning design for Times Square makeover', *Inhabitat*, 25 May 2010, retrieved from http://inhabitat.com/cool-water-hot-island-winning-design-for-times-square-makeover/ (accessed 31 January 2011).

E. Randolph, 'The best seats in Times Square', the *New York Times*, 7 June 2009, retrieved from www.nytimes.com/2009/06/08/opinion/08mon4.html (accessed 20 January 2011).

109

Case Study **#6.12** | Permanent Breakfast
WORLDWIDE

Permanent Breakfast is an initiative of architect Ursula Hofbauer and artist/film maker Friedmann Derschmidt. The initiative began as a public art performance and urban critique in Vienna, in 1996. The group set up a table in a public space and offered coffee and breakfast to anyone who cared to join in. The only requirement for participation is that their guests agree to organise another similar breakfast the next day. As with a chain letter the idea, in theory at least, should spread exponentially. It has since taken root in many cities around the world, including New York and Taiwan. The point of Permanent Breakfast is not only to surprise and delight, but to directly engage in a discourse about the limitations of the use of urban space. The response of passers-by acts as a gauge to assess how accessible a space is perceived to be.

SOURCES: www.guerrilla-innovation.com/archives/2008/04/000651.php.
www.p-breakfast.net/ (both accessed 23 February 2011).

London Festival of Architecture (London Architecture Biennale)
LONDON

The London Festival of Architecture (LFA) was launched in 2004 as the Clerkenwell Biennale by architect Peter Murray, as a response to the Venice Architectural Biennale. Clerkenwell is a centre for many younger architectural practices and the Biennale aimed to explore how architects could actually impact on an area to change people's perception of place. The festival focused on reclaiming streets and public spaces with events, installations and temporary structures. The main street was grassed over and cattle were herded in to graze (to echo the area's history as a livestock market). Buildings were also opened up for exhibitions and lectures attracting a huge response from architects, designers, students and the public at large.

The first year was such a success that it developed beyond Clerkenwell to take in areas of change across London. The 2008 festival included a temporary lido on a small area of wasteland in Southwark (Case Study 4.1) and a temporary 'Skywalk' that transformed a street at the back of the British Museum (otherwise used as a coach park). In another project in South Kensington, traffic was removed from Exhibition Road to gain support for a more permanent landscaping project that is now being implemented.

The London Festival of Architecture is now an established event in London's calendar and has pioneered alternative uses of public space and temporary installations. In the process it has learned valuable lessons about dealing with government machinery. Always non-confrontational, it has negotiated access, sometimes in highly creative ways. When presented with theoretical arguments from city officials on the practicality of bringing cattle into Clerkenwell, it used two architects dressed as a pantomime cow to demonstrate that the project could be accommodated within the street environment. The ever-present danger, however, is that the vociferous individual can scupper an innovative proposal through appealing to risk-averse politicians. To counteract this, the LFA has cultivated the role of local politicians as champions, and there is now an effective network to ensure the festival's continued success.

SOURCE: Interview with Peter Murray, New London Architecture.

CLOCKWISE FROM TOP LEFT

Driving cows into Smithfield, London Festival of Architecture, 2004
ST JOHN'S STREET, CLERKENWELL, LONDON

Temporary landscaping, London Festival of Architecture, 2010
STORE STREET, LONDON

The 'Skywalk', London Festival of Architecture, 2008
MONTAGUE PLACE/BRITISH MUSEUM, LONDON

Outdoor sitting room, London Festival of Architecture, 2008
SOMERSET HOUSE, LONDON

Case Study
#6.14

Paris Plages

PARIS

For one month every summer Paris Plages transforms the banks of the Seine into sandy beaches complete with deckchairs, parasols, fountains, palm trees, ice cream sellers and cafés, and a dazzling array of activities – dance lessons, aerobics, volleyball, climbing, concerts and swimming (in floating pools). The beaches are spread across three spots (Louvre/Pont de Sully, Port de la Gare and Bassin de la Villette). The first beach opened on the Rive Droite in 2002, and spans three kilometres through historical Paris. It uses 3,000 tons of fine sand to transform the tarmac of the Georges Pompidou Expressway into a pedestrian refuge. A second beach was added on the Rive Gauche in 2006. The latest addition, Bassin de la Villette, opened in 2007 and stretches from Rotonde de Ledoux to the former Magasins Généraux in Rue de Crimée. It features a water-sports complex (with rowing boats, kayaks, pedal boats and dinghies and aquagym classes), alongside boule and volleyball courts, and quayside restaurants.

The Paris Plages scheme was instigated by Mayor Bertrand Delanoë, to relieve the misery of those Parisians forced to remain in the city during the heat of August. After some initial criticism as a costly frivolity, the scheme has become a permanent fixture in the Parisian summertime scene and new features are added every season. Visitor numbers have grown each year reaching over four million in 2010. Its enormous popularity reflects both strong management and innovative programming. The scheme costs around €2m (£1.3m), mostly covered by commercial sponsors.

SOURCES: http://news.bbc.co.uk/1/hi/world/europe/3914649.stm.

http://goparis.about.com/od/events/p/Paris_Plage.htm.

www.paris.fr/portail/english/Portal.lut?page_id=8208&document_type_id=5&document_id=34146&portlet_id=18969.

www.pps.org/great_public_spaces/one?public_place_id=997.

L. Tennyson, 'Will urban beaches become the norm?', retrieved from www.rudi.net/node/16422.

http://en.wikipedia.org/wiki/Paris-Plages (all accessed 25 January 2011).

Rebar: Civic Center Victory Garden
SAN FRANCISCO

The Civic Center Victory Garden was built by Rebar in collaboration with the Garden for the Environment's Victory Garden Program and Slow Food Nation. Victory Gardens 2008+ was a pilot project funded by the city of San Francisco to support the transition of back yards, front yards, window boxes, roof-tops and unused land into organic food production areas, echoing the Victory Garden programmes of the First and Second World Wars. In July 2008 volunteer gardeners removed 10,000 square feet of turf from San Francisco's Civic Center Plaza and transformed the site into a temporary food producing garden. Within weeks, the garden was producing around 100 lbs of fresh organic produce a week, all of which was donated to the San Francisco Food Bank, and distributed to meals programmes throughout the city. The project, part of a broader effort to reconsider the way we think about urban open space, was a great success and, at the request of the mayor, its life was extended to Thanksgiving 2008.

SOURCE: www.rebargroup.org/projects/victorygarden/ (accessed 16 June 2011).

113

Civic Center Victory Garden by Rebar
SAN FRANCISCO

Rebar: Walklet

SAN FRANCISCO

Inspired by PARK(ing) Day and other efforts to convert parking spaces into people places, Rebar has created Walklet, a modular, flexible sidewalk extension system designed to create new public spaces for people by extending the pedestrian realm into the parking lane. The installation of 22 modular units at 22nd and Bartlett in San Francisco in 2010 was part of a pilot project supported by the city. The collection of benches, planters, bike parking and tables, sheathed in stained bamboo and red wood, was in place for six months, and if successful could remain indefinitely. Walklet is extremely adaptable and each three-foot-wide module can be mixed and matched with others to create the right design combination for each site.

SOURCE: www.rebargroup.org/projects/walklet/ (accessed 16 June 2011).

Walklet: flexible sidewalk extension system by Rebar
SAN FRANCISCO

Case Study
#6.17

Rebar: Showplace Triangle
SAN FRANCISCO

San Francisco's streets and public rights-of-way make up 25 per cent of the city's land area, more space than in all of its parks. Many are excessively wide and much of the space is wasted. The Pavement to Parks projects seek to temporarily reclaim these unused sites and turn them quickly and inexpensively into new public plazas and parks. Rebar designed Showplace Triangle (in collaboration with the city of San Francisco, Recology, Flora Grubb Nursery, California College of Arts, Wolfe's Lunch and Axis Café and Artist Ramad) to be a neighbourhood gathering space. Almost entirely built of re-used or re-purposed materials, the project demonstrates that ingenious re-use can also be stylish.

SOURCE: www.rebargroup.org/projects/pavementtoparks/ (accessed 16 June 2011).

115

Showplace Triangle by Rebar
SAN FRANCISCO

Graffiti girl by unknown artist
SHOREDITCH, LONDON, 2011

7: Culture and counterculture

WHILE THE INVESTMENT lavished on public buildings, grand spaces, galleries, theatres or opera houses generally reflects the values of the ruling elites, cities also provide a less formal stage for the arts. The stage may be commercial, or it may be space used for popular entertainment by buskers, performers and pavement artists. It is apparent though, that expectations of culture and of the way it is manifested in the city, are changing and that temporary activities are a reflection of this change. As Stern and Seifert note, '(t)he arts are no longer about going to the symphony, the ballet or a Broadway musical. They are more active, more accessible, and more polyglot'.[1] People increasingly expect to be engaged in rather than merely watch a performance passively. The assumption that art is the preserve of a critical elite has all but disappeared, while the boundaries between culture and counterculture are increasingly difficult to locate.

The changing patterns of cultural consumption

This expansion and diversification of the creative scene reflects a number of underlying trends. One factor is the increasing integration of aesthetic production into commodity production generally. As Jameson states, '(t)he economic urgency of producing ever more novel-seeming goods (from clothing to aeroplanes), at ever greater rates of turnover, now assigns an increasingly essential structural function and position to aesthetic innovation and experimentation'.[2] In consequence, there are now many more commercial cultural businesses ranging from galleries to studios offering courses and space. The means of producing, circulating and exchanging arts and culture have also expanded dramatically through new technology and the information revolution, giving wider, easier access to a larger number of practitioners.[3]

Sultan's Elephant, Royal de Luxe Theatre Company
THE MALL, LONDON, MAY 2006

118

On the demand side, the industry has been fuelled by greater prosperity and disposable income, especially among the young. Compared to previous generations many people also have more leisure time in which to explore arts and culture, and this leisure time is less fixed. The flexible working day has created new time niches within which cultural activities can operate. The blurring of leisure and business time and diversification of the workplace to include the home, the gallery, the member's club or the café, have brought a proliferation of opportunities, and an expanding consumer market. The arts have become a consumer experience to be explored, sampled and even discarded. The transient nature of temporary use is ideally suited to this condition. For the consumer, the experience can be compressed into a condensed lifestyle. For the producer there are more openings available.

The nature of creative output has changed too, reflecting the wider changes in society. MacRitchie writes about the growth in live or performance art, that often breaks down the boundaries between other media (film, TV, video, computer technology, photography, theatre, music, dance and art), and makes some interesting observations about its immediacy and impermanence. She argues that performance art has emerged most powerfully 'at moments when formal aesthetic or social structures were perceived to be inadequate or had actually collapsed'.[4] In the wake of the property collapse of the 1990s, for example, live art animated many empty spaces. When everything else seemed to be shifting and uncertain, the process of doing the work, and its live nature became almost more significant than what was actually done: 'the purity of the moment was all that could be relied on, the

Pavement lighting
LA CROISSETTE, CANNES

119

promise of performance the only one that had not been broken'.[5] She continues: 'By appearing not to care about permanence, performance art made immanence its watchword, its immediacy a guarantee of the purity of its intentions.'[6] The role of the audience, not as a spectator, but as a participant, or even a witness, is vital, and the work is often 'an invitation to be here and be immediate, to feel exactly what it is to be in this place at this time'.[7] Thus, the immediacy of emerging culture echoes the prevailing state of uncertainty in society.

Spontaneous urban culture

Klanten and Hübner's book *Urban Interventions* provides an inspiring photographic record of the informal, unsolicited, playful, often anti-authoritarian artworks that have hit our streets in recent years.[8] In an introductory essay to the book, Feireiss notes that for a 'young generation of urban creatives ... the city in all its chaotic beauty and challenging diversity not only represents their natural habitat, but also their prime area of operation'.[9] He argues that such works are another manifestation of the shift that has occurred in the contemporary art world away from conventional showroom space, towards space in general, and towards performance approaches in which the audience's response, to what are often alien art works, 'becomes the main event'. Bieber, too, views such anti-authoritarian interventions as a grassroots democratic reaction against the elitism of the art scene.[10]

120

Street artist
SOUTH BANK, LONDON, 2011

In *Urban Interventions* nothing is sacred. The interventions transform road markings into space fighters, and manhole covers into fish, or show plastic piping conduits apparently breaking free of the pavements. Glass recycling containers, parking ticket dispensers and utility boxes become faces struggling to escape confinement in the structures, or are painted as if transparent. Blank brick walls are decorated with mosaics and lost mortar is repopulated with miniature street or farmyard scenes. Monotonous expanses of filthy concrete are 'painted' in projects of 'reverse graffiti' using high-pressure water jets. Graffiti for the blind is provided in Braille, and political commentaries are spray-painted onto façades with light-emitting ink that fades slowly over time. Light sculptures transform the vapour emissions from household waste incinerators into luminous green clouds. Posters of real doors and windows are pasted over the boarded-up doors and windows of derelict buildings turning them back, temporarily, into seemingly active spaces. Urban waste is gift-wrapped and massive pieces of chewing gum are erected on the piazzas of Venice. The problem of dog faeces on the street is marked by strategically placed toy train engines as if to freight it away. Sculptures are inflated by the air flow from subway ventilation shafts, and coloured balloons mock CCTV cameras.

These works are all meant to be temporary. They have no intrinsic long-term value, as they cannot be collected, curated or exhibited except through photographic records. They can only be experienced. Such work spans the boundaries between political protest and avant-garde art. In a reference to Hakim Bey's work (discussed in Chapter 3) Bieber declares that such '(u)rban interventions, then, are de facto temporary autonomous zones'.[11]

Bieber argues that unauthorised urban interventions make a stand against the functionalism of the modern city through temporarily 'de-purposing' its furnishings, making everything potentially into a work of art.[12] Such artists are exploring the hidden potentials of the city, creating new ways of reading it and actively refreshing the urban landscape. Their works 'continuously contribute to the subversive face of the city today'.[13] They represent a bottom-up experience of the city, adapting and manipulating the landscape, in the face of the 'functionalistic top-down strategies of traditional urban planning'. The idea is often to change familiar environments overnight, to provide a fleeting, and always temporary, insight into alternative possibilities.[14] As Bieber states, 'The ephemeral and anonymous artworks also match the rhythm of the modern major city, which demands constant renewal and a day-to-day urban praxis'.[15] Some of the temporary projects that are an explicit protest against the increasingly controlled and privatised public space or indeed against society in general are discussed further in Chapter 8.

To some these installations are a symbol of unruly youth without respect for 'society', but the predominant public response appears to be that they are challenging, unexpected, witty and above all, playful. As Rachel Dixon notes, '(g)rafitti is either the scourge of the city or part of what makes it unique, depending on your viewpoint'.[16] She describes the Crono Project in Lisbon, where rather than clamping down on graffiti, the council has turned derelict buildings over to street artists. The project is 'based on the premise that we are all as ephemeral as all our creations – a way of reflecting upon time and enhancing a new dimension of the city: the city as a living organism that is built and created in a spontaneous, natural and free way'.[17] Cities as diverse as Melbourne, Sao Paolo and Stavanger in Norway have similarly recognised that good quality street art can be an asset, and are even organising tours and exhibitions to promote it.

In a similar vein, Malloy makes the connection between temporary uses and radical grassroots community development efforts, and argues that it is possible to formulate 'temporary interventions as a way of interjecting a subversive element into the urban fabric and discourse on urban processes'.[18] Temporary uses can challenge the dominant culture and the 'dominant frame of the city as an avenue for competition and exchange' and demonstrate new ways of building community and social capital

121

122

Graffiti, Queen on motorbike by unknown artist
ISLINGTON, LONDON, 2011

and producing art: 'Temporary use is not only associated with the fleeting use of an urban site, it also incorporates the very concept of temporality as a way of approaching and generating projects that have to do with how we choose to live, work and interact with urban spaces'.[19]

Malloy cites the example of Hotel Neustadt in Halle, Germany in 2003. This was a year-long project, based on extensive community development work, to provide training and generate confidence in all the skills necessary to run the 'hotel' on a shoestring. The temporary hotel was established within an abandoned building, and guests experienced interactive staged productions as part of their stay. The project aimed to reanimate the building and stimulate creative ways of dealing with empty socialist-era housing within a shrinking economy and city. It also represented the potential of temporary activity as a radical form of social cooperation which demands spaces run by the people who use them, and which allow learning, sharing and a redistribution of any surplus.

Malloy argues that cities like Chicago are 'filled with examples of people taking over their productive selves' – independent bakeries, alternative craft stores, arts collectives running alternative spaces, radical artists, educational projects and micro-finance schemes which are part of a 'neighbourhood-based creative economy'.[20] Such alternative forms of art and culture are often popularised, co-opted and commodified, but Malloy sees evidence of resistance emerging in some community-building projects. She cites the work of a group of radical artists, Mess Hall, an experimental cultural centre located on the north side of Chicago. This project is based fundamentally on collective decision making and action, generosity and sharing, experimentation, the creative distribution of surpluses and the generation of culture through social interaction. Her conclusion, that temporary urban practices can be seen as 'a resistant strain of radicalism stubbornly changing form in appropriated cracks within the façade of capitalism',[21] finds support from other examples cited in this book. LaFond similarly found that many of the temporary activities in Berlin were experiments in new forms of urban living, often aiming at sustainability or self-sufficiency, communal living and collective decision making.[22]

123

Temporary art installations

There is a long tradition of art and design pop-ups. At the end of the 1980s the property crash and recession drove many New York art dealers to give up expensive premises and operate temporary shows and exhibitions from old warehouses or their own apartments. Many artists as well, such as Damien Hirst of the Young British Artist movement, started by selling work from temporary spaces. More recently, international art festivals, such as Frieze in London, are not just temporary events in their own right, but also provide the focus and publicity around which other temporary exhibitions can operate (Case Study 7.5). Temporary venues for art, dance and theatre productions have also flourished in recent years.

Nelson's Ship in a Bottle by Yinka Shonibare
FOURTH PLINTH, TRAFALGAR SQUARE, LONDON, APRIL 2011

124

The success of the temporary art installations on the Fourth Plinth, in London's Trafalgar Square illustrates their popularity. There are four plinths in Trafalgar Square and bronze statues (to General Sir Charles James Napier, Major General Sir Henry Havelock and King George IV) stand on three of them. But today few people could name these solemn historic figures; most interest centres on the fourth plinth. This was originally intended to hold an equestrian statue of William IV, but remained empty until 1999, when the Royal Society of Arts (RSA) conceived the idea for a new work. Mark Wallinger, Bill Woodrow and Rachel Whiteread received commissions but as there was no consensus on which work to select, a revolving programme of temporary works evolved instead. In 2005 the

Greater London Authority (GLA) revived the temporary exhibitions with work from Marc Quinn, Thomas Schütte and Yinka Shonibare. Antony Gormley's work *One & Other* in 2009 featured 2,400 selected members of the public who spent one hour each on the plinth, as a temporary work of art in their own right. The installations have not only become a very popular feature of the capital's cultural life, and an important tourist attraction, but have established an international reputation in the art world.[23]

In 2010 a number of established names in the UK arts scene used short-lived venues for exhibitions, dance, theatre and film, reflecting a link between the pop-up 'fad' and an increasing creative interest in '"site-specific" theatre and dance projects'.[24] For example, a platform at the former Eurostar terminal at Waterloo Station, London was transformed into a 1,000-seat venue for the York Theatre Royal production of E. Nesbit's novel *The Railway Children*, complete with a 66-tonne steam locomotive. This project, and others such as Sadler's Wells production, the Electric Hotel, at King's Cross, the Hannah Barry Gallery Pop-Up Sculpture Exhibition in Peckham, south London and Theatre Absolute in Coventry, have negotiated short-term access to vacant sites or buildings with the owners (Case Studies 7.1, 7.2, 7.4 and 7.5). Others, such as Theatre Delicatessen in London's West End, have been given permission to occupy buildings on a peppercorn rent, pending their redevelopment (Case Study 7.3). Other groups, such as Oubliette Arthouse in London, have chosen to squat vacant buildings as temporary venues for their exhibitions and performances (Case Study 7.6). And in many other instances, as we explored in Chapter 6, the free space of the urban realm itself is increasingly becoming a venue for street theatre, art and other fleeting cultural events.

125

Temporary cultural events and performances are also being used increasingly as a stimulus for regeneration. In the case of the Electric Hotel, the initiative was supported by developers Argent as a way of starting to create a 'sense of place' at the new King's Cross development. Similarly, in 2009, Berlin-based multi-disciplinary practice Raumlabor transformed the much-vandalised Eichbaum station (located between Essen and Mülheim) into a temporary opera house, Eichbaumoper, as a way of changing the prevailing perceptions of the area away from fear and foreboding.[25] In many other examples, brief arts events provide the avenue by which local communities are encouraged to engage in consultation processes about the options for regeneration or the future of local facilities or spaces.

In conclusion

There is now an almost indistinguishable line between culture and counterculture, especially when the sophisticated urban elite is open to new experiences and eager to commodify everything from pop-up restaurants to street theatre or even to purchase graffiti. The cases in this chapter are just some illustrations of the breadth of activity and the energy that temporary uses are bringing to our cities. There can be no generalisations here, but wider sections of society now have the luxury of consuming culture in its various forms. Our changing work and leisure lives facilitate this, as does the fabric of cities, especially its voids. In uncertain times, the immediacy and impermanence of performance art seems to be striking a chord as it moves out from traditional venues to colonise the city.

126

Stunt cycling and graffiti
SOUTH BANK, LONDON

Case Study
#7.1

Theatre Absolute
COVENTRY

An internationally recognised theatre group, Theatre Absolute, opened a professional 40-seat theatre in a former chip shop in Coventry city centre's shopping precinct in December 2009. The building was provided rent-free by the council for 18 months, and the company secured support from the Arts Council, England, Art in Empty Spaces project (see Chapter 5).

Theatre Absolute was inspired by companies such as Chicago's Steppenwolf who were at the forefront of pioneering theatre in disused spaces in the late 1970s. It aims to give independent theatre a physical presence at the heart of the community. Integral to the company are participatory performance and literacy development activities for young people, particularly those at risk. In the run up to Christmas the company hosted lunchtime readings from Dickens' *A Christmas Carol*, for shoppers, office workers and families. Over the August Bank Holiday weekend it presented tales from Coventry's history at a series of free outdoor performances. For Coventry Council the initiative was a positive development in an area hard hit by the recession, and they persuaded the company to extend its opening hours to the lunchtime in a 'bring-your-own-sandwiches' programme.

SOURCES: Arts Council, 'Theatre Absolute opens the doors to its Shop Front Theatre', 3 December 2009, retrieved from www.artscouncil.org.uk/news/theatre-absolute-opens-doors-its-shop-front-theatr/ (accessed 14 June 2011).

Arts Council, 'Art in Empty Spaces: turning vacant spaces into creative places', retrieved from http://press.artscouncil.org.uk/content/detail.aspx?releaseid=800&newsareaid=2 (accessed 14 June 2011).

Coventry University, 'ICE tenant Theatre Absolute open their doors for the Shop Front Theatre', Institute of Applied Entrepreneurship, retrieved from www.coventry.ac.uk/researchnet/ice/News/Pages/NewsDetail.aspx?ItemQuery1=20 (accessed 14 June 2011).

H. Hanra, 'Art's great squatting revolution', *The Times*, 16 January 2010, retrieved from http://entertainment.timesonline.co.uk/tol/arts_and_entertainment/visual_arts/article6988391.ece (accessed 24 January 2011).

www.theatreabsolute.co.uk/home.asp (accessed 25 January 2011).

127

Case Study
#7.2

Sadler's Wells: the Electric Hotel

KING'S CROSS, LONDON

The Electric Hotel, a theatrical performance, appeared in London in June 2010 in a four-floor building constructed from recycled shipping containers that resembled a piece of 1920s Bauhaus architecture. The creative team behind the project included Sadler's Wells, Without Walls and Fuel Theatre Company. The result was a unique demonstration of dance theatre. The audience witnessed the unfolding drama from outside the building through floor to ceiling hotel windows, as voyeurs into 'do-not-disturb' private rooms, and wearing headphones in order to eavesdrop. Adding to the drama was the dramatic backdrop of the last remaining Victorian ironwork gas holder at King's Cross Central. The temporary production was encouraged by Argent, developers of the King's Cross site.

SOURCES: www.sadlerswells.com/show/Electric-Hotel.

www.theatretickets.co.uk/theatre-news/406/Sadlers+Wells+with+The+Electric+Hotel.html

(both accessed 16 June 2011).

The Electric Hotel pop-up theatre by Sadler's Wells, Without Walls and Fuel Theatre Company
KING'S CROSS, LONDON

The Electric Hotel pop-up theatre by Sadler's Wells, Without Walls and Fuel Theatre Company
KING'S CROSS, LONDON

Theatre Delicatessen
LONDON

Theatre Delicatessen (established by Roland Smith, Jessica Brewster and Frances Loy in 2008) is currently occupying its second vacant building in central London on a short-term peppercorn rent. The group of actor/director/producers were motivated by a desire to explore the possibilities of non-theatre space as a venue for theatre, and a more urgent, even headstrong desire to create and stage their own theatre without having to wait to break in to established venues or compromise their ideas. Their quest for a cheap, temporary space was not only an economic and artistic necessity, but has also proved to be a huge amount of fun.

Finding an appropriate space was relatively easy through an existing contact at the Property Management Group (PMG) which had previously loaned empty properties for rehearsals. Their contact identified the empty ground floor of an office building in Regent Street for their first production, *A Midsummer Night's Dream*. PMG also helped to promote the show through its own PR company and eased cash flow by booking the show for corporate events, which proved to be a resounding success.

At the time, PMG were managing the building on behalf of P&O Properties but the proposed redevelopment was stalled in the recession. Part-way through Theatre Delicatessen's tenure, P&O sold the building to Great Portland Estates (GPE). Fortunately GPE looked kindly on their venture and allowed them to stay to complete their second production, *Fanshen*. With demolition work on the building due to start early in 2010, GPE offered them another vacant property on a peppercorn rent for 12 months just off Oxford Street.

In its second temporary venue, a five-storey building, Theatre Delicatessen has been able to realise its interest in mentoring talent in young theatre companies. From its start as a pop-up *performance* therefore, it has now developed into a pop-up *venue*. Its first production in the new space, *Theatre Souk*, presented performances from 14 different companies in spaces throughout the building. The reviews were very positive and towards the end of the run there were audiences of over 200 a night, with queues at the door.

A Health and Safety Certificate is required for a License as a Place of Entertainment, and health and safety issues can prove to be the major headache and expense. Roland Smith displays a well-thumbed copy of the 'yellow book' of *Technical Standards for Places of Entertainment* that sets out everything from the number of people allowed in rooms of different sizes, to where to put emergency lighting and automatic door closers. Theatre Delicatessen is now on first name terms with the Fire Officer and the local council's Health and Safety Officer who, while enforcing standards strictly, strives to make the project a success.

As an unpaid company, the theatre must minimise its costs and the availability of space on a peppercorn rent is therefore crucial. Costs are kept low through recycling materials, scavenging and hiring out space for rehearsals. Buildings insurance is covered by the landlord but Theatre Delicatessen must pay Public Liability Insurance. As a charity the group receives a significant discount on council tax. Roland believes that such temporary use has a negligible impact on the finances of large property companies; it can reduce maintenance costs, protect the building from squatters and even provide leverage with the local council through demonstrating that the property company is supporting the arts. Theatre Delicatessen is committed to continuing to use non-theatre spaces for its productions, and is optimistic that when the time comes to refurbish the present venue, the landlord will find the company alternative premises.

131

SOURCES: M. Shepherd, 'Great Portland makes its development Marcol', *Property Week*, 12 February 2010, retrieved from www.propertyweek.com/great-portland-makes-its-development-marcol/3158109.article.
Interview with Roland Smith.
www.theatredelicatessen.co.uk/blogs/tag/reviews/ (both accessed 16 June 2011).

The Hannah Barry Gallery Pop-Up Sculpture Exhibition
LONDON

In the emerging Copeland Cultural Quarter in Peckham, south London, the historic Bussey Building is home to almost a hundred artists and small businesses, evidence of Peckham's burgeoning creative activity. Cheap rent and large empty buildings are the classic lure for young artists, and Peckham's creative boom has also been helped by a stream of graduates from nearby Camberwell and Goldsmiths art colleges.

For three summers (2008–10) the Hannah Barry Gallery, located next to the Bussey Building, has held a very successful outdoor pop-up sculpture exhibition on the normally deserted top three floors of the nearby Peckham Rye multi-storey car park. The exhibitions have focused on the work of young artists who would not normally have the chance to exhibit in mainstream galleries. As grassroots events, they have attracted help and resources from many local artists and have created a sense of energy and possibility. As a result the event has blossomed.

SOURCES: H. Hoby, 'Peckham raises the roof', the *Observer*, 5 July 2009, retrieved from
www.guardian.co.uk/artanddesign/2009/jul/05/art-goldsmiths.

SallyB2, 'Art preview: rooftop sculpture park in Peckham', 30 June 2009, retrieved from
http://londonist.com/2009/06/art_preview_rooftop_sculpture_park.php?gallery0Pic=2.

'Top-level art in a Peckham car park', 1 July 2009, retrieved from
http://realcycling.blogspot.com/2009/07/top-level-art-in-peckham-car-park.html
(all accessed 25 January 2011).

Case Study
#7.5

Gallery Libby Sellers
LONDON

Libby Sellers left her post as curator of contemporary art at the Design Museum in London to set up an itinerant gallery. Its mission is to provide a platform for emerging designers. The first premises in Exhibition Road were provided by the Brompton Design District, an initiative operated by South Kensington Estates who could see the complementary nature of this type of temporary use to their business as estate managers in one of the wealthiest districts of London. They fill temporarily empty shops with interesting and alluring content that draws customers into the area. The collaboration has continued since 2007, with Gallery Libby Sellers moving to other shop locations in the area, including a disused car park.

The launch of the gallery in September 2007 was timed to coincide with the London Design Festival, and it continues to 'piggy-back', for its publicity and profile, on other arts and design events in London. As a commercial enterprise it does pay a small rent to the Brompton Design District for its various premises, but operates on a simple and flexible lease or license agreement. While the pop-up design gallery has been successful, the model does have disadvantages. Purchasers, especially of high-value items, can be nervous of a business that is clearly transient. And artists often prefer a more permanent location for the display of their work if they are offering an exclusive contract with a dealer. Ironically the gallery still requires permanent premises to store its work and basic equipment when not operating from a temporary shop. Planning such a business can also be very difficult given the uncertainty of finding the right premises, in the right location, at the right time. Like many temporary enterprises the curiosity of its founder is also starting to focus on other possible creative outlets. That said, however, pop-ups like Gallery Libby Sellers are sustainable business models with low overheads, operational flexibility and the ability to seize the moment and respond to, and capture the excitement of, whatever is happening in the creative world at a given time.

SOURCE: Interview with Libby Sellers.

133

The Oubliette Arthouse
LONDON

The Oubliette Arthouse is an itinerant, autonomous arts group based in London. It squats empty properties to showcase the work of new artists, and in fact developed from the squatting scene. Its founder Dan Simon has been a squatter for nearly 10 years and many of the 35 premises he has occupied to date have provided an outlet for those working at the cutting edge of art, music and theatre. For struggling artists without affordable space in which to create or display their work, the existence of long-term vacant property is both a frustration and a tantalising opportunity. By 2009 Simon was increasingly interested in the potential of vacant property for showcasing arts, but was becoming exasperated by the problems of organising events within an essentially anarchist culture. Many creative ideas had fizzled out through a lack of clear leadership. It has taken hard work and experimentation to find an organisational model that works as a vehicle for fringe arts productions, but the Arthouse is now a recognised arts promotion group, regularly attracting positive reviews from the mainstream press. Several of its 'discoveries' have subsequently been taken up by mainstream venues.

Simon sees the Arthouse as 'a group of serious grown-ups running a proper organisation, not a bunch of anarchic chancers daubing graffiti on the walls'. He points to the long tradition of squatting in England and the massive contribution to culture that this 'way of life' has made. The Arthouse is committed to minimal interference with the property and maintains that it always returns property in a better condition. Having entered a building the Arthouse inform the owner, the police and relevant authorities and ask for permission to stay. In some cases, they have been allowed to remain for a limited period. Their presence can save the owner £200 or £300 a week in security and maintenance costs, and can prevent fly tipping and damage from break-ins by kids. Squatting is a civil dispute between the owner and the squatter and generally it takes several months to get an eviction order through the courts, which provides just enough time to organise and deliver an arts programme. The first task for the live-in community of volunteers is to clean the building from top to bottom. They install their own basic health and safety systems and invite the local Fire Officer or Building Inspector to ensure basic compliance with the regulations; otherwise they could be closed down. The Arthouse provides entirely unregulated and unlicensed venues, and in this sense operates as a private house and its audiences are 'guests'. Simon is clear that occupying such spaces comes with a massive responsibility – to the volunteer crew, the art, the artists and the public – and is highly stressful. Its most celebrated squats to date, the Mexican and Tanzanian Embassies in Mayfair, empty since 2004, attracted considerable press attention in 2009.

The Arthouse enjoys financial self-sufficiency, principally through donations. With no extramural objectives or targets, it is able to focus on offering both free space and considerable creative freedom to its artists. The artistic programmes are put together from a database of over 5,000 independent artists. In an average two-month squat there may be two or three programmes of work. As well as arts promotion, the Arthouse also acts as a 'hub', bringing together people from different media to collaborate on new ideas. The shows are promoted through Facebook and Twitter posts to over 2,000 supporters. It is a model that works and it achieves its objectives, but not without immense stresses, and Simon would be the first to admit that the offer of a long-term but free home with no strings would be seized with both hands.

SOURCES: Interview with Dan Simon, Oubliette Arthouse.
http://theoubliette.co.uk/ (accessed 2 November 2011).

135

The Oubliette Arthouse
LONDON

Sculpture, NDSM

AMSTERDAM

8: Activism and community use

IN THEIR STUDY of temporary uses in Berlin, Urban Catalyst suggest that temporary users of space, or 'space pioneers', are 'evidence of a trend to greater social commitment, to more participation, to active networks and the desire to try out something new'.[1] The report also pointed to growing insecurity and the poor prospects for permanent employment, as factors that are leading 'a growing number of people to seek a niche in which they can dare try out their own social experiment and strike a balance between material prosperity and social well-being'.[2] We must therefore consider the possibility that the growing interest in temporary use reflects a greater number of people who are prepared to act to achieve their desires. This chapter looks at some of the underlying trends that may be contributing to a growth in grassroots activism and some of its manifestations.

There is certainly evidence in the UK that the prospects for today's youth are worsening. The *Guardian* newspaper reported unprecedented competition for university places in 2010 with demand for university places hitting a record high for the fourth year in a row.[3] By May 2010, there were over 640,000 applications for places, an increase of nearly 14 per cent on 2009. Despite government funding for extra places in 2010, it is forecast that record numbers of school leavers may miss out on a place. In future, the rise in tuition fees means there is also a real risk that many individuals from poorer backgrounds, who have been at the heart of the drive to uplift aspirations and increase social mobility, will be denied a place.

At the same time, graduates are facing an intense scramble to get a job. A recent poll of employers revealed that the number of applications for each vacancy has surged to nearly 70 while the number of available positions is predicted to fall by nearly seven per cent.[4] Competition in the jobs market is fierce for the 'post-crunch' generation of students. Looking at the wider picture, the number of young long-term unemployed people is still rising across two-thirds of the UK.[5] Young people still face particular hurdles to getting jobs and the youth unemployment rate at 17 per cent, is more than double the national rate.

A similar picture is apparent elsewhere in the world. A report from the UN International Labour Organisation in 2010, states that global youth unemployment has hit a record high and is expected to rise further. Of around 620 million economically active 15 to 24 year olds, 81 million were unemployed at the end of 2009, the highest number since records began in 1991.[6] The global youth unemployment rate of 13 per cent was up from 11.9 per cent just before the global downturn in 2007. The agency warns of the 'risk of a crisis legacy of a lost generation' with a disillusioned youth trapped in a cycle of working poverty or in danger of detaching from the labour market altogether (Case Study 8.1). The implications for governments are significant, as illustrated by the popular uprisings in Tunisia, Egypt, Libya and elsewhere in 2011.

Such trends are likely to force more people to opt out of conventional society and seek an alternative entrepreneurial outlet for their ambitions. There is some evidence that the rise in temporary uses is partly a manifestation of this. For example, the Raumpioniere study in Berlin found that a small proportion of space pioneers saw temporary activities as an opportunity to drop out of traditional social structures and create alternative forms of living and working.[7] There are also signs that more young people than ever before may have the confidence and drive to *act* to realise their dreams, rather than waiting for opportunities to come their way. For example, a report by the Carnegie UK Trust identified a rise in individualism as one of the key drivers shaping the future of civil society in the UK,[8] while Evans and Saxton found evidence that affluence is linked to a greater desire for self-fulfilment and self-expression.[9] At the same time, this affluence provides a degree of security within which it is safe to experiment. Similar research by Brooks found that many young people in Europe today are self-actualising individuals who are motivated by a sense of individual purpose rather than an obligation to the state.[10]

138

Encouraging local participation

Across the globe, we have witnessed an explosion of interest, over the past decade, in 'public participation'.[11] Participation is almost universally seen as a 'good thing' by democratic national and local governments. Voting and political party membership have been in marked decline particularly in the West, and involving individuals directly in decisions that affect their lives is seen as a way of strengthening the legitimacy and accountability of democracy. Various initiatives have sought to encourage formal participation (such as postal voting, citizens' juries etc.) but, in the West at least, it still remains at an all-time low. While people are turning away from formal political involvement, there is little evidence that they are any less active in local community groups or campaigning organisations.[12] People remain willing to engage in issues that are perceived to concern them directly, and are no longer willing to be the passive recipients of government services or decision making, however benign. From the community perspective, local involvement offers an outlet in the face of this perceived remoteness and irrelevance of central government.

Public consultation
WHITECHAPEL ROAD, LONDON

139

Public sector reform has been strongly influenced by market principles. Increasingly the citizen is seen as a consumer who needs to be empowered to make informed choices, and enabled to hold service-deliverers accountable for their performance. Participation can help to ensure that services are designed so that they are more responsive to people's needs. It is recognised that the previous practice of relying exclusively on 'specialists' neglected the local knowledge and experience that is vital to the design of places and services that 'work'. Citizens now expect to be consulted on issues that affect their lives. In fact, apart from encouraging action by local communities in their own right, many temporary installations and interventions have been established with the express purpose of providing a focus for community engagement around the future of an area. For example, Park Fiction in Hamburg (see Chapter 9) used a 'planning container' that could be moved around the neighbourhood to collect residents' wishes. A similar temporary building Hullabaloo by Fluid Architects, provided a focus for consultations on the future of Shoreditch Goods Yard, London. In addition, involving people in decision making and bringing them together around a common cause has been shown to empower communities, foster ties and shared norms and help build social cohesion, as well as providing benefits to personal development such as increased self-esteem and new skills.[13]

In the UK, local authorities have been required to inform, consult and involve local residents since 2006,[14] and in 2009 a 'Duty to Involve' came into force that requires local authorities to embed a culture of engagement and empowerment in service delivery and decision making.[15] Such measures have been accompanied by strategies of devolution, decentralisation and the involvement of citizens at grassroots level generally. All the UK political parties now declare themselves in favour of social entrepreneurship and there are initiatives that encourage local authorities to pass their surplus assets to third sector organisations – charities, community groups and social enterprises – with the local roots, support and drive to get them into productive use, even temporarily. This has been encapsulated within the UK government's 'Localism Agenda'.

At a time of significant cuts in public expenditure such government policies also help to justify the abolition of directly funded social programmes. The independent community is meant to cost as little as possible and simultaneously help to diminish state intervention and funding. A central policy of the UK government, the 'Big Society', sees devolving power to citizens and communities ostensibly as a way of generating social responsibility, civic pride and innovation. The Big Society will introduce reform to the planning system to give more powers to neighbourhoods, train a new generation of community organisers, encourage volunteering, devolve power to local authorities and support the creation and expansion of co-operatives, charities and social enterprises.[22] The advent of the Big Society spells the end of widespread government-planned interventions, and will be accompanied by sharp and draconian cuts in state expenditure. By 2014–15, £81 billion worth of spending cuts will be made in the UK, reducing the fiscal deficit from 10 per cent of GDP in 2011–12 to 1.9 per cent in 2014–15.[23]

140

In Chapter 3 we noted that entrepreneurship and freelancing in the UK grew by 20 per cent between 1998 and 2008 (Case Study 8.2).[16] This has been accompanied by a remarkable growth throughout the world in social enterprise, which Feiss defines as a 'for-profit/non-profit or hybrid business, using private investment to work on common-good social problems'.[17] According to government figures there are currently 55,000 social enterprises in the UK with a combined turnover of £27 billion.[18] The Monitor Group suggests that the sector could have a global value of over £500 billion a year within 5 to 10 years.[19] In the UK, the Social Investment Task Force was established in 2000 to stimulate and improve the efficiency of social investment.[20] Partly as a result of its recommendations, the last decade has seen a significant increase in social investment funds and growing interest from the mainstream financial sector. In parallel, a more entrepreneurial culture is emerging among many voluntary sector organisations. A number of new social investment vehicles have appeared providing grants, loans, risk and venture capital (such as Charity Bank, Bridges Social Entrepreneurs Fund and Triodos Social Enterprise Fund). These have attracted new investors from private equity funds, wealthy individuals, institutional investors and charitable foundations as well as government funding. In May 2010, Charity Bank announced record lending to social enterprises and charities during 2009 of £8.5 million.[21] Investment by Socially Responsible Investment Funds has seen strong growth over the decade, to over £760 billion in 2008. In the UK, Community Investment Tax Relief was introduced in 2003, providing tax relief to investors in accredited Community Development Finance Institutions. Social enterprises now deliver a huge range of products and services: day-care, home-care and rehabilitation services, vocational training, affordable housing, regeneration projects and wind- and water-powered energy generation.

It would be wrong at this stage to attempt to draw general conclusions from long-term economic uncertainty, the growth of the third sector and the flourishing of temporary activities. What .is becoming clearer, however, is that many individuals are coming together, forming new enterprises and participating in new forms of work and self-expression. The manifestation is sometimes a temporary structure, event or activity, and many of these enterprises involve architects, designers and a wide range of professionals from other disciplines working collaboratively.

Temporary architectural projects

Rowan Moore, on a mission 'to uncover the brightest of the newest generation of British architects' for the *Observer* newspaper, was struck by the fact that some really young, recently qualified architects had not only designed, but also built, often with their own hands, some very exciting temporary structures, 'things the PR world has called pop-ups, whose short lives leave an impression on the memory'.[24] Moore cites these as part of a 'lineage of temporary installations fuelled by the "power of enthusiasm"', that 'share a mood, of getting back to the basic pleasures of building' and which are a reaction (even an antidote) to the computer-dominated design processes of the large architectural offices. They demonstrate the desire to actually create something, and to do so in the spirit of adaptation. They could also be seen as a reaction to the limited prospects of highly paid architectural work in today's climate and an expression of the energy of the 'can do' generation (Case Studies 8.3, 8.4 and 8.5). Popupcity.net similarly notes that many architects have coped with the recession through finding temporary projects to work on and 'broaden their professional scope'.[25]

141

Many of the temporary structures that are emerging from architects exploit the availability of new building technologies and materials from laminated timber, to woven plastic bags, plastic water tanks and storage boxes,[26] that allow rapid and cheap assembly, disassembly and transportation (Case Study 8.6). For example, at the 'beach' at Amsterdam's suburb Almere, DUS Architects built an illegal temporary summer house/hotel, Gecekondu, constructed entirely of woven plastic bags filled with sand.[27] The project was a protest against the over-regulated and formal Dutch planning culture and a plea for greater spontaneity. In Parque da Cidade, Porto, two designers built a semi-translucent bar out of 420 IKEA storage boxes fixed on a metal frame, for a competition organised by the Universidade do Porto. By opening one of the walls the cube transforms into a bar, and at night the boxes are illuminated by LED lights that change colour in response to music.[28] Similarly, the Knot, developed by Berlin-based multi-disciplinary practice Raumlabor, is a mobile inflatable space that provides a platform for artistic production, exchange and experimentation. It is capable of housing a wide range of uses – workshop, kitchen, café, laboratory, classroom, stage, dormitory, disco, exhibition space and archive – and in 2010 was erected for a few weeks in Berlin, Warsaw and Bucharest.[29] A giant 145-foot inflatable is planned as an add-on to the Hirschorn Museum in Washington D.C. It is proposed that the translucent structure will be installed twice a year, transforming the building into a luminous landmark.[30] Meanwhile, Tim Pyne Associates have created the 'm-hotel' a temporary apart-hotel for use on vacant sites. The 500 square feet units slot into a steel frame and the outside is decorated using bus-film technology that can be tailored to the character and needs of particular sites. The hotel is designed to last for between seven and ten years, after which it is broken down and removed.[31]

Environmental activism

As a manifestation of environmental activism, temporary projects have often sought to use discarded materials both to highlight the waste associated with modern living and to demonstrate the potential for recycling. Raumlabor's House of Contamination was an experimental museum/cultural centre created for Artissima 17, the International Fair of Contemporary Art in Turin in 2010. Walls were made out of rubbish intercepted en route through the recycling process: crushed plastic bottles, compressed bales of paper, fabrics and discarded wood. The furniture was produced from old fridges, washing machines, doors, dressers, bookshelves and chairs. Located inside the vast space of the Oval Linghotto, which was built for use at the 2006 Winter Olympics, the large temporary structure hosted a number of spaces for dance, cinema, literature, design, urbanism and education.[32]

In a similar project designed to raise awareness of the shocking levels of plastic in our oceans and the growth of the 'Great Pacific Garbage Patch', Corona has launched a Save the Beach campaign.[33] To give visual expression to the project, German sculptor H.A. Shult, who is known for his garbage art, designed a hotel made out of 12 tons of garbage found on beaches (from cans and car parts to socks and soccer balls). The unusual temporary accommodation was open to guests for just five days.[34] The hotel was launched in Rome for World Environment Day and the campaign has travelled to places as diverse as South Korea, Brazil, Pakistan, Canada and Vietnam.

Protest

The right to demonstrate lies at the heart of the democratic state and is one of the litmus tests of the stewardship of public space. Political protest is often a temporary activity that occupies and transforms the street for a brief period before melting away. However, the concept of protest is moving from the temporary to the permanent and this is posing new questions about citizen rights to the public realm. An early example of the permanent protest was the women's peace camp at Greenham Common in the 1980s. A more recent example has been the peace camp in Parliament Square in London beneath the flag poles of the Commonwealth nations. This somewhat unstructured protest has grown up over the past three years and despite repeated attempts to remove or close it has stubbornly hung on.

Activism has always had an impact on the fabric of the city, which is the canvas on which the political message of the excluded or alienated can be expressed. Graffiti as an artistic and countercultural

142

Peace camp
PARLIAMENT SQUARE, LONDON, 2009

143

Mural
FALLS ROAD, BELFAST

expression was considered further in Chapter 7. Many murals are, in contrast, officially sanctioned and if they succeed in gaining the support of their communities, as in Belfast, they may become semi-permanent.

Urban agriculture and gardening projects

Some of the most common forms of temporary community project are concerned with urban agriculture (Case Studies 6.15, 8.7 and 8.8). The practice of small-scale, localised urban gardening or farming has long been popular in Europe and elsewhere, but the use of surplus urban land for allotments, orchards, gardens, nurseries or farms has grown into a significant movement in recent years, and is one of the most widespread temporary interventions. The economic downturn, rising living costs, advocacy by popular TV chefs as well as a growing interest in organic food and sustainability have all served to fuel interest. Some gardens spring up and later disappear as the land is reclaimed for development, but many are designed to be moved and reinstalled elsewhere as the need arises. Most food growing initiatives are community inspired and instigated, although there are examples that are public or even private sector-led. Apart from growing food, waste land is being used temporarily for the production of nursery stock for planting permanent landscapes, for grazing sheep and bee-keeping (bees produce some of their best honey from urban flowers). In Sheffield, a project run by the city council in partnership with the Whirlow Farm Trust (an educational trust) has even grassed over the sites of demolished housing areas and installed moveable electric stock-proof fencing to allow the temporary grazing of cattle.[35]

London and other major cities have also seen a growth in recent years in 'guerrilla gardening'. Enthusiasts, frustrated by urban eyesores or lacking access to gardens of their own, colonise vacant plots to grow flowers, thereby brightening the street scene for all. The term was coined by artist Liz Christy and her Green Guerrilla group in 1973 in the Bowery Houston area of New York. They started by scattering seeds on empty spaces and planting disused tree pits, and then transformed a derelict private lot into a garden.[36] Since then the movement has blossomed throughout the world.

In 2009 the New Local Government Network estimated that 100,000 people were on waiting lists for allotments in the UK. Since the Dig for Victory campaign during the Second World War when there were 1.4 million allotments, the current supply has declined to around 200,000 plots, well below the level of demand. The report notes that '(i)n order to increase supply in areas of high demand, more innovative approaches need to be adopted. As the supply of land is finite, these approaches largely involve converting under-utilised land into more productive allotments'.[37] Allotments bring a wide range of benefits: health (from physical exercise, a healthier diet and stress relief), education (on healthy food and environmental issues), sustainability (on carbon footprints, packaging waste, composting and biodiversity) as well as facilitating social interaction and building social capital. Communication and mediation between landowners and potential temporary users is important and many cities are now developing simple programmes to do this.[38]

144

Some cities have formally recognised the new role that urban agriculture can bring. The crossover between the economic, health and environmental agendas, linked to the evident popularity of food cultivation programmes, can yield considerable political capital for very little public funding. Cities such as Groningen and Middlesbrough have developed strategies for urban agriculture that are embedded in their land-use plans (Case Study 8.9). In other cases such as Detroit, urban agriculture is a community response to significant population decline and dereliction. Here the city's response is more one of tolerance and tacit acceptance rather than active involvement through planned programmes (Case Study 8.10).

Allan Correy, writing as early as 1978, advocated the creation of 'ephemeral landscapes', arguing that the technology exists to experiment with trees, fountains, paving, grass, even shelters, kiosks and play equipment as moveable elements.[39] In the last decade the range of such temporary spaces equipped with moveable elements has expanded greatly. Plants can be grown in moveable containers of all sorts from wheelbarrows to shopping trolleys, or, as with soil bags and beds on pallets, they may have to be moved from site to site on fork-lift trucks. There is now a growing collection of case studies to show how this can be put into practice. The Union Street Urban Orchard in Southwark was designed in containers that were wholly transplantable (Case Study 4.2). The ECObox garden initiated by atelier d'architecture autogérée (aaa), in the La Chapelle area of northern Paris in 2001, was assembled on pallets that could be moved to new sites as and when the need arose.[40]

What if: projects seek vacant and neglected spaces around London's housing estates and develop their use for food production and social space. The first Vacant Lot project established an allotment garden in Shoreditch, London in May 2007 using 70 half-tonne bulk bags filled with soil.[41] Such bags are not only breathable and provide space for roots to grow, but are also moveable. Over 60 households from the surrounding housing estates were given a Vacant Lot plot.[42] The What if team is now working to establish 20 new allotment gardens in inner-city housing estates by 2012 based on this model.

145

Community recreation projects

There is a long history of temporary urban events such as festivals, carnivals and sports fixtures that are organised in parks and streets in fine weather. Children and young people have always colonised under-used spaces for play and adventure: BMX bikers and skateboarders build their own tracks using whatever materials are at hand. However, the number and range of temporary recreation projects has grown considerably. Parks, riding centres, adventure parks, urban beaches, ice rinks and swimming pools have all been established on a temporary basis (see pp. 91–3 and Case Studies 4.1, 6.7, 6.8, 6.14 and 8.4). The new communication technologies are playing an important role in enabling the development of online communities that can share their enthusiasms, ideas and initiatives. Just-in-time events and spontaneous activities such as yoga in a park, a cinema in an abandoned petrol station or a rave in a vacant office, can now be organised with ease. People have even organised a pool party in someone else's outdoor pool, located via Google Maps.

The Sunday Adventure Club (which originated in Amsterdam) is a temporary club of self-organised urban pioneers, who realise their personal passions through initiating activities in public spaces.[43] ExperimentaDesign, which hosted an exhibition of such projects in 2008, argued that they are a response to 'over-regulated cities (which) provide little room for their citizens to play freely, conduct experiments, and be adventurous'.[44] The Club identifies vacant or under-used plots, dead ends and corners of public squares, and matches the space with an unmet need from a club that would otherwise have no space in the city. Examples include a space for boat building, another for outdoor cooking, an outdoor beauty parlour, a dog training space and a study area for urban flora and fauna. Such projects convert 'no-mans lands into everyman's land', and transform near-abandoned plots into public places with a strong identity and communal value.

Krasny provides a case study that illustrates the immense delight that temporary play spaces can bring.[45] In 2005 a temporary vertical playing field was located on Wallensteinplatz in Vienna. Twenty metres tall, it was a hybrid of architecture, installation and sculpture that was not only usable for play but was also inhabited by artists and architectural students. The physical use of the tower was much greater than had been anticipated. The creators were astonished by the intensity with which the children and young people climbed 'their' tower and participated through adding things to it. The intensity of use was heightened by the time limit for the installation.

146

Squatting and community uses

One of the most enduring forms of activism resulting in temporary use is, of course, squatting and there are a number of case studies in this book that illustrate how this can play a positive role beyond the original purpose of bringing an empty building back into short-term beneficial use (Case Study 7.6). The relationship between squatting and political activism has led commentators to take very different stances in assessing its role as either a constructive or disruptive element in urban renewal. We do not intend to delve deeply into this area, but the activity has spawned some very interesting projects.

The very 'threat' of squatting is a catalyst leading landowners, developers and city authorities to consider pre-emptive strategies to promote or sanction similarly short-term occupations that they can control (see Chapter 4). As early as the 1970s, city authorities responded to the perceived threat of squatting by initiating 'homesteading' schemes, originally pioneered in North America. Empty houses were transferred to community groups or individuals with the will and finance to refurbish them. Many cities are currently developing programmes along similar lines. For example, the Save the House project in Leipzig is an effort to stem the loss of some of the estimated 1,000 empty Gründerzeit buildings in the city. The programme offers five years without rent for people willing to live in these vacant buildings. Tenants undertake basic maintenance and small repairs, and notify the landlord of larger problems. A non-profit organisation receives funds to market the initiative and helps match owners and users.[46]

Europe and to a lesser extent, North America have a long history of buildings that have been squatted for use as social centres, community cafés, bars, libraries, free shops, swaps shops and gyms. Such community centres often combine a range of activities within one space to act as a non-commercial social hub. Most exist or existed in countries where squatting is legal, such as the Ernst-Kirchweger-Haus in Austria, the RampART Social Centre in England, OT301 in the Netherlands and Ungdomshuset in Denmark. Some of these centres, such as ABC No Rio in New York (Case Study 8.11), gained ownership of the property after a lengthy battle, while others lost the battle and were evicted.

Many other temporary uses have provided facilities or services for the community (such as crèches and nurseries, laundries, heritage centres, and spaces for informal learning and teaching) (Case Study 8.12). They are often set up and operated by volunteers, and use the initial period of low overheads to gain a sound footing as a community or even a commercial business. The Raumpioniere study of temporary uses in Berlin found that many space pioneers run some kind of public venue: '(b)arely half of the temporary use projects studied in Berlin chose to identify as a business, be it an exclusively commercial or cultural venture, or even a "community-minded" business' and '(o)ne third of the temporary users documented run their project on a voluntary basis'.[47] In other more established community centres (such as Bromley-by-Bow Centre in London), the role and reputation as a community hub has been established incrementally over time, through a sequence of temporary activities.

147

In conclusion

This chapter has demonstrated that temporary uses and activities are one of the manifestations of personal and community activism. The expressions of this vary from squatting, to urban agriculture, sports and street parties. The examples and case studies cited merely scratch the surface of this vast grassroots activity. A common thread in many of these examples is that they occur largely outside the control of business or government. They are usually small-scale, are initiated by groups of committed enthusiasts and most are either temporary or started temporarily.

Greater community activism is likely to be an increasingly important influence on the shape of twenty-first-century cities. The empowerment that activism brings can reinvigorate political systems, social structures and local economies. Politicians and city planners ignore this force at their peril, but can also find it very difficult to get this particular genie back into the bottle. The energy that it brings can not only add delight to the urban landscape through its fleeting manifestations, but can reinvent the city with a creativity that is often lacking in the city authorities themselves. There are many ways in which such activity can be encouraged and fostered. The overarching lesson from most of the best practice in this area, though, is that intervention works best when it is genuinely enabling and activism and community enterprise work best in a lightly regulated environment.

Scumoween: The Squat Monster's Ball

LONDON

A combination of available vacant property, a deepening disenchantment on the part of youth with the new coalition government in the UK, together with rapid communication enabled by the internet, were factors cited by the *Observer* newspaper in November 2010 to explain the re-emergence of urban raves reminiscent of the wave that swept Britain in the late 1980s and early 1990s. On 30 October Scumtek, a grassroots movement that grew out of the squatting scene, organised a rave at a disused parcel sorting office on London's Shaftesbury Avenue. Shortly after 7 pm a pay-as-you-go mobile number with details of the event was posted on a rave blog, and within minutes the digits were circulating through cyberspace via texts, Facebook and tweets. By 9 pm a huge crowd was assembling outside the building, catching the police by surprise. Heavily outnumbered, they were reluctant to exercise their powers under the Criminal Justice Act 1994, that was introduced to close down such gatherings, and the rave continued well into the following afternoon.

The *Observer* noted that '(c)ommentators on youth culture believe that deepening disenchantment with the government could result in a generation turning to illegal raves in an echo of the backlash against the Thatcher government in the mid-1980s'. Some of the partygoers spoke of a feeling of 'self-entitlement' among youth, and a sense that if they want to do something, then why not do it. Some saw the doom and gloom of the recession simply as a good justification for a party, especially a free party. The underground illegal club scene has always flourished at times of recession, filling urban vacuums.

SOURCE: M. Townsend, 'Return of underground rave culture is fuelled by the recession and Facebook',

the *Observer*, 7 November 2010, p. 36.

Begin Space
CAMBRIDGE

Begin Space is an incubation centre for social enterprises which is located in a disused bank in the centre of Cambridge. The recession has caused a surge in social enterprises, and Begin Space was created to inspire and enable would-be entrepreneurs. Its services include mentoring, hot-desking, shared work spaces, meeting rooms and event spaces. The project also aims to connect would-be entrepreneurs with each other and with other sources of support and resources. So far over 15 different organisations have been established such as a radio-controlled racing facility for young people, and a business developing software for emergency services.

The project developed from a recognition by Cambridge City Council that, with over 60 empty shops in the city, it needed to take action to address the problem. Begin Space is supported by an existing Social Enterprise Centre, *City Life*, and provides an opportunity to experiment with different models of enterprise support in a high-profile location within the city. The landlord, PRUPIM (the property management arm of Prudential Assurance Company), provides the space rent-free, while Cambridge City Council has given a discount on the local business rates. A grant of £10,000 from the Meanwhile Project (established by the UK Development Trust Association) covered start-up costs, and allowed the project to operate through its early months.

149

SOURCES: *Cambridge News*, 'Now retail needs therapy to survive', 28 October 2009, retrieved from
www.cambridge-news.co.uk/Home/Now-retail-needs-therapy-to-survive.htm.
Cambridge News, 'Growth den for social enterprise', 17 November 2009, retrieved from
www.cambridge-news.co.uk/Business/Test/Growth-den-for-social-enterprise.htm.
www.meanwhile.org.uk/showcase/begin-space-cambridge (all accessed 1 February 2011).

Case Study
#8.3

Studio East Dining
LONDON

Studio East Dining was a restaurant designed to last three weeks on a site adjacent to the Olympic Park that will be redeveloped as a car park for a new Westfield shopping centre. The restaurant was created by Bistroteque, pioneers of a number of other pop-up eateries in London, and was housed in a pavilion designed by young architects Carmody Groarke. It was made almost entirely from materials already to hand on the site – a scaffold frame, lined with rough boards and weatherproofed with the kind of plastic more usually used to shrink-wrap steel for transport.

SOURCES: R. Moore, 'Let's put on the chow right here …', the *Observer*, The New Review, 20 June 2010, p. 35.

R. Moore, 'Meet Britain's most promising young architects', the *Observer*, The New Review, 9 January 2011, pp. 12–15.

150

Case Study
#8.4

The Cineroleum

LONDON

In the autumn of 2010, a derelict petrol station in Clerkenwell, London was transformed for 15 brief screenings into a hand-built cinema (with a programme of off-beat classics from Buster Keaton to *Barbarella*), that celebrated the extravagant and decadent interiors of cinema's golden age. The Cineroleum was conceived and built by a collective of young artists, designers and architects called Assemble, which is committed to the creative re-use of urban spaces. It grew out of a 'general idea that it would be nice to do something', to actually create a building. It was put together on a budget of just £6,500, in just three weeks, primarily constructed from donated and found materials and drawing on free labour from networks of friends and supporters. With 4,000 petrol stations currently lying derelict in the UK, the project demonstrates their potential for transformation into exciting and unusual spaces for public use. See also Folly for a Flyover, a follow-on project, 2011 (p. 93).

SOURCES: www.cineroleum.co.uk/info/.

www.follyforaflyover.co.uk (both accessed 17 June 2011).

151

The Cineroleum: temporary cinema
LONDON

Case Study
#8.5

Frank's Bar

PECKHAM, LONDON

The Hannah Barry Gallery's highly successful outdoor pop-up sculpture exhibition has been established for three years (2008–10) on the normally deserted top three floors (levels 7–10) of the Peckham Rye multi-storey car park (Case Study 7.4). In 2009 the gallery opened a pop-up café, Frank's Bar, on the roof-top. Designed by Practice Architecture (recent architecture graduates Lettice Drake and Paloma Gormley), it was built by volunteers in 25 days for just £5,000 from scaffolding boards and lorry tarpaulins. It offered some of the best views in London in a panorama stretching from the Houses of Parliament to the O$_2$ Arena and proved hugely popular.

SOURCES: H. Hoby, 'Peckham raises the roof', the *Observer*, 5 July 2009, retrieved from
www.guardian.co.uk/artanddesign/2009/jul/05/art-goldsmiths.

SallyB2, 'Art preview: rooftop sculpture park in Peckham', 30 June 2009, retrieved from
http://londonist.com/2009/06/art_preview_rooftop_sculpture_park.php?gallery0Pic=2
(both accessed 25 January 2011).

152

Case Study
#8.6

Temporary buildings: de Rijke Marsh Morgan Architects (dRMM)

ENGLAND AND THE NETHERLANDS

For a number of years dRMM have been experimenting with cross-laminated timber, a material that is carbon negative and versatile. More importantly perhaps, it lends itself to prefabrication and allows structures to be disassembled, dismantled and reassembled quickly and easily. After initial innovative work on school design, they developed an installation for Modern Art Oxford that converted a loading bay into a gallery extension, café and meeting place. The room was open to the street and blurred the distinction between entrance and gallery, increasing the sense of this being a truly transient space. It was designed with a life of five years. Using similar techniques dRMM have designed and built the Naked House out of prefabricated timber. It sits cantilevered on a foundation of the container it is delivered in and can be moved and reassembled in a few days.

Developing the theme further, dRMM were commissioned by the Tate Galleries to produce a mobile art exhibition that can tour Britain. The same laminated wood panel technique has been employed, to be capable of rapid assembly in numerous shapes and combinations to fit various exhibitions and sites. dRMM are currently designing an office for their own practice in an old Dutch cargo barge. The wooden office can be craned in and out of the barge. It includes a café, exhibition space and workshops, and will move the architectural practice from city to city depending on their commissions.

SOURCE: Interview with Alex de Rijke and Sadre Morgan, dRMM Architects.

Loading bay, café, gallery space, Modern Art Oxford, by dRMM Architects
OXFORD

Case Study
#8.7

Community gardens
NEW YORK

Temporary land use in New York is strongly associated with the Community Garden Movement where groups of volunteers create gardens in areas of the city that have been abandoned. By the mid-1990s due to a building boom, many of these gardens came under intense development pressure and there were a number of high-profile evictions. Today, though, many receive assistance through organisations such as GreenThumb, a subsidiary of the City's Parks Department. GreenThumb was established in 1978 in response to the city's financial crisis of the 1970s that resulted in the abandonment of large areas of public and private land. It remains the nation's largest urban gardening programme, assisting over 600 gardens and nearly 20,000 garden members throughout New York City. Many community gardens have developed a strong role in building community: they have transformed into community centres that run courses, educational workshops, children's activities, food pantries, host parties and exhibitions and provide a venue for baptisms and weddings.

SOURCES: http://greenthumbnyc.org.

A. McSpadden, 'Instant cities: a memo to our times', retrieved from www.ciutatsocasionals.net/
englishEXPOCOWEB/archivocastellano/centrodocumentacion/textosdocumentacion/DAMn%B016_
p90_Post-It_Cities.pdf (both accessed 3 March 2011).

Case Study
#8.8

Skip Garden
KING'S CROSS, LONDON

The King's Cross Central Partnership is developing 67 acres of brownfield land north of St Pancras for nearly 8 million square feet of mixed-use accommodation, as well as new streets, major public spaces, restored historic buildings and up to 2,000 new homes. Behind the hoardings on a site adjacent to the new St Pancras International Station, the charity Global Generation has created portable allotments in a series of construction skips. The project was part of Argent's corporate social responsibility programme and is also seen as an opportunity to start place-making on the development site. The project is also supported by the Guardian News & Media, whose headquarters are nearby, and for whom it is an opportunity to support and develop links with the local community. In August 2009, the skips produced an abundant first harvest. Since then a composting and worm skip has been constructed and the project is extending into intensive polytunnel food production. It shows the potential of small-scale temporary projects alongside major development initiatives. As different areas of the King's Cross regeneration scheme are developed, the skips will be moved to new locations within the overall site.

SOURCES: www.globalgeneration.org.uk/living-food.

www.kingscrosscentral.com/index.

www.kingscrosscentral.com/skip_garden (all accessed 17 June 2011).

155

Skip Garden
KING'S CROSS, LONDON

Community Food Project

MIDDLESBROUGH

Middlesbrough in the north-east of England built its wealth on steel, heavy industries and shipbuilding. These industries collapsed in the 1980s and the city entered a period of decline with high unemployment, low incomes and little development activity. The city shrank and hollowed out as old industrial buildings were demolished and the sites grassed over. Abandoning traditional policies to re-establish its economic prosperity, the city sought new plans and strategies to address its problems.

One response was a joint initiative from the Design Council and the Regional Development Agency (One North East). Designs of the Time (DOTT 07) Director John Thackara was commissioned initially to set up a design biennale for the region, with a sustainability brief. Out of this initial idea a group came together, led by urban regeneration advisor and social entrepreneur David Barrie, and the project developed into an initiative around community agriculture, food and health. Middlesbrough's agricultural hinterland is some of the most productive in the UK. The supply chains have, however, been broken, with most of the produce shipped away to wholesale markets in other parts of the country. Paradoxically, the city had the reputation as one of the unhealthiest in Britain with high levels of obesity and heart problems. Food growing did have a resonance with the local community, although most of the allotments were on the city edge, inaccessible to the poorest communities and under-used. This provided the starting point for the initiative.

The city council had the advantage of a strong mayor, good community infrastructure and staff who were keen to engage in the project. The Education Department had already been promoting healthy eating in schools and the Parks Department had been promoting allotments. The council also recognised that a community food growing programme had the potential to diversify the blandness of swathes of the city given over to grassland and reduce their maintenance costs.

The project was structured in three parts. First was a growing project, delivered by charity Groundwork South Tees. This worked on three plot sizes, small (window-box-sized), medium (one square metre) and large (two square metres). The initial 250 community gardening sites were supplemented by an eager Parks Department who were only too happy to switch from growing flowers to vegetables. The city art gallery also set up its own allotment. The second part was a cookery project which was run in partnership with Sure Start (a government initiative aimed at the very young and parents) and the Primary Health Care Trust. The final aspect was a 'town meal' organised by the city council, Arts Council and other public agencies. This brought the elements together into a one-day community food festival with mobile kitchens and open-air dining.

The success of this programme lies in the fact that although the original instigators have moved on, the city council has adopted it and the initiative is now being delivered through a local organisation, Middlesbrough Environment City. They have produced a spatial landscape plan for the city to retrospectively map food producing areas and have involved their business and community partners through the Local Strategic Partnership in making food and health key elements of their corporate strategy. The final move in the project has been the decision by Middlesbrough Environment City to shift the emphasis of the initiative from activity of aggregated community groups to families as the sustainable building foundation for its future.

157

SOURCES: Interview with David Barrie.

www.seeproject.org/casestudies/Dott07 (accessed 28 October 2011).

Case Study
#8.10

Urban agriculture

DETROIT

Detroit is one of the most widely discussed examples of the shrinking city. The collapse of the motor industry has resulted in a 60 per cent decline in the city's population, which is now less than 800,000. This is extreme even compared to other American cities facing a similar sharp post-industrial decline (Pittsburgh –51 per cent; Cleveland –48 per cent). The flight of the population and the outflow to suburban satellites has resulted in unemployment of over 24 per cent and over 40 square miles of vacant land within the city limits. Nearly 500 acres of this land is now in public ownership as the city implements plans to demolish another 10,000 abandoned homes. In total there are 125,000 vacant housing plots in the city. There is, however, nothing tangible to replace them with. The city's problems have been compounded by falling tax revenues, in some districts by as much as 75 per cent. This places a further strain on public services, creating a downward spiral of decline.

Detroit's vacant land – termed the 'urban prairie' by John Gallagher of the *Detroit Free Press* – also represents an opportunity that is allowing the city to accept the development of urban agriculture as a 'temporary' response to urban decline. Urban farming evolved in Detroit mainly as a community initiative, through volunteers and individuals, sometimes with the assistance of the non-profit Detroit Agricultural Network. Typical of these enterprises are the Capuchinian Friars who operate the Earthworks Urban Farm and Soup Kitchen. Started in 1997 by Brother Rick Samyu, the project links urban agriculture with a mission to feed the poor and hungry. It has expanded from a small plot and now includes itinerant markets, the supply of produce to community centres through project FRESH sales, 40 hives for honey production and a 1,300 square foot greenhouse that produces seedlings for other community agriculture projects.

The debate in Detroit is now centred on whether urban agriculture should extend to embrace commercial farming. There is certainly interest from business, but there is suspicion from the community who fear that this would represent a move away from local control. For some it is also associated with a return to the poverty of agricultural labour and slavery that the forebears of many of Detroit's African American citizens came to the city to escape. Other ideas are also developing for the use of the city's vacant land resource including wind farms, solar energy, bio fuel and forestation.

Whether the example of Detroit sits comfortably in a book on temporary use is open to question. In many areas the urban agriculture movement is a response to catastrophic levels of decline, and as such it is different from the European examples around urban pioneers and entrepreneurs. Unless Detroit's fortunes take a dramatic turn, there is also likely to be a degree of permanence about the emergence of urban agriculture. The city is struggling under a new mayor to address its deep problems of urban decline, but although it has been willing to see urban agriculture develop and has indeed facilitated it in certain districts, there is, unlike Middlesbrough (Case Study 8.9), no discernable plan to actively develop it as part of a coherent city strategy.

SOURCE: *World Architecture News* Event, London–Detroit Dialogue, February 2011.

Volunteers working at Earthworks Urban Farm
DETROIT

Case Study
#8.11

ABC No Rio

NEW YORK

In the late 1960s, the Lower East Side of Manhattan experienced massive disinvestment by absentee landlords, and by the late 1970s was home to a growing squatter movement and arts scene. ABC No Rio itself grew out of the 1979 Real Estate Show, in which a group of artists turned an abandoned building at 123 Delancey Street into a gallery with a theme critical of the city's land-use policies. The show opened in January 1980, but was promptly shut down by the New York City Department of Housing Preservation and Development (HPD). In subsequent negotiations with HPD, however, the organisers were granted the use of a building at 156 Rivington Street that became ABC No Rio.

The centre was in a legal limbo for years, sometimes as a squat, sometimes paying rent to the city. In 1994, when the city revoked the lease in order to sell the building, a group of activists squatted the upper floors and stalled the eviction proceedings for several years. Meanwhile the organisation started to fundraise and to reform its image to be a more legitimate organisation in the eyes of the city. In 1997, the city agreed to sell the building to ABC No Rio for $1 provided ABC could raise the money to renovate the building and open it for public use. Ultimately it was agreed that renovation could be divided into three phases and that the property would be sold to the collective when it had the funds for phase one in place. The sale was completed in 2006, and in 2009, ABC No Rio was awarded capital funding of $1,650,000 from New York City for a development project.

ABC No Rio remains true to its roots. Known internationally as a venue for oppositional culture, it seeks to facilitate 'cross-pollination between artists and activists and provide a place where people share resources and ideas to impact society, culture, and community'. It is both a community centre for the Lower East Side, and a centre of radical activism. It features a gallery space, a library, a darkroom, a silkscreening studio, the Books Through Bars Collective (that sends books to people incarcerated in US prisons) and a public computer lab.

SOURCES: www.abcnorio.org/about/about.html.

http://en.wikipedia.org/wiki/ABC_No_Rio (both accessed 17 June 2011).

160

Maritime Heritage Centre
SCARBOROUGH

The Scarborough Maritime Heritage Centre opened in November 2009, and aims to build up an archive of material regarding maritime life on the Scarborough and Yorkshire coast and to raise awareness of local heritage. The idea originated in 2004 and found considerable local support, but struggled to find a home and start-up funding. The council's Civic Pride Steering Group established a Windows to the Borough project group following concerns over the increasing number of empty shops in the borough. An old apothecary building was transformed into a temporary home as part of the Shop Lift arts programme. The ability to pilot the idea for minimal cost, and with support from the Meanwhile Project, gave the project the momentum it required.

SOURCES: Civic Pride Windows to the Borough, New Scarborough Maritime Heritage Centre, 5 November 2009, retrieved from www.scarborough.gov.uk/default.aspx?page=14816.

www.scarboroughsmaritimeheritage.org.uk/index.php (both accessed 1 February 2011).

Art installation, NDSM

AMSTERDAM

9: Creative cities and the gentrification dilemma

MANY OF THE BUSINESSES in the creative sector are small (employing less than five people), and their development, in a field that is vulnerable to the changing winds of fashion and taste, is often unpredictable. Such businesses are also highly reliant on networking, co-operation and face-to-face contact since they often work freelance or on project-based assignments, and this helps to manage the inherent riskiness. These enterprises therefore tend to form clusters, or 'creative milieus'. Often they operate on very limited budgets and therefore need cheap space on flexible terms to gain a foothold. They are naturally attracted to urban fringe areas where space is available and rents are cheaper. The 'edginess' of such areas may be an additional attraction, as is the fact that they may be less regulated than more established central business districts.

Charles Landry defines a creative milieu as a place (a building or neighbourhood), that has both 'soft' infrastructure (social networks and connections) that encourages the flow of ideas, and 'hard' infrastructure (buildings, educational and research institutions, cultural facilities, meeting places and support services).[1] Other researchers emphasise the indefinable 'buzz' that makes up the creative milieu and suggest that creative entrepreneurs often start as part of a localised 'scene', as active consumers, drawing on a vital local knowledge.[2]

Much of the research into the role and potential of temporary use has been carried out in relation to such creative milieus, where clusters of artists and other entrepreneurs have been shown to act as a power-house of creativity and a force for regeneration. This is not a new phenomenon, but in recent years culture and creativity have been recognised as essential components of the vibrant, competitive post-industrial city. In consequence, many cities now have policies aimed at attracting or stimulating such cultural industries. In an increasingly competitive global market, the creative industries are seen as offering high added value and a competitive edge over the emerging 'tiger' economies of Asia. This is particularly true where creative clusters are fed by a steady flow of graduates, or linked to universities and established design or fashion markets. Research into the value of creative milieus and appropriate ways of supporting them, is now a substantial field. We are not experts and can only touch on aspects of this body of work here. Our aim is to emphasise the importance of temporary activities in the inception stage of creativity, to explore some of the contradictions and problems of *spatial* interventions in this field, and to highlight through the case studies some of the more successful approaches.

The terms 'creative' or 'cultural' industries raise complex definitional issues that have been debated extensively by academics.[3] For the most part the arguments revolve around the line between culture and cultural commodities, whether the 'creative industries' should include all those covered by intellectual property rights, and whether 'digital' culture and software development should be included. Increasingly, studies define the creative industries as those that have creativity (in content, service or product) as the focus of their activities. We are in no position to adjudicate the debate. For the sake of clarity the Department of Culture, Media and Sport (DCMS) definition of 'creative industries' that includes 'advertising, architecture, the art and antiques market, crafts, design, designer fashion, film and video, interactive leisure software, music, the performing arts, publishing, software and computer games, television and radio' has been adopted here.[4] In the past 20 years the boundaries between these activities have in any case been blurring.

It has long been observed that creative entrepreneurs are often early entrants to marginal areas and untested property markets, either squatting or occupying vacant buildings on short-term leases, adapting them and helping to change the image of an area. As pioneers, creative entrepreneurs may have to contend with unclear planning or zoning issues, poor infrastructure, difficult access and the costs of basic refurbishment. But they do so because the rents are low, and the spaces are large and offer the kind of flexibility that art making, craft production, performance, installations or exhibitions require. As Nowak states, 'artists are experts at uncovering, expressing and re-purposing the assets of place – from buildings and public spaces to community stories'.[5] Thus, arts and culture related space 'is an adaptive re-use vehicle well-suited for an uncertain market, precisely because artists value the process of remaking a space as well as a finished product'.[6]

Over time this colonisation has been shown to spark intricate social and physical changes across whole neighbourhoods. The typical gentrification process might see clubs, bars, cafés and galleries moving into the area, followed by art dealers, designer shops and other creative small businesses. In other words the cluster of creative producers evolves into a place for creative consumption (Case Study 9.1). Property developers, recognising the increasing commercial success of the area, follow, together with more affluent residents and established creative companies and cultural institutions. At this point the 'alternative cachet' of the area diminishes and lower-income-generating activities are forced out by the process of gentrification.[7]

Creative milieus present a dilemma for those interested in promoting economic development through the creative industries, since the evidence suggests that they are not created through top-down initiatives, but happen in the absence of formal planning. There is no shortage of creative enterprise in cities such as London, but there is a shortage of easily available, low-price and therefore low-risk space. As Urban Unlimited state, 'booming creative cities and metropolises often prove to be devouring their very economic basis'.[8] Jane Jacobs similarly recognises that the spatial, social and economic diversity that is the key to creative urban environments is often a victim of its own success.[9] In the sections which follow we review different aspects of this policy dilemma by reference to Berlin, Hamburg, Amsterdam and Hoxton/Shoreditch in London.

Berlin

The impact of temporary uses on the development of cultural industries is exemplified in Berlin, and it is worth exploring the conditions that nurtured the sector there. Berlin has a long history of squatting that, after the Second World War, 'became part of the counter-culture of the time and had a mildly illicit reputation'.[10] In Kreuzberg and Friedrichshain in west Berlin, the city renewal programme of 1964–5 planned to demolish most of the nineteenth-century residential blocks. Anticipating state intervention, many private owners ceased to repair their properties, and left them vacant (or let on short licenses to students and foreign workers). Squatters moved in on the basis that the buildings would fall apart otherwise, and called this 'maintain-squatting'.[11] In 1981, there were over 150 squatted buildings in Kreuzberg alone. Bounded by the Berlin Wall, and with poor connectivity, Kreuzberg was very much a 'city edge', overlooked by the property market and an ideal location for temporary uses to flourish.

165

The concentration of temporary uses in Berlin today reflects its history of immense social, economic and political upheaval, its division, stagnation and radical de-industrialisation. More than 50 per cent of the city's structures were destroyed in the Second World War and the urban renewal projects of the 1970s and 1980s added to the devastation and urban dysfunction.[12] There are extensive abandoned railway depots, stations and maintenance sites, disused docks and riverside areas, former military training grounds, an inner-city airport (356 hectares), the no-man's land along the former Berlin Wall, superfluous cemeteries (143 hectares), schools and sports facilities, demolished housing estates, gap sites (170 hectares) and an estimated 500 hectares or more of space in former industrial sites, many of which are centrally located.[13] While Berlin experienced a building boom post-unification, a sluggish economy and severe fiscal crisis since then has meant that vast areas remain unoccupied. As Oswalt *et al.* note, '(i)t is no accident that temporary uses sprang up throughout the countries of central and eastern Europe after the collapse of the socialist system, since government authority only continued to operate to a limited extent'.[14] Following reunification, large-scale economic transformation and high unemployment also led to a massive population movement from East to West.[15] In Berlin though there was a small but significant counter-flow of individuals who saw the potential of east Berlin with its cheap housing and vacant buildings as an ideal locality for a freer, less regulated lifestyle. A high proportion of housing with index-linked rents,[16] a generous social welfare system and exemplary childcare were an added lure. As Arlt notes, Berlin 'became a Mecca for everyone involved in art and culture, attracting many involved in these areas as well as others who had contacts in the scene'.[17]

This critical mass enabled a marginal scene to evolve into a vital cultural movement affecting the city as a whole.

Lange reports that over 90,000 people were working in Berlin's creative economy in 2005, mostly in single person businesses, and there was a 40 per cent increase in the number of self-employed artists between 2000 and 2004.[18] Many were helped by state support through a job-seekers allowance, enterprise allowance or start-up loans schemes. They found mutual support through clustering in creative milieus that evolved into a fashion-setting 'scene' with a growing commercial market. This 'scene' then drew in creatives from outside the city. Its capital status and multi-cultural atmosphere made it highly attractive, not just to small firms but also corporate media companies. In 2002, leading music companies Bertelsmann Music Group (BMG) and Universal decided to move their headquarters from Hamburg to Berlin due, in part, to the vibrant subculture in Berlin's up-and-coming east.[19]

The concept of Berlin as a creative metropolis has become significant for promotion and regeneration. In recognition of the value of the creative economy (that had a turnover of over €8bn – over 10 per cent of the city's GDP, in 2002),[20] the state has adopted a cultural development strategy,[21] has commissioned a number of studies of temporary activities and is exploring new ways to support them.

166

Many of the creative enterprises, such as the underground clubs and galleries that clustered in Berlin Mitte in the 1990s, started temporarily and managed to consolidate. Internationally renowned galleries now cluster around Auguststrasse, while the music and club scene has shifted towards Friedrichshain and the fashion scene towards Prenzlauer Berg. The current wave of temporary uses in the city was documented by Phillipp Oswalt and Klaus Overmeyer in their work *Urban Pioneers*.[22] The number and range of activities is astonishing, from temporary beaches with volleyball courts and beach cafés, to bars, art and flea markets, sightseeing balloons, theatres, cabaret tents, swimming pools, BMX and skateboard tracks, ski schools, adventure parks, golf driving ranges and courses, children's play centres and farms, creative studios, start-up enterprise centres, exhibition spaces, sculpture parks, gardens, pasture, allotments, wildlife parks, labyrinths, camp grounds and caravan villages. As LaFond points out, many of the initiatives in Berlin also represent experiments in new forms of urban living. They are often more sustainable (with low energy use and minimal carbon footprints), co-operative or collective and participatory. They 'embrace everything from anarchist trailer communities to eco-coop condominiums', as well as organic bakeries, free schools, energy generation systems and community centres.[23]

As the *Lonely Planet* travel guide notes '(w)hen it comes to fashion, art, design and music, the German capital is the city to watch. A global influx of creatives has turned it into a cauldron of cultural cool … What draws them is Berlin's legendary climate of tolerance, openness and experimentation infused with an edgy undercurrent that gives this "eternally unfinished" city its street cred'.[24] However, there are growing signs that 'Cool Berlin' may be a victim of its own success. Beaumont, writing in the *Observer* newspaper, notes that 'a new generation of monied professionals is buying run-down properties and threatening the cultural and bohemian heart of the capital'.[25] Buildings that have long been squatted by cultural industries, to the extent that they have come to symbolise all that is 'cool' about the city, are now being redeveloped, while in other parts of the city run-down blocks of flats are being turned into New York-style lofts. In keeping with the long tradition of resistance in Berlin, a counter-movement is developing, but the tensions between the forces of gentrification and the creativity of cultural milieus are strongly biased in favour of the former.

Richard Florida has famously promoted 'creative class' strategies whereby cities compete for creative talent by developing urban environments that are open, diverse, dynamic and 'cool'. The message is that cities must be 'talent magnets' for young mobile professionals in order to succeed in today's knowledge economy.[26] His work has attracted immense interest internationally, but is not without its critics.[27] Some argue that his approach proposes a creative meritocracy and smacks of the elitist ideology of gentrification. Others are critical that making somewhere appear 'cool' can place undue emphasis on the consumption of the 'bohemian' lifestyle. This can lead to a focus on investment in superficial physical improvements rather than long-term social infrastructure, and may also deflect political priorities and resources away from investment in the education required to produce local talented individuals. For our purposes it is useful to note that Florida appears to be concerned with strategies to *attract* creative talent, over those that might seek to nurture home-grown creative start-ups. As Pratt points out, cultural production is often the driver creating a trendy area which is then taken over as a venue for cultural consumption by the 'creative class'.[28] The two approaches can be complementary, but as the example of Hamburg demonstrates they can also clash, and gentrification has met with intense opposition from the well-organised and radical local creative sector.

167

Hamburg

Hamburg is a major trading port, whose economic success has positioned it as one of the wealthiest areas in the European Union. With the restructuring of global trade and port technology, however, the city has had to adapt. The attraction of a creative class, based on the theories of Richard Florida, was championed by the city administration in a report entitled 'Hamburg – City of Talent'. According to Florida there are three criteria that are crucial to the attraction of 'creative professionals' to a city: technology (a high capacity for technological innovation), talent (creative talent wants to be where other smart, creative people are) and tolerance (cosmopolitan, inclusive and open-minded).[29] Florida, therefore, seems to be more concerned with the consumption of culture than with its production. In contrast to the policies of the 1990s, the argument is that cities should no longer aim to attract companies, but people. The Hamburg authorities aimed to reposition the city and increase its competitiveness through developing a city that would attract the creative class through a top-down policy approach. This called for the adaptation of the residential and leisure situation to the tastes of the 'creators of new industries and services'.[30] Plans for the regeneration of the harbour, HafenCity, one of the largest urban planning projects in Europe, were presented in 1997. The abandoned site of the Hamburg free port was envisioned as a symbiosis of event culture, service industry and lifestyle retail. Incorporating a private university, it would expand the current city centre by nearly 50 per cent.

For many commentators, the HafenCity (masterplanned by the Dutch architects KCAP) is an exemplar of port regeneration that is creating a successful new business and cultural quarter adjacent to the historic core. However, the city's plans have also met with local opposition from a broad coalition of groups in the arts and creative sector and those campaigning for more affordable housing. For example, Park Fiction, a loose network of artists and local interest groups, is based in the St Pauli neighbourhood, an area that has a history of dissent, and where the squatter movement of the 1980s was prominent. Following the prolonged neglect of the area by the authorities, the group campaigned for a public park rather than private development. It organised a parallel planning and design process based on extensive local outreach and engagement, and drew up plans. Their most successful strategy was not just to campaign for a public space but to act as if one already existed. To this end, they hosted an extensive programme of temporary public events on the site (Infotainment), including talks, exhibitions, open-air screenings and concerts. This continual use of the 'park' helped to make it a social and physical reality.[31] The park was finally implemented in 2005 and features artificial palm trees, an elegant 40-metre-long bench, an open-air solarium and a wave-shaped lawn. Other aspects have yet to be financed but Park Fiction is clear that the 'fiction' is still far from being fulfilled, even when the park is finished.[32]

168

In 2009 about 200 artists squatted buildings in Gängerviertel, one of the oldest areas in Hamburg, much of which had already been torn down. The focus of their opposition was a redevelopment that had been delayed by the economic crisis. Similar opposition was again simmering in the St Pauli district where artists' studios were also threatened by commercial redevelopment. In the city's Altona neighbourhood too, over 100 artists squatted the Karstadt department store as a protest against development plans. In 2010 the protestors formed a broad alliance called Right to the City (echoing a movement with the same name in the USA), that promotes temporary uses and artists' studios and opposes 'gentrification'. Many of its members represent the respectable middle classes for whom the high rents in new housing developments and the shortage of affordable housing in the city are a cause for concern.[33] Oehmke maintains that Hamburg characterises the conflicts of the coming decade that 'will pit change against preservation, private property against the community and, most of all, economic interests against social considerations'.[34]

The reaction of the city authorities to these events has been ambivalent. It still wants to attract regeneration through developments like HafenCity, and has recognised that the local creative class also has real economic potential. Offers of alternative 'creative spaces' elsewhere in the city have been rejected, and whereas in the past the police might have been asked to clear the occupied premises, the city has sought to co-opt and legitimise the activity through suggesting that the squatters sign tenancy agreements. Significantly, Hamburg's 'city of talent' slogan has been quietly dropped, and the city authorities do recognise that the squat has evolved from the anti-authoritarian counterculture of the 1970s into a potential seedbed of tomorrow's urban prosperity.

The relationship is uneasy, but it is clearly symbiotic. Without the freedom of temporary uses, the city risks its ability to renew and regenerate. If it loses this, then it could face slow long-term economic stagnation.

The experiences of the authorities in Berlin and Hamburg illustrate the importance of creative milieus and the temporary activities that can initiate them. There is no doubt that interventions in this field can be difficult, especially when a city has a long tradition of radicalism. The contrasts with Amsterdam, Helsinki and London are interesting in this respect.

Amsterdam

Since 1998, the municipality of Amsterdam has earmarked €2.8m annually for the promotion of 'breeding grounds' for creative enterprises.[35] To date it has allocated almost €40m to the Art Factories Programme, and as of mid-2008 the fund had over €5m at its disposal. The policy arose from the recognition that gentrification was reducing the number of affordable living and working spaces for the city's informal arts and culture sector, to the detriment of the life, variety and economy of the city.[36] Under the policy, the municipality has provided rent subsidies, developed studios and workspace, and encouraged provision by others. So far, over 40 buildings have been turned into 'art factories', providing 1,250 spaces for more than 2,000 artists and creative entrepreneurs.[37]

The city of Amsterdam's Art Factories Programme 2008–12 sets out an impressive commitment by the city and its partners to build on this work in the coming years. Significantly, it is based on a clear view that the

> presence of artists can improve an area's image, thus improving public interest in buying or renting homes there. If that in turn pushes up local property prices, then it goes without saying that the artists themselves expect their facilities to remain affordable in the long term.[38]

Thus Amsterdam, in contrast to many other cities, does not view artists as a force for regeneration to be used and moved on as market conditions demand, but as a presence that can continue to build social capital in a neighbourhood in the longer term.

The programme aims to identify at least five buildings in Amsterdam suitable for conversion to studios or studio housing each year, and to create 100–150 new workplaces annually with a total area of 10,000 square metres. A number of property developers and estate agencies have joined forces with the city to help provide accommodation for creatives. Reflecting the current conditions in the property market, vacant office space is being made available for projects. In most cases this is done on a temporary basis for a period of between two and five years. The city has also recognised that strict planning regulations form another obstacle to the creation of arts factories, stating that '(a)fter all, creativity calls for freedom'. It has launched a pilot project in the Hogehilweh area that suffers from high rates of vacant office space. As part of a strategy to transform the area into a mixed-use district, it will experiment with leasehold arrangements, temporary and flexible use of buildings and a more flexible interpretation of the local zoning plan in conjunction with revised environmental impact regulations.[39]

Apart from such projects, the city is encouraging art factory users to purchase their properties in partnership with the Culture Fund managed by Triodos Bank. For example, in 2003 Xpositron, originally a squatters' group, transformed itself into a formal organisation and began to pay rent for the building it occupied in Elektronstraat. When the opportunity arose to purchase the property, Triodos Bank provided the majority of the funding, with the city's Art Factories Fund just making up the shortfall. The NDSM project (Case Study 9.2) is one of those encouraged through the breeding ground policy. Through granting a 25-year lease to a community group to develop the area for creative industries, the city has created the largest incubator in Amsterdam.

While some research promotes public investment in arts and culture largely on economic grounds, Stern and Seifert's work for the Reinvestment Fund emphasises place-based benefits in broad terms.[40] They maintain that the arts 'revitalise cities not through their bottom-line but through their social role. The arts build ties that bind – neighbour-to-neighbour and community-to-community. It is these social networks that translate cultural vitality into economic dynamism'. As Nowak notes, in a paper from the same research project, the arts 'reinforce and build social capital; they facilitate connections across urban and regional boundaries; they help to construct quality public space; and they provide educational opportunities for residents'.[41]

The city of Amsterdam has also recognised that with so many creative people working in one building or area, there is potential to join forces with local communities in a range of neighbourhood initiatives: 'The art factory can thus become a binding factor in all kinds of cultural productions and events.'[42] Many Art Factory groups are recognising the advantages of forging such links with local communities, which can reveal hidden skills, resources and qualities in the neighbourhood that artists can incorporate in their own activities.

Stern and Seifert assert that '(c)ulture is the right tool for urban revival because it flourishes in the new urban reality of the 21st century'.[43] They use the term 'natural cultural district' to describe a neighbourhood that has spawned a density of assets (organisations, businesses, participants and artists) that sets it apart from other neighbourhoods. These areas are of interest because of the side-effects of the density. Clusters encourage innovation and creativity, and a cluster of cultural assets often acts to push an area to a 'regeneration tipping-point', attracting new services and residents. Their research has shown that ethnically diverse areas are more likely than homogenous areas to be associated with high levels of cultural engagement and high densities of cultural assets. So too are 'prof-pov' areas (those where a higher than average proportion of the population has a degree and also a higher proportion has no qualifications at all) and areas with a high proportion of non-family households. Diverse neighbourhoods seem to have a level of energy and vitality that is conducive to creativity, and, of course, may well attract creative people. Natural cultural districts offer particularly attractive alternatives for developing the arts because they are already sustaining a vital cultural scene and present an opportunity for time-limited, strategic interventions to expand their effectiveness. And because they are already established they can generate spill-over effects on less dynamic areas of the city. As Malloy argues, their model attempts to address the shortcomings of creative economy strategies that frequently result in gentrification, displacing the very residents who helped to revitalise the neighbourhood.[44] This idea for using the arts to build community lay behind the work of *muf* architecture/art in its project for the regeneration of Dalston in London (Case Study 10.3).

Hoxton / Shoreditch, London

London has successfully developed and attracted creative industries over a long period. There were nearly 800,000 creative workforce jobs in London in 2007, around 32 per cent of the UK total for the sector,[45] and one in five of all new jobs in London are in this sector.[46] London's creative and cultural industries accounted for 6.4 per cent of national GDP in 2010.[47] The capital also attracted more than 200 new creative industry foreign direct investment (FDI) projects between 2003 and 2010; Paris in second place attracted just 100 over the same period.[48]

Areas such as Soho, Notting Hill, Clerkenwell, Covent Garden and, more recently, Hoxton/Shoreditch have acted as creative milieus at different times. Through their very success the sector has been driven out to seed in other areas with lower land values and available floorspace. Hoxton/Shoreditch, located to the north of the City of London, has always been 'on the edge'. As Pratt notes, '(i)ts early good fortune was to be outside the regulatory control of the City which led to the location of various "undesirable" activities (social, economic and environmental) being located there: from noxious manufacturing to illegal trading and prostitution'.[49] At the time of its colonisation as a creative milieu it was home mainly to 'small manufacturers making buttons and engaged in specialised tailoring', who recognised that their properties were worth more than their businesses and were happy to move on. Space available in the predominantly nineteenth-century building stock, with low rents, made it ideal for designers, architects, artists and photographic studios. In the early 1990s members of the group which became known as the Young British Artists (YBA) set up their studio and living spaces in the area in and around Hoxton. The network extended into music (with punk labels such as Stiff Records located there), and film and video, stimulated in large part by the dynamic Lux arts cinema on Hoxton Square. In just over a decade the area had become almost mythically 'cool', and attracted an influx of bars, clubs and cafés. Some of these were temporary by intention, others through the perils of the market. By 2000 prices had risen and the artists moved to areas like Borough, Hackney and Bankside, where rents were still lower. Many of the studios and vacant buildings have since been redeveloped or converted to residential use, many as 'pieds à terre' for City workers.

There was no cultural or spatial strategy behind the area's success. However, as Pratt notes, '(i)n a remarkable rearguard action to avoid what was feared to be mass demolition of Shoreditch the planning authority declared the whole a Conservation Area in 1986'.[50] This illustrates the potential impact of building conservation in helping to create the conditions for temporary use. The main zoning issue at the time was resistance by the local planning authority to office uses in an effort to protect more traditional 'blue-collar' jobs. However, changes to the Use Classes Order in 1987 (which merged the separate use class definitions between offices and light industrial) did not bring about the expected office speculation, but instead facilitated the informal mixed-use activity that was already afoot.

Although many London local authorities and the Mayor of London purport to support cultural enterprises through worthy policy documents, unlike the situation in Amsterdam, it is difficult to discern any real government spatial intervention that has proved pivotal in nurturing creative milieus. In Hoxton/Shoreditch as in the rest of London, the provision of affordable workspace has largely been carried out by charitable organisations and trusts such as the Shoreditch Trust,[51] SPACE and ACME (who specialise in short-life buildings that are let to artists). Sculptor David Nicholson was also instrumental in Shoreditch where his company Glasshouse Investments set up several studios in the 1990s.

172 While the bubble in the artistic colonisation of Shoreditch may have burst, some temporary uses are still evident. For example, Village Underground, which was born to address the need for affordable studio space for artists, is located in a series of disused London Underground carriages on a section of the Broad Street Railway Viaduct. The viaduct, derelict for over 20 years, provides the perfect location for the carriages, now used as studios. The enterprise also makes use of an adjacent Victorian warehouse leased from Hackney Council and customised recycled shipping containers. It has grown into a multi-disciplinary cultural space supporting a wide range of creative practitioners including artists, designers, film makers and musicians.[52] The Village Underground premises provide a canvas for several lively examples of street art, the building next door is almost entirely concealed behind a temporary advertising hoarding, while the large site to the rear is a temporary car park also used for a night market. This part of Shoreditch is also on the more down-market fringes of the Sunday market at Brick Lane when the street is filled with vendors selling a diverse range of personal possessions and bric-a-brac displayed on blankets and in suitcases. Ironically, the backdrop to this flea market was the shipping container used for marketing Boxpark, 'the world's first pop-up mall' (photo p. 61, Case Study 4.10), that opened on the nearby Bishopsgate Goods Yard in 2011. Thus temporary activities continue to capitalise on the 'buzz' even in established creative districts.

Elsewhere in London there are some indications that the public sector is starting to take a more active role in relation to the creative sector. The work of *muf* architecture/art in Dalston for Hackney Council and the London Development Agency (LDA), for example (Case Study 10.3), demonstrates the scope for small-scale incremental interventions to consolidate this 'natural cultural district'. Similarly, the pop-up shop initiatives instigated by the Business Improvement District (BID) in Camden

Village Underground: artists' studios and arts venue
SHOREDITCH, LONDON

173

Three temporary activities: Village Underground, a temporary car park and a temporary art installation
SHOREDITCH, LONDON, 2011

Town provide start-up retail space for creatives (Case Study 4.9). More recently Design for London/ the LDA has started to intervene to try to foster creative clusters directly. Design for London, again working with *muf,* has produced a strategy for creative industries in the Hackney Wick area of east London as part of wider work on the long-term legacy for the 2012 Olympic Games. Situated adjacent to the Olympic Park, the area has flexible but old building stock, high vacancy and low rents, and already accommodates one of the highest concentrations of artists in Europe. The proposals build on this advantage by reconfiguring the area's poor quality public spaces and creating a new local centre around the railway station. The project also negotiated a lease on a vacant warehouse building for studio use, and has worked with the Barbican Theatre to use premises in Hackney Wick for rehearsals and performances.

In conclusion

Creative milieus exemplify the potential of temporary uses. The policies and approaches used to nurture creative milieus in different cities are not necessarily transferrable. There are, however, some simple things that cities can do to assist, such as taking head leases on buildings, providing databases of vacant properties, encouraging the establishment of intermediary organisations and supporting networking, marketing and promotion. Most researchers will agree that creative environments cannot come into being purely as a result of top-down measures sponsored by city authorities. They are bottom-up spontaneous happenings that principally require cheap space and freedom from constraints.[53] The principle assistance is probably for governments to have the courage to leave areas relatively loosely defined in planning terms, and to use quite specific interventions to make land, buildings or small start-up finance available. In this respect there is an argument for the creation of zones of tolerance where government planning and regulations can be more permissive and flexible. This concept is explored further in Chapter 11.

In comparing the experiences of Berlin, Hamburg, Amsterdam and Hoxton/Shoreditch, London, the approach to the dilemma of gentrification differs considerably. Creative industries can be seen just as a dynamic stage in the regeneration of an area, as a catalyst for change that is dispensable in the face of market forces; in other words just as transitional or temporary uses. The problem with this view is that it overlooks the evidence that the arts also have a long-term community-building role. This role is explicitly acknowledged in the approach in Amsterdam, where creatives are artificially protected through subsidies to become a permanent component of neighbourhoods. This is a dilemma for planners and policy makers and the solutions that are adopted will inevitably reflect the political and cultural conditions of individual cities. Whether the institutionalisation of temporary activities is able to sustain their vitality in the long term remains to be seen. Perhaps, though, in the creative melting pot of open outward-looking cities both approaches can co-exist.

| The Cable Factory
HELSINKI, FINLAND

The Cable Factory is the largest cultural centre in Finland (covering a total area of over 53,000 square metres), and provides a highly successful creative milieu. It houses three museums, 13 galleries, dance theatres, art schools and a host of artists, bands and companies. Spaces are also available for rent on a short-term basis for concerts, exhibitions, festivals and fairs. It has over 250 tenants, around 900 people work there daily and each year over 200,000 people attend events.

It occupies the premises that once produced Nokia's telephone and electrical cables. In the last few years of its ownership, recognising that it would soon be relocating, Nokia started renting the premises at affordable rates to artists and other creatives. The potential of the factory was therefore proven before any official decisions on its future were made. In 1987 the city of Helsinki and Nokia agreed redevelopment plans for the former factory. In response, the concerned tenants founded an association, Pro Kaapeli, and campaigned to save the building. In 1991, the city council agreed to preserve the Cable Factory, and its milieu, as a diverse and independent cultural centre. The council founded an estate company, Kiinteistö Oy Kaapelitalo, to take responsibility for renting, maintaining and developing the facilities. It finances its own operations and in 2005 had a turnover of over €3.5m.

SOURCE: www.kaapelitehdas.fi/en/factory (accessed 17 June 2011).

175

NDSM Wharf
AMSTERDAM

Separated by the Ij waterway from Central Station and the tourist districts, North Amsterdam is a very different world. As a working-class district based on heavy industries, it faced crisis in the 1980s when the shipbuilding industries collapsed and the docks and wharves moved. Over 1,500 workers were made redundant, and large areas of contaminated and derelict land were left behind. Initially, the Municipality of Amsterdam North (SDAN) sought to encourage new industrial development and manufacturing, but with very limited success. The vacuum was partly filled by artists who found free workspace through squatting in some of the buildings. It also became a venue for parties and events that began to establish the location within Amsterdam's counterculture scene. This was not endorsed by SDAN which had to respond to the sometimes hostile reaction of the local communities, and still had to cover the costs of the maintenance of the area and its buildings, some of which became protected for their historic interest. Their solution, however, was radical.

In 1999 SDAN launched an open competition for ideas for the area with a strong brief in favour of creative industries. The council wished to both re-establish a degree of control over the area, and at the same time bring forward new jobs and regeneration. The competition was won by a team from Kinetisch Noord, an alliance of artists, performers and architects. Their winning concept anticipated dividing the 20,000-square-metre hall into thematic zones: ArtTown, SkatePark, Noordstrook (exhibitions, cafés, galleries and apartments) and DazzleVille (outdoor performance area). The group provided the basic infrastructure for studios and workshops which were completed by the end users, saving costs and allowing participation in the design of the space. Artists, craftspeople, youth projects and creative commercial ventures can apply to rent these reasonably priced spaces.

SDAN made some shrewd strategic moves to support NDSM in its early days. First, in order to establish it as a destination in its own right, it lobbied the city of Amsterdam to provide a

176

Temporary café, NDSM
AMSTERDAM

Temporary student housing in containers, NDSM
AMSTERDAM

passenger ferry to link it to the central area, and subsidised the ferry itself for the first two years. Second, the council renovated the former wharf canteen to provide a restaurant and office space, that helped to put the area on the map. Third, it introduced temporary student housing in a development of shipping containers. Containers are a common feature of many temporary interventions, but the interesting aspect here is that the rigidity of Dutch land-use zoning would not have allowed permanent housing development; therefore the public authority had the boldness and imagination to subvert its own plans and policies. In 2003 the municipality also commissioned STEALTH.unlimited to prepare a strategy for the application of temporary use in the area as part of a long-term vision for regeneration. This identified gaps across the site, and provided new planning tools and a database linking users to potential sites. The plan was part of the EU funded research project by Urban Catalyst.

NDSM is a good example of how temporary use can be used to serve longer-term planning targets. The complex now hosts over 250 jobs, a skate park, café and support facilities, as well as a vast outdoor area that attracts over 150,000 visitors a year with regular flea markets and cultural events. It has become the largest creative industries incubator in Amsterdam. The council still operates to keep rents at low levels to encourage a mix that includes small start-ups and provides access for the local community. The NDSM Wharf is one of the most prestigious projects funded by the Broedplaatsfond Amsterdam (BPA) and run as a means of promoting the urban creative economy. The municipal policy of providing subsidised space is intended to compensate for the drop in social and cultural provision that resulted from a building boom in the early 1990s. The project has cost an estimated €25m of which €10m has come from the public purse, €5m has been loaned and €10m is user-funded. For the completion of the complex, at least another €5m is needed. Initially the group's future was uncertain, but it has now been granted a 25-year lease.

Pieter Klomp, the head designer of the urban plan in the area, considers the NDSM experiment a success. Polluted and contaminated land has been tackled and several thousand people are now employed in the wider area that was recently largely empty and derelict. But the council does still lose money on the project and has found that vacant buildings within the site have been a lot easier to re-use than land. Traditional development activity remains at a very low level, but the area is starting to attract a wider range of more established film and television companies such as MTV. They are attracted by the area's 'authenticity', which, of course, they may ultimately jeopardise by forcing up rents.

SOURCES: Interview with Pieter Klomp.

www.stealth.ultd.net/stealth/.

Urban Catalyst, *Urban Pioneers: Temporary Use and Urban Development in Berlin.*
Jovis, Berlin, 2007, p. 110.

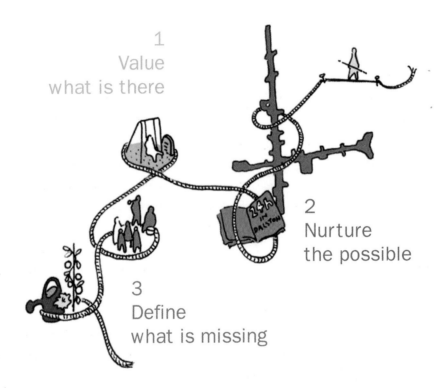

1
Value
what is there

2
Nurture
the possible

3
Define
what is missing

Masterplanning principles: 'Value, Nurture, Define'[1]

10: Re-imagining the city: planning for temporary activity

THE PRESENT PERIOD of urban planning and development is a watershed. It is possibly as significant as the end of the nineteenth century when the growth of democratic city government ushered in a century of urban planning based on an active public sector with sufficient power and resources at its disposal to physically shape cities. The fragmentation of political consensus, loss of faith in 'big government' and, in the Western economies at least, the economic downturn affecting business confidence and public expenditure amount to an almost 'perfect storm' in relation to the usefulness of many traditional masterplans. In their place an alternative approach to masterplanning is beginning to emerge. This proposition utilises phased development often as a range of temporary stages along a more flexible path that moves towards a loosely defined end vision, rather than a fixed end state. Phased packages of small initiatives are better suited to unlock the potential of sites now and sequentially, rather than in the longer term. This approach will often include deliberate strategies around temporary uses. By procuring, enabling or cooperating with interim activities it may be possible to stimulate economic activity, change the image and feel of an area, stabilise weaker neighbourhoods and reactivate vacant sites, without significant expenditure. Temporary uses can create momentum and a market profile for a site that can even hasten its eventual 'permanent' development.

Defined good practice in masterplanning has been arrived at through a long process of trial and error, and in response to an increasingly sophisticated understanding of the processes that need to be considered in long-term planning. Any critique of masterplanning must therefore take into account its evolution over a long period of urban experimentation. We must also emphasise that it is not our intention to write off traditional masterplanning as a technique. Where the resources, power and control do exist, as, for example, in the planning of the Olympics site in east London, the well-executed masterplan can play a vital role. It provides an opportunity for professionals from all fields to work together, to consider the complex forces for change acting on an urban area, to anticipate future pressures, and identify a clearly defined end state.[2] The ultimate aim of masterplanning is to create value, whether defined in terms of financial return, social capital, civic worth, physical beauty, urban efficiency or successful commercial or residential neighbourhoods. Some or all of these motives have been at the heart of masterplanning over the ages whether the sponsor/client has been a ruler or ruling elite, a democratic state, a private individual or a commercial corporation.

The success of different types of masterplanning is illustrated by the alternative approaches taken to the redesign of Rome and London in the sixteenth and seventeenth centuries. In the late sixteenth century, Rome was a medieval slum and the papacy was effectively bankrupt. It had no means to transform the city into a fitting stage for the Papal See. While Domenico Fontana's plan of grand avenues and piazzas could not be implemented due to a lack of resources, he did recognise this and commenced work by symbolically placing six obelisks salvaged from the ruins of

180

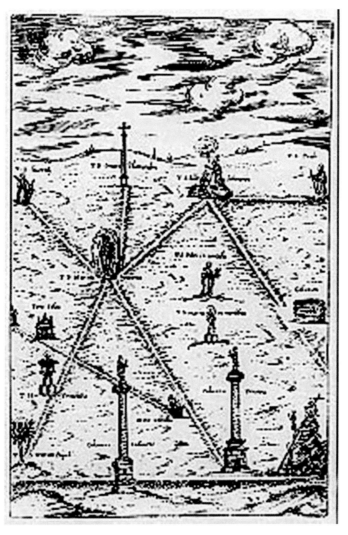

Domenico Fontana's concept plan for Rome, 1585

Ancient Rome. These marked the key new piazzas and intersections of the plan. Subsequent rulers used this framework to implement the plan gradually over the next 200 years, empowered but also controlled by the architect's vision.

In contrast to this stands Wren's masterplan for the rebuilding of London after the Great Fire of 1666. Prepared within a few days of the fire it represented a rational and idealised vision for the city. But, along with other plans submitted at the time, it was divorced from any means of realisation, in particular the dynamics of landownership and finance. The actual rebuilding of London was instead overseen by a Royal Commission that pragmatically set detailed parameters for construction, effectively abandoning a masterplanned approach. London was rebuilt largely respecting the medieval street plan and existing landownerships, completely ignoring Wren's vision.

181

Wren's plan for London, 1666

Flexible masterplanning

Whether or not an individual masterplan presents an effective framework through which to produce an efficient, beautiful and sustainable piece of city will only be judged over time. A more basic measure of success is whether the masterplan is implemented at all. The basic requirements for implementation – continuity of power, resolve, market certainty, finance and the immediate availability of land – are absent in many masterplans, and they fail as a result. Whether they result from the idealism of politicians, the optimism of developers or ill fortune, failed masterplans are a costly waste of resources and a source of cynicism in the communities affected.

Another problem is the length of time involved in the formulation, approval, adoption and implementation of masterplans. Rigid masterplans cannot easily adapt to changes in the financial, social, environmental and technical context that can occur during the period of their realisation. Even Haussmann admitted that his plans for Paris were outdated before they were complete. The process of implementation therefore needs to be embedded into a masterplan as firmly as the vision. Sophisticated and flexible phasing strategies need to sit alongside the three-dimensional vision. This is leading to the emergence of *four-dimensional* design that seeks to understand and plan the temporal as well as the physical element. Such adaptive strategies can open up new opportunities for thinking about short-term, temporary and meanwhile uses, especially where they serve to create excitement, a destination and a new image for the locality.

182

Masterplanning can be far more effective when it is concerned with loose 'visions' and has sufficient inbuilt flexibility to allow development to occur in layers over time. This approach recognises that the implementation of one phase will both have an impact on the surrounding area and interact with subsequent phases of the plan. In the example of the King's Cross development, Argent and the local planning authority placed great emphasis on the need to manage change over the 20 years that it would take to complete the development (Case Study 10.1). This entailed considering what the area would look like year-on-year as different phases were completed, and how these would be relevant to local communities. For example, the primary school and doctor's surgery were required for the completed development, but were also intended to serve a wider clientele. By being provided earlier rather than later, they would help to integrate the new development with the neighbouring communities.

Another important element of successful masterplanning is that the planning vision aims to use the existing social and physical characteristics of an area, rather than eliminate them. Many practitioners now agree that urban projects should begin with a survey of all existing elements, planned or not, and that the individual qualities of a place should be enhanced by sculpting new programmes and places out of what is already there.[3] This is shown very clearly by *muf*'s work in Dalston (Case Study 10.3) where a comprehensive survey of the area developed into a sophisticated regeneration programme that 'valued what is there, nurtured the possible and defined what is missing'.[4] In a similar way,

Bankside (Case Study 10.2) illustrates the way in which a long-term vision, based firmly on an appreciation of the characteristics and potential of the existing urban form, can be implemented flexibly, as and when the resources are available.

Tactical masterplans

Where the conditions of market certainty, financial and legislative control do not all exist, masterplanning has to take a more tactical approach. De Certeau defines strategy as the work of systematising, and imposing order. Its ways are set, and it cannot break up and regroup easily, something that a tactical model does naturally. Tactics are the ways we negotiate the strategies that are set us, or the creative intelligence that we employ to ensure our environment works to meet our needs. Tactics allow us to assert our individuality and autonomy. Tacticians rely on timing and are always on the watch for opportunities that must be seized 'on the wing'.[5] There are strong links between the tactical approach in masterplanning and Bauman's 'liquid modernity' referred to in Chapter 3.

Many writers on temporary use refer to their key role as tactics in planning. Kirshenblatt-Gimblett refers to the tactical, as the 'vernacular' – what ordinary people do in their everyday lives – that is often outside, or in spite of planning regulations. And because the vernacular is tactical, its practices have a temporal character, arising and melting away at short notice.[6] Rebar, the San Francisco-based collective of artists, activists and designers (Case Studies 6.8, 6.9, 6.15, 6.16 and 6.17), define tactical urbanism as 'the use of modest or temporary revisions to urban space to seed structural environmental change'.[7] Similarly, Temel argues that urban revitalisation needs to 'proceed tactically rather than strategically, reacting to existing situations by attempting to locate the fulcrum that makes it possible to achieve large effects with limited means, by making arrangements with other actors or by cooperating with them'.[8] Since urban planners no longer have the resources to act as strategists they must act increasingly tactically, or ally themselves with *other* tacticians to achieve their ends.

Masterplanning for the commonplace

Masterplans also overlook what John Chase, Margaret Crawford and John Kaliski have called 'everyday urbanism': 'Banal suburbs, shiny but empty downtowns, formal office parks and abandoned districts result from policies that neither recognise the everyday nor allow it to assert and reassert itself.'[9] The masterplan, based primarily on physical design, tends to produce coarse grained layouts of buildings, blocks, spaces and streets and can overlook the subtleties of function, usage and activity that will take place within this physical framework. Masterplans are too controlling and leave little space for the whimsical or the unexpected. It is often the unplanned activities that provide the diversity and dynamism that make urban areas attractive and liveable. While plans and planning processes have grown increasingly sophisticated, they have never been able to create the spontaneous, unexpected, diverse and often fleeting activities that make cities exciting.

The everyday urbanism proposed by Chase, Crawford and Kaliski is concerned with interventions that reinforce the heterogeneous qualities of small, temporary, not-intended, undistinguished though well-used spaces. It takes ordinary places, 'the nooks and crannies of existing urban environments', thinks about them in new ways, and makes small changes, that may accumulate to have a transformative effect on the wider locality.[10] It aims to reconnect urban design with ordinary human and social meanings and thus strengthen 'the connective tissue that binds daily lives together'.[11] When *Everyday Urbanism* was first published in 1999, its ideas attracted a lot of interest, but as Crawford notes in the second edition, 'in retrospect, it seems clear that rather than inventing a new idea, *everyday urbanism* actually encapsulated a widespread but not yet fully articulated attitude towards urban design'.[12]

Elsewhere in *Everyday Urbanism*, Kaliski provides an analysis of the evolution of urban design in the twentieth century that, while based largely on the American experience, illustrates the fundamental dilemma between 'modern architecture's quest for the conceptually pure and the plurality of the modern city'.[13] Successive approaches to urban design have veered from a rigorous separation of uses and people at one extreme, to attempts to recreate or extrapolate the complex patterns of everyday life at the other. However, such unilateral design theories have tended to produce homogenous spaces with little urban vitality, through processes that 'deny the multiple human voices that comprise the everyday city'.[14] Kaliski argues that as 'urban environments continue to evolve, designers must find new means of incorporating the elements that remain elusive: ephemerality, cacophony, multiplicity and simultaneity'.[15] He calls for a practice of *city design* that 'reconciles the intellectual abstraction of urban design and the formalism of architecture with the plural forces of the everyday city'.[16] Such city design would need to recognise that the city is in a process of continuous creation. The problem is that architects and urban designers are generally taught to design for static or stable situations.[17] In the traditional city, simultaneity has only been achieved after years of gradual, step-by-step change, so city design needs to generate, rather than simulate such simultaneous situations.[18]

Collaborative masterplanning

Applying the approach of everyday urbanism to practical urban design projects inevitably involves close collaboration with the potential users of spaces to define their needs, and to attempt to meet these through small-scale, innovative interventions. As Speaks states, '(w)ithout sufficient resources to provide necessary housing or jobs, and unable to redevelop blighted neighbourhoods, cities are forced ... to develop strategies ... that encourage entrepreneurial action initiated by local communities'.[19]

Many masterplans do seek, through extensive processes of stakeholder engagement, to reach a wider consensus about the end product. But even the most ardent advocates of such community involvement would admit that the process is often difficult. A key adage of community engagement is that you can only ever engage people around their concerns. Large-scale long-term planning, by its very nature, finds it difficult to engage the concerns of the majority of people that focus on issues that happen in their immediate neighbourhood, or affect their daily lives or interests directly. The masterplan is often too remote, in terms of both time and scale, to reflect such concerns. There is greater scope to engage local stakeholders in interim planning, and from there to engage their interest in longer-term scenarios. Interim-use charrettes can help to demonstrate to stakeholders that there can be a transitional stage between what exists on a site now, and what might evolve as a semi-permanent state sometime in the future (Case Study 10.4). Importantly they can also demonstrate that this transitional or phased process offers a role for a far wider group of stakeholders than might normally be involved. It is the neighbouring communities who are most likely to understand the fine grained dynamics and existing characteristics of a locality and the type of uses that might be grown to colonise an area.

Temporary uses are, of course, of far more interest to local communities than a promised utopia some 20 years hence. As Haydn notes, there is a need to stimulate, reveal and take more account of potential demands and new opportunities to use the city, and to stimulate social development, through a more participatory approach to planning. Thus, '(i)nitiating and supporting temporary uses is part of a new, alternative practice of urban planning that creates potential space by means of experimental demand'.[20] Such a bottom-up approach, informed by the desires of the community, and harnessing its energy through immediate action, within a long-term vision is well illustrated by the approach of *muf* architecture/art in Dalston (Case Study 10.3).

185

Community and social networks

The *traditional* masterplan cannot of itself build community. Communities consist of a multiplicity of activities that are interconnected and these can only be nurtured through fine grained planning. It can take many years to build up networks of activities from scratch, and this is another reason to work from existing activities and build outwards from successful areas. This calls for a particular type of planning, one that encourages diversity and supports the connections between people and one that builds inclusion and social capital as an integral part of the design process. The work of entrepreneur Teodor Frolu in Bucharest illustrates the absolute centrality of community building or rebuilding as a precursor to longer-term change (Case Study 10.5).

Reflecting the complexity of building complementary social networks, a new generation of 'smart city' masterplanning thinking is now emerging that is concerned with issues wider than the physical fabric of the area. The smart city is about the connectivity of everything, at all levels – systems, data, people and organisations. Investment in connectivity is essential to build up trust, intelligence and opportunity. In this regard, the example of North Fulham and Newham (Case Study 10.6) illustrates the way in which a masterplan for 'community infrastructure' can sit alongside a physical plan, and start to build the social connections that underpin it. This is a tacit recognition of the fact that the physical renewal of urban areas, especially the more deprived ones, is often less of a concern to the communities involved than addressing the day-to-day issues of poverty, crime and unemployment.

186

Evolutionary planning

The emerging characteristics of this 'alternative masterplanning' resonate with the approaches advocated by other researchers. Stephen Marshall, for example, suggests that we can draw on the lessons of evolution to help understand urban change and inform planning and design.[21] His 'evolutionary planning' approach aims to apply the best aspects of evolution to overcome the worst aspects of planning (plans that are fixed and inflexible tend to go too fast, make too big leaps, allow too little variation and settle on a fixed process). At the risk of over-simplifying his approach, its principles include: not sacrificing things that are currently viable, or disturbing existing symbioses; proceeding by small innovations and avoiding major departures from tried-and-tested formats; encouraging spontaneity and unsolicited novelty; discarding 'visions' expressed through zoning and instead using more flexible development guidelines; and devolving decision making as far as possible, incentivising individual initiative. Or in other words, 'if it ain't broke, don't fix it; if it don't fit, adapt it; if it's new, try it small; if it's small, let the people do it; if it works, run with it' (Case Study 10.7).[22]

Masterplanning around temporary activities

The approach to urban regeneration followed by the London Development Agency (LDA) and the London Borough of Newham in the Royal Docks illustrates how temporary use can form part of a longer-term strategy (Case Study 10.8). Here traditional masterplanning had failed to deliver any coherent or sustained change in the area since the docks closed at the end of the 1960s. The alternative solution was: first, to produce a clear concept and to remarket the wider area for green businesses; next, to remove the clutter of all the preceding planning documents and masterplans; then to build political commitment and development credibility; finally, to bring in temporary uses to act as a catalyst for change. In effect, the final element of the strategy for the Royal Docks entailed turning it into a 'Temporary Creative Zone', allowing a sense of place to emerge from temporary activities that may in turn inspire the confidence required by longer-term investors.

The promotion of temporary use is still evolving as an approach to urban development in which government initiates instead of regulating, pays more consideration to what is on the land, takes smaller steps, gives more serious consideration to the input of all players and focuses on *process* rather than *product*. Misselwitz *et al.* liken the process to open-source software development in which the programmer defines a concept that is to be developed with the aid of a programme that has yet to be written. They argue that the 'primary task of process-oriented planning is to actively configure the development itself. Discussion about the ultimate formal look of a city is not paramount here but, rather, the question of opportunities to activate the city and use the city'. Such an open-ended approach 'necessarily involves a suspension of planning's traditional perception of its role'.[23]

187

Beyond the masterplan

The parallels between the characteristics of open-source software development and the kind of urban planning that we now require have been picked up by a number of other writers in this field, and suggest that there is one further model for masterplanning that we should consider. Kelly provides a fascinating exploration of the *communal* aspects of digital culture and the implications of this for our economic, social and political systems. Sites like Wikipedia and many others represent vast numbers of communal contributions and are effectively a growing form of community action. Sharing what we are doing, thinking, reading, spending, learning is becoming a foundation of our culture and the number of people doing it, or benefiting from it, 'has reached millions and counting'. People not only share work but cooperate, collaborate and work collectively, with the amount of coordination increasing at each step. The thousands, even millions of contributors gain status, satisfaction and experience rather than money. The products are free, and ownership remains 'in the hands of the workers'.[24]

Kelly argues that 'these developments suggest a steady move toward a sort of socialism uniquely tuned for a networked world', a 'socialism without the state', where 'peer production' replaces 'national production'. As he notes, when 'masses of people who own the means of production work toward a common goal and share their products in common, when they contribute labor without wages and enjoy the fruits free of charge, it's not unreasonable to call that socialism'.[25] This virtual 'third way' or 'digital socialism' goes way beyond social enterprise as an alternative to conventional private or public sectors.

David Barrie suggests that place-making needs to complement the way in which the internet is influencing social exchange. It needs to provide adaptive, flexible frameworks within which sociability, 'social capital' and entrepreneurial networks can grow. He suggests that since social enterprises (discussed further on p. 140) prioritise human relationships and social transactions, not just those with commercial value, they 'shift the narrative of renewal from the provision of space to services, with sites acting as places that enable change, rather than dictate them via a masterplan'.[26] Such an approach would embrace 'citizen demand' and use it 'to make places that unfold over time through programmes of low-cost capital investment'.[27]

Such 'open-source place-making' aims to maximise opportunities for self-organisation and the interactive use of a site. The physical space becomes much like a web page that is shaped through collaborations between its users. Rather than create facilities for long-term occupation, sites would be treated as a utility, made available to creative, social and business communities to populate and repurpose. Essentially a very basic planning framework is established for a site, rather than a masterplan. Incremental occupation mobilises demand and creates 'a narrative and personality for the place'. In effect it is the physical equivalent of 'digital swarming'. The role of the developer or planner changes to 'theatrical manager' or 'creative impresario', creating opportunities for spontaneous activity, collaborative shared risk services, self-build, barter, and the development of networks and internal trading for goods and services between tenants. It may involve scouting for and nurturing talent, building projects around individuals' skills or potential markets, even recruiting entrepreneurs (Case Study 10.9).

'Open-source place-making' has some similarities, superficially at least, with the proposals of the UK government for 'open-source planning' to solve the negative, adversarial, inflexible and bureaucratic problems of the present planning system.[28] Just as open-source software can be programmed in a flexible and adaptable way, 'open-source planning' would be more responsive to the needs of local communities. The key difference is that Barrie talks in terms of 'place-making' rather than 'planning'.[29]

Temporary use can change the future development options

In conclusion

The new approach to masterplanning that is beginning to emerge has a number of characteristics. It promotes looser visions rather than idealised end states; it aims to be implementable through having flexible phasing, an open time frame and a tactical approach that can respond to changing conditions; it values and seeks to build on what is already on site; it nurtures the 'everyday'; it is based firmly on user collaboration; and it proceeds through smaller projects, many of which will be temporary but which may have a significant cumulative impact over time. These characteristics mean that it is better able to build community during the process. And inevitably it entails a greater role for transient activities. These may or may not grow into substantial activities, but will almost certainly permit involvement and experimentation by the communities concerned.

King's Cross
LONDON

The approach adopted by Argent to the redevelopment of King's Cross was based on an explicit recognition of the difficulties presented by end-state masterplanning. The catalyst for the development was the construction of the high-speed rail link into central London that resulted in the transfer of 57 acres of land into the ownership of London and Continental Railways (LCR). LCR held a development competition and selected Argent as their development partners. Argent was the only prospective developer not to submit a detailed masterplan. Instead they submitted the principles that would guide the development and the delivery process, one of which was that the development should not be restricted by a rigid detailed plan. Argent then developed a flexible masterplan that allowed various parts of the site, and the component uses and buildings, to be built in different combinations of phases as market forces dictated. Although the basic infrastructure was fixed in the plan, individual building volumes and heights had sufficient latitude to allow variations during the 18-year timetable, enabling the scheme to weather two or even three economic cycles. Crucially Argent recognised the importance of establishing a 'place' or 'destination' early in this development process. The introduction of new activities, the management of public spaces and encouragement of temporary art installations and activities all formed part of their strategy. In consequence Argent continued active development at the King's Cross site throughout the extreme slump in the UK development industry from 2008.

190

Masterplan, King's Cross, by Allies and Morrison – Urban Practitioners
KING'S CROSS, LONDON

Case Study
#10.2

Bankside
LONDON

Bankside is an overlooked area of London, sandwiched between the river and large estates of post-war public housing. An old warehousing and industrial area, it is bisected by railway viaducts, and still exhibits, in its vacant and derelict sites, the randomness of the bombing raids on London in the Second World War. It is in essence a patchwork of broken and accidental spaces with no apparent urban structure.

The popularity of London's South Bank area, the opening of Tate Modern in 2000 and the conversion of Borough Market into the farmers' market par excellence have started to change the area. Witherford Watson Mann Architects were engaged to examine how this change could be harnessed and how the footfall of the Thames riverside could be drawn deeper into the hinterland. Their strategy grew out of the morphology of the area. With fragmented landownerships and a tiny and insecure budget, a masterplan in the traditional sense would have failed. The only viable approach was to embrace the unplanned informal nature of the place, engage with its residents and develop a flexible strategy based on incremental improvement of informal spaces. This strategy bridged the potentially difficult gap between major institutions like the Tate and local residents. It could also engage, experiment and build local confidence in the process. Like any good urban strategy it was robust and could be implemented opportunistically in pieces, as conditions allowed. By using a combination of temporary and permanent interventions within a clear strategic framework, it was able to build intensity into the area.

191

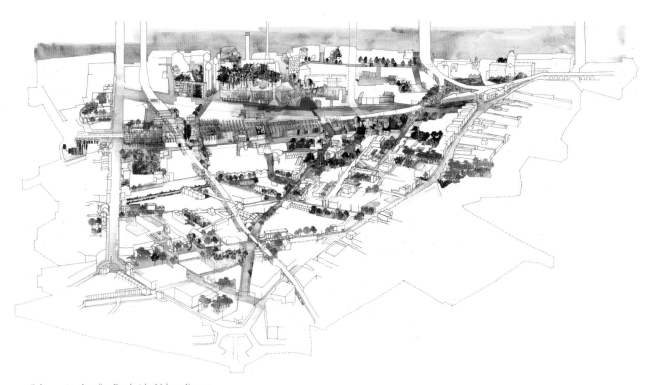

Schematic plan for Bankside Urban Forest
BANKSIDE, LONDON

Despite severe cutbacks in public spending, the project is now underway and the first phase of new public spaces is being completed. The whole approach has generated public support. The use of temporary interventions such as the Union Street Urban Orchard (Case Study 4.2) have reinforced this by giving something back to the community early on. There is no absolute end state to this project. The working title Urban Forest was chosen to illustrate the organic nature of the area, with the public spaces as clearings within a new urban fabric where the individuals can make their own discoveries.

SOURCE: Interview with Stephen Witherford, Witherford Watson Mann Architects.

192

southwark bridge road

Drawing of redesigned public spaces
BANKSIDE, LONDON

union street ⟶

Dalston
LONDON

The study *Making Space in Dalston* (sponsored by Design for London and carried out by *muf* architecture/art and J&L Gibbons LLP) provides an example of both the principles of the meanwhile plan, and the immediate possibilities that can be released by it.

Dalston in Hackney, north-east London is undergoing intense physical change. The East London line has connected the area to the London Underground network for the first time. As the line was being built the London Development Agency (LDA) underwrote the construction of a slab over the railway in Dalston town centre and brought in development partners to provide a new centre with housing, shops, a library and a new public square. While this development project had the potential to regenerate Dalston, the LDA recognised that it was site-specific and did not address the connectivity with the wider area.

Dalston is among the most deprived wards in London with over 20 per cent of residents on benefits, and it has very little green space. It has a long history of social activism and a strong entrepreneurial tradition. Importantly, there is also political commitment to involving the community. The area is very diverse culturally and its distinct social groups provide a vibrant social and cultural scene. It has a higher than average proportion of the population with university degrees and also a higher proportion with no qualifications at all. This 'prof-pov'

Wheatfield and mill installations in Dalston
DALSTON, LONDON

relationship is one of the characteristics of what Stern and Seifert call a 'natural cultural district', and their research was important to the thinking behind the *muf* proposals (see p. 170).

The six-month study by *muf* started in September 2008, and was intended to inform and complement a more formal masterplan for Dalston by the Matrix Partnership. The lack of green spaces, but abundant cultural life were the two main characteristics that informed the study brief that sought a linked approach to public realm and cultural initiatives. The objectives included open dialogue with community representatives; demonstrating how regeneration could benefit existing communities; improving the quality and accessibility of the public realm; identifying existing assets and how to secure them; ensuring a coherence of design approach; and demonstrating how projects could be linked, programmed and funded. A cultural programme of events was embedded into the physical redesign of the area. The concept was to use these to open up areas hitherto closed and, through these events, for local people to explore and rediscover their area.

In seeking to nurture Dalston's inherent creativity and diversity, the study placed as much importance on the *process of engagement* as on the delivery of an enhanced urban setting. The study methodology was based on three clear principles: valuing what's there; nurturing the possible; and defining what's missing.

Most importantly, however, the study did not just produce a final report. By breaking up the 'masterplan' into a series of 76 projects, implementation could take place immediately and visibly. A temporary installation (in collaboration with the Barbican Centre and installed by French group EXYZT) animated the area alongside the Peace Mural Square. The Dalston Mill, a five-storey windmill and pizza oven, was erected adjacent to a field of wheat that was later harvested and milled (an artistic installation, *Wheatfield*, by the artist Agnes Denes). It opened in

195

Harvesting wheat to make local bread
DALSTON, LONDON

July 2009 and provided an opportunity for between 400 and 1,500 people daily, to experience the potential of the area as a green host space for planned and unplanned activities. Dalston Barn followed on from the Mill as a more permanent meeting place, part tithe barn and part Scandinavian summer house. There were other speedy outcomes: a hoardings scheme for young people; a dossier on the potential for cultural programming; gardening workshops on housing estate spaces and discussions with the community and managers about the maintenance regimes of such spaces; beautiful stencilled signage; and temporary soft play equipment in Gillett Square that is packed away after use (photo, p. 93). The project also provided flower beds and trees, and a community garden planted with vegetables. The phasing is flexible and has allowed funding packages to be stitched together from different sources. Not all of the projects are essential, but each phase builds on the previous one and the sum is always greater than the individual parts. Critically, the community is involved in each phase and can see the visible improvements in their area.

SOURCES: Interview with Lisa Fior, *muf* architecture/art.

J&L Gibbons LLP, *muf* architecture/art, *Making Space in Dalston*, prepared for London Borough of Hackney and Design for London/LDA, July 2009.

K. Long, 'The Big Society begins in Dalston', *Evening Standard*, 30 June 2010, p. 31.

M.J. Stern and S.C. Seifert, *Cultivating 'Natural' Cultural Districts*, Creativity and Change: A collaboration between the Social Impact of the Arts Project and the Reinvestment Fund funded by the Rockefeller Foundation, 2007, retrieved from http://trfund.com/resource/downloads/creativity/NaturalCulturalDistricts.pdf (accessed 17 November 2010).

196

Colonising the street
DALSTON, LONDON

Interim-use charrette
PHILADELPHIA

In November 2009 a charrette was held in Philadelphia to explore interim uses for industrial sites around the city as part of the annual Design on the Delaware event. It represented a partnership between the Community Design Collaborative (CDC), the American Institute of Architects (AIA) Urban Design Committee and the Philadelphia Association of Community Development Corporations. The charrette was part of the CDC's Infill Philadelphia initiative that started in 2007. There are thousands of acres of vacant land in Philadelphia that have a major impact on the vitality of neighbourhoods and the city overall.

Teams of designers, architects, landscape architects, planners and public artists were charged with designing temporary uses for four vacant industrial sites. They proposed a wide range of options: public art installations, performance spaces, outdoor markets, a roof-top urban campsite with areas for stargazing, rainwater capture schemes, vine-covered green walls, an outdoor band shell or theatre and designs for a sequence of sites along 10th Street in Chinatown. The event illustrates the growing interest in temporary use in the city and the immense enthusiasm and wealth of creative ideas that the topic stimulates. Infill Philadelphia will use the event to continue its work on design solutions for unused industrial properties in the city and help foster a discussion on temporary use and redeveloping industrial land.

197

SOURCES: Designing for Temporary Use, Infill Philadelphia, 2 November 2009, retrieved from http://blog.cdesignc.org/designing-for-temporary-use/.

J.W. Thomas, *Infill Philadelphia: Boldness Redefines 'Community Center'*, PlanPhilly, 4 November 2009, retrieved from http://planphilly.com/boldness-can-redefine-community-center-infill-philadelphias-design-charrette (both accessed 17 June 2011).

Rahova district

BUCHAREST

From the 1970s a major programme of reconstruction was commenced in Bucharest under Nicolai Ceauşescu. Inspired by North Korea, it imposed a completely alien urban form and scale on the city, with construction of the Palace of the People and a series of grand boulevards, squares and new public and government buildings. The vision was never fully completed, but by the time of the revolution in 1989 some eight square kilometres in the historic centre of Bucharest had been levelled, including three monasteries, 20 churches, three synagogues, three hospitals, two theatres and a sports stadium. Some 40,000 people had been displaced and the functionality of the city centre was seriously damaged. A report drawn up soon afterwards by a group of non-profit organisations summed up the situation in its title *Bucharest: An Urban Disaster*. In the absence of a well-grounded private or community sector, power passed seamlessly to a succession of mayors who set about remodelling the city to respond to the rapid growth and power of the motorcar-owning classes. Grandiose traffic and highways solutions have, in many cases, continued the tradition of top-down imposed city masterplanning solutions. But there have been some interesting exceptions.

In 2005 the architect and entrepreneur Teodor Frolu purchased a disused and semi-derelict Commodities Exchange building on Va Urma Street in the Rahova district. Once a thriving commercial quarter of the city, the works of Ceauşescu had severed it from the rest of the central area and left it an impoverished neighbourhood, characterised by vacant land and marginalised uses. The concept was to create an urban 'room' or 'lounge' meeting place between the local populace and the emerging creative sector, urban thinkers and architects. Of course, this is in direct contrast to the Palace of the People that towers over the area, barely 800 metres away. The urban lounge opened in 2008. On the ground floor is a café and community space available for events, concerts and conferences. Above it are offices occupied by media, PR and architecture and design companies. The 'Ark', as it is now termed, is a place of refuge and exchange. It now boasts a 'Peasant's Market' and runs an intensive programme of events. But it is essentially a place of debate and the exchange of ideas, often focused on the future direction of Bucharest.

This bold intervention has now raised questions about the relationship of the Ark and Rahova with the cultural area of Bucharest. Working with General Public Agency and Space Syntax, Teodor Frolu has set about exploring the spatial relationship between Rahova and the historic centre. The solution is a proposition of a new cultural axis, using simple interventions to construct pedestrian and cycle links through the dead areas of Ceauşescu's city and to use a series of cultural nodes and activities to invite people to rediscover the lost city centre. At the end of this axis will be the Ark at Rahova. This has led inevitably to the exploration and temporary appropriation of unused space. Projects such as 'we open the yards to the public' sought to utilise, on a temporary basis, abandoned space for public markets and cultural events.

This project is sophisticated and ambitious, and there are parallels with grassroots movements in London (such as the Covent Garden Community Association that saved Covent Garden in the 1970s and the Coin Street Community Builders that has transformed 13 acres of the South

198

Bank since the 1980s). It goes beyond the narrow confines of space occupation and temporary activity to providing an urban manifesto that challenges the outdated urban planning practices of the city. Teodor Frolu states: 'our project aims to transform the Uranus-Rahova area into the socio-economic avant-garde of the new Bucharest, a city that would reach, through cultural and urban interventions, the status of a true European capital'. It has now spawned a wide variety of temporary uses and interventions. A flower market has been established, the community development project Jarustea has begun to engage with residents of some of the housing neighbourhoods and educational projects have started in local schools. Local projects have been initiated to plant trees, design local parks and even establish a Speakers Corner.

The interesting distinguishing feature with project Rahova is the understanding of incremental urbanism, the stimulation of debate as an alternative to the sterile City Hall policies and the projection of that debate outwards to reshape the city.

SOURCES: Interview with Teodor Frolu.

www.hotnews.ro/stiri-2565788-bucharest-urban-disaster-with-9-000-people-pre-square-kilometer.htm (accessed 1 April 2011).

http://en.wikipedia.org/wiki/Systematization_(Romania) (accessed 5 April 2011).

199

Community bakery, part of the Rahova project
BUCHAREST

| Newham and North Fulham
LONDON

North Fulham in west London is a neighbourhood that, over recent years, has lost much of its vitality, vibrancy and community identity. For local people, the neglect and under-investment has gone on for too long. They have seen the quality of the environment worsen with growing traffic congestion, litter, fly-tipping, graffiti and dog fouling. Their streets have become less safe as crime, street drinking, drug abuse and racial harassment have become more prevalent and visible, and they have suffered high levels of unemployment and have correspondingly low household incomes. The delivery of their services appears confusing, remote, fragmented, uncoordinated and unresponsive. For those in poverty, or with complex health, social or family problems, or language or cultural barriers, access to services is even more difficult and impenetrable. In the late 1990s the area was designated under the New Deal in the Communities (NDC) initiative and regeneration programmes were formulated.

Alongside a spatial masterplan for the area, the architectural practice Fluid produced a complementary 'community infrastructure' layer. This described the potential social geography for the district and created a structure for information and communication. A proposed intranet collated all forms of service delivery and offered the scope for online community support, a diary of events and an A–Z of local businesses. As with intranets being designed for east Manchester and Newham NDC, a purpose-built website is to be assembled to act as the portal through which all of these services would be accessed.

In a parallel piece of work in a very similar community in Newham, east London, Fluid established a broadband intranet tying four principle community support buildings together, each of which offers a particular service tied to prosperity, learning, health and crime control. One of these proposed buildings is a pavilion equipped as a community radio station (FM and internet) that, at a later stage, could be developed into a small TV studio. All of these interventions will complement the website and local newsletter as a means of building social capital and, through training programmes, community capacity. A digital job search agency will be built into the website, as will a local employment trading scheme and time bank. The information infrastructure will also facilitate better neighbourhood and town centre management.

This represents a radical development of the masterplanning process into multi-dimensional design within a framework where the city is understood as the complex web of people's lives. The changing patterns of these lives comprise a multitude of temporary transient states. Physical interventions can be planned, designed and inserted into these frameworks, often after experimentation and trial and error, in a way that the more static physical masterplans of the twentieth century could never achieve.

SOURCE: Interview with Steve McAdam, Fluid Architects.

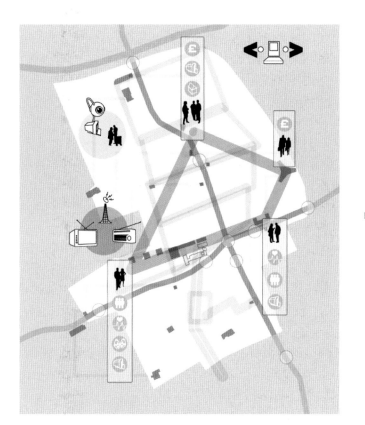

NDC area

broadband information infrastructure

webcam & ICT cable system

principal roads

transport information points

community radio station, television, webcam

menu of site-specific and intranet services
(linkages to theme initiatives)

community support / public buildings

201

Masterplan, the Smart City, by Fluid Architects
NEWHAM, LONDON

Case Study
#10.7

South Shields
SOUTH TYNESIDE

South Shields on the River Tyne near Newcastle brought in Studio Egret West in 2007 to produce a masterplan and regeneration framework for its waterfront. Although the conventional approach would have been to develop the waterside for high-value uses such as residential, Studio Egret West instead proposed clearing the area to create a new 35-hectare People's Park – the New Shore – to encourage local enterprise in the form of events, businesses and activities.

There was a precedent for this. Close by, the Ouseburn Valley joins the Tyne near Gateshead. It is an area that has remained largely unplanned and has in a sense always provided a meanwhile space, accommodating urban farms, pigeon lofts, allotments, workshops and music events. This unregulated environment creates the space for the city to breathe, not just physically, but economically and socially as well. The problem with recreating the Ouseburn in South Shields was simply how could the unplanned be planned? Studio Egret West's concept was understood and fully supported by the council, but they did not initially have the government culture or entrepreneurial infrastructure to implement it. They have now commissioned the next stage, the detailed landscape strategy, and are working with Studio Egret West to foster some of the conditions required to make the concept a reality. To achieve this they will have to take a sizeable step for local government and relinquish some of their own control in order to just allow good things to happen.

202

SOURCE: Interview with David West, Studio Egret West.

The Royal Docks

LONDON

The Royal Docks in east London were the largest enclosed dock area in Europe before they closed at the end of the 1960s. The London Docklands Development Corporation invested in site clearance and road infrastructure and a series of brave individual investments established the London International Convention Centre (EXCEL), London City Airport and the University of East London. These bold investments were unfortunately accompanied by a mix of inward-facing residential developments often of mediocre architectural quality. Despite its proximity to the business district at Canary Wharf and good communications into central London, the Royal Docks failed to establish itself as an area where London's development industry was willing to invest further.

The 2008 property recession forced the London Development Agency (LDA) to rethink its strategy. The response was to abandon any attempt at masterplanning (there had been 73 masterplans and strategies for the area over the past 30 years) and consider looser strategic frameworks instead. The principle initiative was the Green Enterprise District (GED) that addressed three pressing imperatives. The first was London's need to diversify from its over-dependence on financial services. The second was the Mayor's desire for a single big idea on climate change, and the third was the need to brand and market an area where development activity had been very weak. The GED brought these together into a very simple overarching

203

The Royal Docks
LONDON

Green Enterprise District: a conceptual plan for east London
ROYAL DOCKS, LONDON

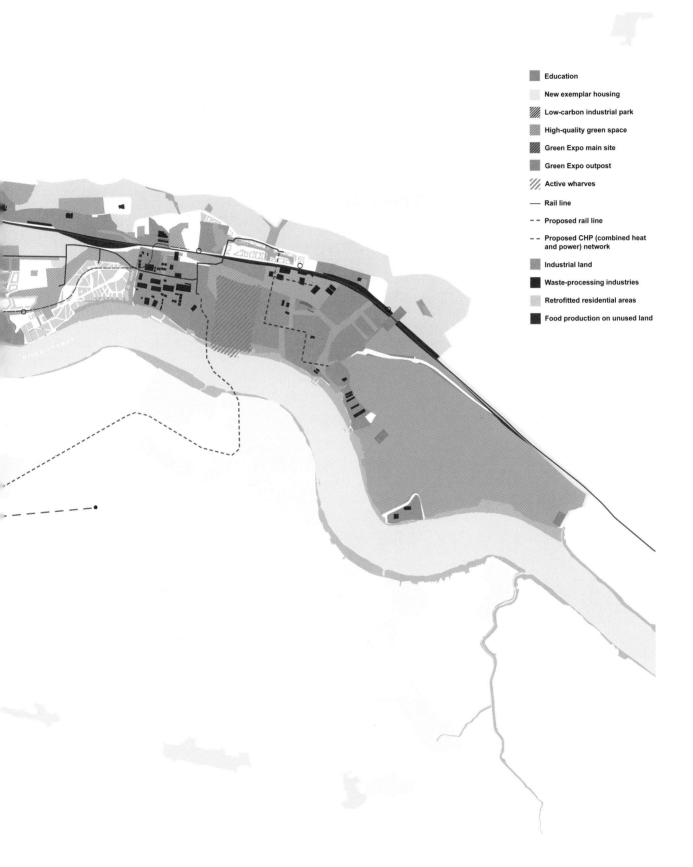

Education

New exemplar housing

Low-carbon industrial park

High-quality green space

Green Expo main site

Green Expo outpost

Active wharves

Rail line

Proposed rail line

Proposed CHP (combined heat and power) network

Industrial land

Waste-processing industries

Retrofitted residential areas

Food production on unused land

205

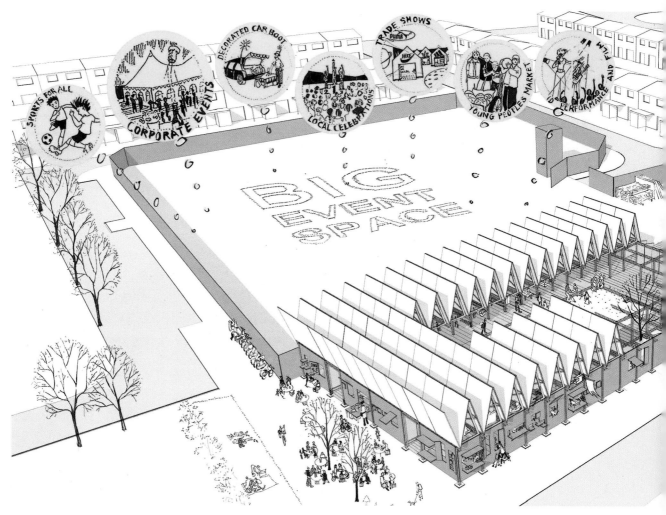

206

Caravanserai: a proposal for retail and workshops, Site Life competition
ROYAL DOCKS, LONDON

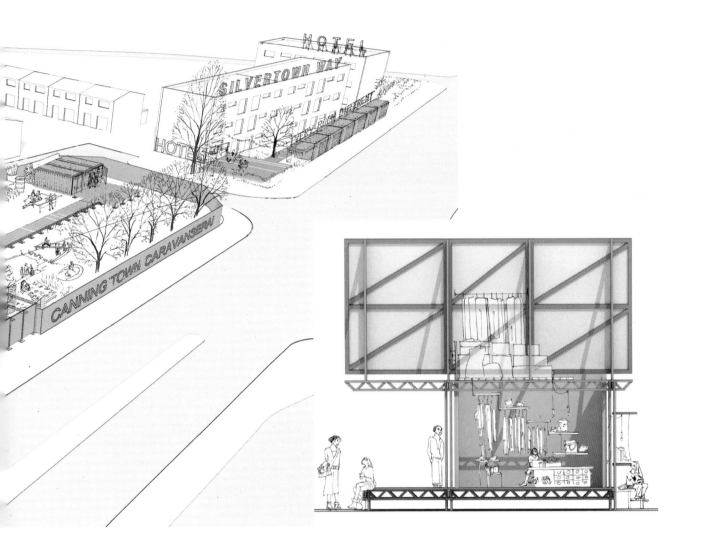

Proposal for an urban honey farm, Site Life competition
ROYAL DOCKS, LONDON

208

Temporary-use proposal, Site Life competition
ROYAL DOCKS, LONDON

strategic framework. It proposed the allocation of land for research, technology, manufacturing and high-end recycling and targeted companies within what was deliberately loosely defined as the 'green economy'. This was to be underpinned by investment in public infrastructure including district heating and energy networks, funded in association with the European Investment Bank via a £100m revolving 'green' investment fund. A planning policy framework established high design and environmental specifications for all new development, and the LDA backed this up with residential and industrial retrofit programmes to improve energy performance. The final element was a proposition to seek a tourist/exhibition centre to showcase climate change and environmental issues.

This was never intended to be a plan. It was an aspiration and a branding exercise and was produced by Design for London in a matter of days. Sitting outside any legal or statutory framework, it was launched via the internet, conferences and exhibitions, including the 2010 Shanghai Expo. Word of mouth did the rest, resulting, for example, in Siemens deciding to locate their London research centre and environmental exhibition centre in the Royal Docks (due to open in July 2012).

The next stage in the process was for the LDA to broker an alliance between the (Conservative) Mayor of London and the (Labour) mayor of the local borough, Newham. The alliance was significant in creating market confidence and was captured in a jointly signed 'vision' document, which was also non-statutory. The vision document swept away all previous masterplans and set out a simple joint objective to develop the Royal Docks as a business, hotel, conferencing, research and logistics district to support the central London economy. In doing this it built on the area's strengths: its international airport, the O_2 Arena and the EXCEL Conference Centre. These are now being linked (across the Thames) by a cable car funded by the Mayor.

The final element of the strategy centred on land development. LDA has substantial landholdings in the Royal Docks, and the next move was to incorporate a temporary-use element into the process. Early in 2010 the magazine *Property Week* launched the Site Life initiative (see p. 43) to promote temporary uses as a means of rejuvenating large urban sites left empty by the property recession. In Meanwhile London, *Property Week* teamed up with the LDA and the Borough of Newham to promote three sites as part of a longer-term regeneration strategy on the back of the 2012 Olympics (another temporary event).

The sites ranged from a 0.5-hectare site adjacent to the centre of Canning Town, to two dockside sites. All were seen as important strategic sites for long-term development, but each had the potential to provide economic activity in the short term. The competition aimed to find ideas that were exciting and would promote entrepreneurial activities, create jobs for local people and reflect the 'green enterprise' ambitions for the Royal Docks. Critically, all projects had to be deliverable and come with a funding partner. Finally, the ideas were also required to be capable of being transferred to other sites in the locality.

The competition, judged by an independent panel of architects, planners and developers, considered 47 responses. These included the Industri(us) by Fluid, David Barrie and John Thakara, a proposal to use all three sites as an 'engine for change' by recycling found materials into new products. Another winner was Caravanserai, a temporary wooden structure by EXYZT

209

to house shops, cafés and workshops along with a small events space. A third project (from Strong and Co and Future Tents, promoters of part of the Glastonbury music festival) was to create a twenty-first-century pleasure garden, Shangri-La. The team proposed a waterside festival and events site, including a boutique hotel, bar, and sculpture garden and restaurants. Another proposal by Studio Egret West proposed a floating swimming pool using redundant Thames barges (lighters). Other proposals included a honey factory, a boatyard and adventure sports.

The significance of this initiative goes beyond the quite extraordinary range of ideas that it generated. In this case study, temporary uses have been deliberately structured into a cogent long-term regeneration strategy. The Borough of Newham and the LDA see them as a vital component in the creation of a sense of place and as a prerequisite for urban regeneration. The uses will be temporary but are expected to evolve and move within the sites. They will also interact with the emerging proposals for permanent use and may seed longer-term initiatives themselves. The involvement of *Property Week* also signifies a major shift of interest in temporary uses from the design and architectural press into the mainstream of property best practice.

There has been a further unexpected spin-off from this project. Studio Egret West has been approached by city authorities in Hong Kong for proposals for a temporary park along the Kowloon waterfront. Whether there is a direct link between this potential commission and the Meanwhile London competition is not clear. What is clear is that interest in temporary activities is evolving fast. If temporary-use strategies start to be taken up formally by countries like China, they will certainly be entering mainstream urban planning practice.

Proposal for temporary uses on Kowloon Waterfront
HONG KONG

Case Study
#10.9

Speirs Locks

GLASGOW

In Speirs Locks, a development site close to Glasgow city centre, the developer (Isis Waterside Regeneration) and Glasgow City Council are exploring an innovative approach to realise the vision for the area as a world-class creative and cultural quarter for Glasgow. The regeneration process is being guided by a flexible physical framework developed by the Glasgow Canal Partnership and 7N architects called Growing the Place and a creative industries action plan prepared by David Barrie and Associates with A+DS called Growing the People.

The place-making plans are based around incremental occupation and the cultivation of the site for social enterprise. Such organic development takes an informal 'open-source' approach to occupation, enterprise and the building of identity. The creative industries action plan seeks 'to build upon the activity of its existing tenants and turn the site into a place about "making" and "doing": the production of goods and services that have social and creative value, a place for new social businesses, manufacturing workshops and new community enterprise'. Over three years a sequence of social, environmental and economic activities is planned to make a market for the settlement of the area and over time attract new occupants.

SOURCE: Architecture+Design Scotland, 'Speirs Locks', 2010, retrieved from
www.ads.org.uk/urbanism/features/spiers-locks (accessed 17 June 2011).

211

'Please keep on the grass' at the London Festival of Architecture
STORE STREET, LONDON, 2010

11: The four-dimensional city

TEMPORARY ACTIVITY represents a reaction to a world where the future is more uncertain and less secure, and a response to rapid economic, societal and technological changes that are shortening the present into smaller and smaller time frames. Our loss of faith in a stable, 'solid' world, our increasing sense of the fragility of our existence, our reluctance to face our uncertain future or to build a more sustainable lifestyle, our growing indifference to the lessons of the past, our short attention spans and our focus on instant satisfaction are all trends which favour indulgence in ephemeral, fleeting experiences. And perhaps they represent an emerging global mind-set in which temporariness in all its forms and experiences will flourish.

Our cities have always been subject to continuous organic redesign, but the new wave of temporary activity is perhaps a manifestation of the acceleration in this process. New technology and communications media certainly have a central enabling role in temporary use. They provide a means of publicising fleeting, illicit or fringe activities, or those with a niche appeal. They also mean that we are less tied to specific locations and thereby free up space for complex mixes of work, consumption, relaxation and play. Temporary activities also reflect a bottom-up current within society whereby people are starting to reappropriate their cities and to colonise them in new ways to suit emerging needs and lifestyles. The growth in activism is both part of a top-down drive to encourage active communities and diminish the burden on the state, and a grassroots desire to 'do something', anything, rather than face long-term unemployment.

Many temporary phenomena appear to occupy a position at the cutting edge of creativity, where the traditional distinctions between different types of activity are less clear. The actors are increasingly multi-disciplinary. Many pop-up shops, restaurants, exhibitions and performances reflect the increasingly diverse nature of culture, and explicitly offer new consumer experiences by blurring the usual boundaries between eating, theatre, music and art. The boundary between culture and counterculture is also far less clear than was once the case. Some temporary interventions have a clear countercultural intent and express discontent with the blandness and sameness of urban areas, or the controls on public space. Others question the way in which the market allocates space to uses that produce economic value, over those that generate social benefits. Temporary activities might therefore signal a growing rejection of the way in which top-down controls and the quest for a utopian end state have stifled the variety, individuality, even the delightful madness of our urban areas.

It could be assumed that anything temporary is not particularly sustainable simply because the term can imply a 'throw-away' attitude. However, an *intention* to be short-lived could also suggest a desire to leave minimal traces on the earth. Many of the temporary activities explored in this book do embody some of the principles of sustainable development. Temporary structures frequently re-use or recycle whatever materials are at hand, while many temporary activities represent a more efficient use of land and buildings. Temporary urban agriculture projects, for instance, reduce 'food miles' and build social capital in the process. Other projects represent experiments in more alternative forms of urban living that seek to minimise their impact on the environment, are cooperative, participatory or prioritise qualitative aspects of life such as building 'community', or providing opportunities for self-expression.

There is still insufficient evidence on which to base any hard conclusions about the conditions that are encouraging temporary activities in some cities but not in others, or that are leading a relatively small number of city authorities to embrace the notion of temporary use. There is no doubt though, that the deep culture of some cities is more likely to generate this type of activity. Cities with long traditions of entrepreneurship, individualism and dissent such as New York, London and Berlin may be more inclined to spawn temporary activities. Multi-culturalism and strong creative industry sectors are other important components as these bring together clusters of people who are inclined to experiment and innovate. Another important factor is crisis, caused by economic or structural decline. This creates a large supply of the basic raw material for temporary-use cheap property, and can force cities to respond with strategies in which temporary use may be the only available agenda to address the needs of a desperate electorate.

Temporary uses appear to seed most easily in particular places. They work best in the intimacy of the inner city where the urban form is fine-grained, where there are voids and cheap or free space. They seem to work especially well on the cheaper fringes of areas of intense activity. They also thrive in areas where there is less regulation and greater ambiguity around ownership of space – civic, private or corporate. For these reasons it does not come as a surprise that there are fewer examples in suburbs or in cities where the overriding urban form is corporate and suburban. Where the motor car rather than the pedestrian dominates the environment, the public realm has effectively been 'confiscated', and the chance encounters upon which many temporary activities depend, just do not occur. For similar reasons corporate space where uses are carefully proscribed or municipal spaces that are sanitised can be equally sterile.

There is no sign that the drivers behind the expansion of temporary activity are themselves transient. This suggests that temporary activity, as both a symptom of these changes and a potential response to them, will continue to grow. Most of the conditions required for a more fluid and organic form of temporary urbanism appear to be in place already. There are a growing number of artists, entrepreneurs, architects, activists and even landowners who are willing to enter the market, innovate and experiment. There is an emerging consensus that if carefully and sensitively managed, temporary uses can add commercial and social value. This is matched by significant public interest in temporary activities and more participants, users, spectators and customers. In consequence there is a considerable body of practice to show how temporary uses can both fit into long-term strategies of urban renewal and stand alone in their own right.

Obviously practice varies from country to country, but in Europe and North America there appear to be no fundamental legal or property management problems militating against temporary activities. The changes in property law that are required to further facilitate temporary uses are relatively minor. The biggest barriers sit with city government. There are plenty of examples of cities innovating in this field, but these still constitute a minority position. To accommodate the unforeseen and unanticipated, cities need, above all, to have the confidence to stand back and 'allow things to happen'. As Pogoreutz argues, it must become 'a task of municipal politics to keep open spaces for such unplanned, spontaneous urban articulation'.[1] This is an immense challenge for city authorities whose historical role has been so strongly associated with the process of control. Crucially, good leadership whether public or private sector needs to be actively curious about what might emerge, and be prepared to hold its nerve against any short-term opposition. Attitudes still need to evolve, particularly among the older generation of professionals, many of whom remain stuck in a quest for 'permanent solutions' and are slower to embrace the spirit of experimentation that is more natural to the young.

215

The characteristics of four-dimensional design

To be truly effective, temporary activities should not be viewed as an experimental prototype for a longer-term use. They are an essential feature of the urban and spatial condition in their own right, not 'a test run that needs to be completed as quickly as possible so that one can focus on stabilisation and codification again'. Spiegl and Teckert argue that many projects only become possible because they are temporary. Not all of them can 'lead the way to the institutional'. 'If temporary use is seen merely as the prototype for a long-term utilisation, then the plea for the temporary runs the risk of inadvertently demanding a right of asylum from the temporary.'[2]

Some of the characteristics of four-dimensional design were alluded to in Chapter 10. One of these is the use of looser conceptual strategies instead of inflexible land zoning and rigid masterplans. Broad but realistic visions can provide the focus around which inclusive stakeholder alliances can be formed. Incremental action is the mechanism for flexible implementation. Many designers are now talking about 'getting stuck in', starting a process and working iteratively. This is not meant to be an alternative to professional rigour, but interminable abstract studies can blight an area just as effectively as unfounded development projects. More immediate outcomes reinforce the resolve of all parties to see the project through. The *process* is at least as important as the end state and needs to be understood in all of its potential complexities. The impact of each stage on the form of that which follows must be subject to continuous review. Effective and continuous local engagement is an essential component and helps to build both ownership and a degree of certainty into the process. It can also help to overcome the 'power deficit' that condemns so many masterplans to the shelf. Despite the unpredictable nature of the journey, the process itself needs to be choreographed. This does not necessarily entail the hard physical design of every stage, but may involve temporary installations, events and activities, brokering, networking or providing information. In choreographing the process, the designer will, at times, have to be prepared to concentrate on creating the conditions rather than the solutions. Spaces need to be configured as the stage upon which time-limited uses and activities are acted out, develop, flourish, move on or simply wither. The contribution of temporary activities is that they give dynamism, even alchemy, to the process and may well, in themselves, have a significant and beneficial effect on the future. Experimentation with time-limited activities can twist and transmute long-term strategies into more interesting and completely unanticipated forms. Temporary uses can develop their own natural energy. In so doing they can bring that vector of surprise. In a world stripped of many of its certainties, temporary activities are life forms that may have separate evolutionary paths leading to a richer urban ecosystem.

This process is a way of thinking about how urban change can be beneficially shaped. It can be applied to neighbourhoods or specific sites that are in public or community ownership. It may also represent a model whereby privately owned sites, developed with private capital, are more sensitively planned, are more relevant to their surroundings and lead to less conflict and delay in the process.

216

The planning framework

Whereas the underlying characteristics and processes that are required for more flexible planning are becoming clearer, the right planning framework is still required. The underlying condition that seems to be most conducive to temporary activity is freedom. The temporary needs to be allowed to happen organically. This raises particular difficulties for urban planning. As the Urban Catalyst study notes, the issue of temporary uses has not yet been addressed or worked out with reference to the statutory framework of legally binding detailed land-use plans.[3]

In relation to planning reform many commentators these days argue that the present planning system in the UK is negative, adversarial, inflexible and bureaucratic. The UK government is now proposing what it terms 'Open-Source Planning'.[4] Just as open-source software can be programmed in a flexible and adaptable way, the government argues that planning should be made more responsive to the needs of local communities. Instead of a whole series of rigid statutory development plans, there should be a basic national framework within which communities and councils produce their own distinctive local policies. In parallel, it is proposed that the present system of development control should be replaced by a system of 'Flexible Zoning' (or 'neighbourhood development orders'), whereby land uses could be changed without planning permission within a range of specified permissible uses. The coalition government has confirmed that it wishes to introduce radical reforms in the Decentralisation and Localism Bill published in December 2010.[5]

The loosening of planning controls is being considered in a number of other countries. There are moves to make temporary permissions easier in San Francisco, Seattle and Germany. In San Francisco, city councillors are considering introducing a Green Development Agreement which will allow approval for temporary uses to be fast-tracked through the planning and legal system and provide financial assistance by offering developers the opportunity to 'lock in' existing entitlements for a five- to eight-year period. The development entitlement process in San Francisco is especially cumbersome, requiring developers to renew on a one- to three-year basis, and projects are at risk as entitlements are always subject to modification. In theory, the savings from not having to hire lawyers and architects to keep entitlements current could be applied to the cost of commissioning temporary uses. In return, the city will ask simply for an interim use that benefits the public. The UK British Property Federation has similarly argued that if developers could be given an extended time to commence development before planning permissions expire, this would encourage better interim solutions (as long as there was a cast-iron guarantee that 'interim' *meant* interim).[6]

Seattle also finalised legislation in the spring of 2010 to provide flexibility to the owners of stalled developments and allow interim uses until market conditions are more favourable. In Germany the '*Baurecht auf Zeit*' (a right to build for a limited time) aims to reduce the inflexibility of German planning law in regard to time-limited developments. It protects the short- and long-term use of the site, as well as allowing the possibility of a progressively more intensive use.[7] There is also great potential for local authorities and regeneration agencies to explore and promote potential temporary uses through competitions, as in London's Royal Docks through the Site Life initiative and the Holding Patterns initiative in Seattle (see Chapter 4).

In the UK there are other possible reforms that could recognise the potential importance of temporary uses. First, the present definition of a temporary use as one lasting 28 days is outmoded and can result in preplanning costs that are prohibitive. Research commissioned by the Department for Communities and Local Government (DCLG) ironically showed that it is temporary uses (such as car boot sales, weekend markets, motor sports and evening cricket matches) that are granted automatic consent for up to 28 days in any calendar year, that figure as among the types of development giving most problems to local authorities. The report reviewed various solutions, but concluded that none of these work: '(u)ltimately, only the removal of temporary use provisions will really address the problems adequately.'[8]

Second, planning policy could positively encourage landowners to think about phased or temporary activities at the planning stage. It is perhaps anomalous that while Environmental Impact Assessments are firmly established within planning requirements, the consideration of phasing and 'interim usage plans' are not. Where major sites are being developed, often over many years, there is scope for local planning authorities to build in a requirement for temporary use as part of the planning permission.

217

There is also the issue around how the planning system controls land uses. In the UK there has been no fundamental reform of the Use Classes Order since its inception, and a strong case can be made for a radical rethink to reflect the economy and social conditions pertaining to the twenty-first century.

Zones of tolerance

Finally there is the option of applying simplified planning legislation to particular areas or zones. In the UK Local Development Orders do give some local flexibility in this respect, but their take-up has been limited, and there are signs that even if adopted more widely, they will still be extremely time-consuming to prepare.[9]

Enterprise Zones (EZs), designated urban areas that benefit from tax breaks, simplified planning procedures, a discount on business rates and super-fast broadband, have just been resuscitated by the UK government in a move to attract new businesses and create new jobs. In their previous incarnation, 38 EZs were established between 1981 and 1996. However, two recent reports throw doubt on their cost-effectiveness and on their relevance today. The Centre for Cities found that they only generated 58,000 additional jobs and that the cost per job was £26,000 at today's prices.[10] The Work Foundation's report found that 80 per cent of jobs created in EZs were displaced from other places and the prosperity they brought was short-lived.

Both reports warn that the model of the 1980s will not work today because urban dereliction is no longer the key issue. The structure of the economy has changed; there are fewer manufacturing firms so large capital allowances are less relevant. Instead the Centre for Cities propose 'Local Growth Zones' where a menu of policy tools focused on employment and skills support would be available and could be tailored to local economic conditions. The options include 'Rapid Planning Zones' with radically slimmed-down controls on development. The Work Foundation similarly argued that the relaxation of planning regulations offered by Enterprise Zones was also much more effective than tax breaks.[11]

There are clear pointers in our own research to suggest that more loosely regulated environments are likely to seed and foster the enterprises and activities that often manifest themselves temporarily in the city. The idea of some kind of flexible planning zone receives support from other researchers.[12] Large zones, if linked to a relaxation of planning controls would almost certainly prove to be highly unpopular with the established residential or business communities that they would inevitably impinge upon. To be workable any area relaxations would need to be tightly drawn and targeted to areas where the right combinations of conditions co-exist. Such 'free zones' already exist informally in many localities from Christianberg in Denmark to the Ouseburn Valley near Newcastle. The conditions that apply are those of tolerance and minimal interference to allow citizens to be creative within the confines of the law.

Perhaps rather than cumbersome and outdated EZs, twenty-first-century cities need small and responsive 'zones of tolerance', scattered throughout their neighbourhoods. These may be very small indeed, perhaps covering just an individual building. Radical deregulation could create areas akin to Hakim Bey's Temporary Autonomous Zones, allowing experimentation outside the confines of conventional practice. They could catalyse and nurture temporary activities and new enterprise, and offer stimulation and delight. They would in effect be the twenty-first-century city's 'erogenous zones'. Kelvin Campbell, for example, proposes 'Free Idea Zones', a form of 'white land' or unzoned part of the city, as an alternative to the traditional business park model, and 'Greyworlds' where industries on the lowest rung of the ladder would be allowed to flourish unmolested by officials.[13] Colin Ward similarly advocates 'reviving the idea of relaxed planning zones associated with some of the New Towns in the 1960s', to provide a more sympathetic environment for experiments in self-help housing. He argues that such an experiment would 'make it possible for those who wanted to, to experiment in alternative ways of building and servicing houses, and in permitting a dwelling to be occupied in a most rudimentary condition for gradual completion'.[14]

The 'Big Society'

Many policy researchers and national politicians now advocate a more flexible and less regulated approach to urban management and planning. For the UK Conservative Party this argument has traditionally been associated with freeing the market from the control of the state. However, the same arguments are now made by the coalition government with the central aim of devolving power to *communities*. The drive to empower individuals and communities has evolved gradually in the UK over the last decade or so, but has never before been the central plank of government policy, as it is in the 'Localism Agenda' or 'Big Society'. The aim now is to devolve power to citizens and communities in order to encourage social responsibility, civic pride and innovation (while reducing government expenditure at the same time). In theory, this could herald an era which is more favourable to small-scale, community or social enterprise and could facilitate its development as the sustainable alternative to both state service provision and private enterprise. Looked at from this perspective it is perhaps an odd policy direction for the Conservative Party to take. However, as we noted earlier, the roles of government and the private and community sectors are becoming increasingly blurred as we move towards a more pluralistic society.

Several commentators have likened the ideas underlying the Big Society to those expounded by Schumacher in the global bestseller of 1973, *Small is Beautiful*.[15] The three pillars of the Big Society – decentralisation of power, public service reform and social/community reform (helping people to collaborate and work for the common good) – are indistinguishable in many ways from the ideas of *Small is Beautiful*. The fact that these ideas are not reconciled with the continued dominance of global capitalism illustrates the fact that the government, in common with the rest of the G20 nations, has still not quite grasped the fact that 'sustainable economic growth' is a contradiction

219

in terms. However, since the Big Society is based on a recognition of some of the underlying trends within society, it could, potentially be an important initiative.

Unfortunately, there are problems with the policy. It ignores the fact that people have little additional free time to spend governing schools or community centres. Many existing bottom-up initiatives are driven instead by charities and social enterprises which have paid coordinators, and this sector is being hit hard by the cuts in public expenditure. The expectation that community action will be able to develop spontaneously to fill in the gaps left by cuts in public expenditure is also unrealistic. Above all, community development requires time. As presently construed, the Big Society is too amorphous or ephemeral to capture the public's imagination; it needs a focus or 'Big Idea' around which to operate. Temporary activities could provide one 'way in' for the Big Society. They empower, are quick and cheap, are experimental and low risk, and can have unexpected spin-offs. The zones of tolerance described above could even be activated by local communities, perhaps through mechanisms such as local Community Development Trusts and interim-use design charrettes or competitions.

In conclusion

220

Temporary urbanism remains a novelty and an idea, and several commentators have commented on the need for more research in this field.[16] Jane Jacobs notes that 'cities are an immense laboratory of trial and error, failure and success in city building and city design'.[17] Urbanists should be documenting experiments in temporary use, before they disappear and before the lessons from these experiences are lost.

Temporary uses represent a latent energy that can be tapped through a four-dimensional approach to urban planning and design. The desire for a better future can be matched with a better present through strategies that adopt an iterative rather than an end-state approach to urban change. This book draws on a wide range of extraordinary case studies but these are only a tiny fraction of the activity in this field, and each day brings more examples from cities across the world. Urban planners, policy makers, architects and designers need to view the city through the prism of the temporary. Projects and plans need to be threaded deliberately into the temporal layers of the city with a greater understanding of their particular time frames and evolutionary processes. The city around us needs to be recognised for what it is, an ever-changing but essentially temporary phenomenon.

For all that, the temporary city is the space designed by the individual. Perhaps it is the future, as disillusionment with rigidly organised cities spreads. Temporary activities empower individuals and allow them space in a dehumanised corporate world. It is still too early to say whether the temporary is starting to define a new approach to urban design or planning. What is clear, though, is that in the twenty-first century, if we want the innovation, fluidity and flexibility that temporary activities can give us, then we will need to relinquish our twentieth-century notions of control.

'Temporary access'
SERVICE STATION CAR PARK, NEWBURY

221

Notes

1: Introduction: the temporary city

1 Between 2001 and 2003, Urban Catalyst (an interdisciplinary team of architects, planners, lawyers, sociologists and local government representatives based in Berlin) conducted research (funded by the European Commission within the Key Action 4 City of Tomorrow and Cultural Heritage Program of the European Union) with 11 partners in six countries that was coordinated by the Technische Universität Berlin.

2 A study, symposium and exhibition on temporary uses in Berlin 2004–5 undertaken by the studio Urban Catalyst and commissioned by the Berlin Senate Department for Urban Development.

3 Urban Catalyst, *Urban Pioneers: Temporary Use and Urban Development in Berlin*, Berlin: Jovis, 2007.

4 F. Haydn and R. Temel (eds), *Temporary Urban Spaces: Concepts for the Use of City Space*, Basel: Birkhäuser, 2006.

5 K. Franck and Q. Stevens (eds), *Loose Space*, London: Routledge, 2007.

6 J.L. Chase, M. Crawford and J. Kaliski (eds), *Everyday Urbanism*, New York: The Monacelli Press, 2nd edition, 2008.

7 G. la Varra, 'POST-IT CITY: the other European public spaces', 2003, retrieved from http://subsol.c3.hu/subsol_2/contributors0/lavarratext. html (accessed 11 November 2010).

8 J. Hou (ed.), *Insurgent Public Space: Guerrilla Urbanism and the Remaking of Contemporary Cities*, London: Routledge, 2010.

9 STEALTH have even produced a 'Constitution for the Interim', modelled on the draft Constitution for the European Union. STEALTH.unlimited (A. Dzokic and M. Neelen) and I. de Kievith, 'Constituting the interim' in *Vacant NL: Where Architecture Meets Ideas*, retrieved from http://en.nai.nl/.../Booklet_Vacant_NL,_where_architecture_meets_ideas (accessed 8 October 2011).

10 See for example: Experiment City, http://experimentcity.net/en/; Pop-Up City, an online magazine by Amsterdam-based design agency Golfstromen, http://popupcity.net/; Templace, www.templace.com/; Spatial Agency (led by Nishat Awan, School of Architecture, University of Sheffield; Tatjana Schneider, School of Architecture, University of Sheffield; Jeremy Till, Architecture and the Built Environment, University of Westminster, London), www.spatialagency.net/ (the site notes that even before it was formally launched, the website attracted over 50,000 visitors, suggesting both a growing interest in the field and a pressing need for such documentation); Urban Tactics, www.urbantactics.org/home.html; The Meanwhile Project, www.meanwhile.org.uk/ (all accessed 14 June 2011).

11 H-L. Hentila and T. Lindborg, *Temporary Uses of Central Residual Spaces as Urban Development Catalysts*. Paper presented in ERSA Congress, Jyvaskyla 27–30 August 2003, retrieved from www-sre.wu-wien.ac.at/ersa/ersa-confs/ersa03/cdrom/papers/242.pdf (accessed 28 September 2010).

12 For example, the definition adopted by the Meanwhile Project 'Meanwhile use: business case and learning points', SQW Consulting (for the Meanwhile Project), May 2010, retrieved from www.meanwhile.org.uk/useful-info/misc/SQW%20-%20Meanwhile%20Use%20Report%20May%2010.pdf (accessed 28 January 2011).

13 R. Temel, 'The temporary in the city', in Haydn and Temel (eds), *Temporary Urban Spaces*, p. 55.

2: The dream of permanence

1 http://en.wikipedia.org/wiki/Ozymandias (accessed 14 June 2011).

2 T. Phillips, 'Urbanism for the masses', the *Guardian Weekly*, 31 December 2010, p. 28.

3 R. Kapuściński, *Another Day of Life*, London: Penguin Classics, 2001, pp. 13–19.

4 www.buildinghistory.org/regulations.shtml (accessed 13 December 2010).

5 www.planninghelp.org.uk/planning-system/history-of-the-planning-system; www.planninghelp.org.uk/planning-system/history-of-the-planning-system/public-health-reform-1800s (both accessed 13 December 2010).

6 www.planninghelp.org.uk/planning-system/history-of-the-planning-system/town-planning-in-the-1900s (accessed 13 December 2010).

7 M. Pearce, *Saving Time: A Review of the Conservation Movement in Britain in the 20th Century*, reproduced from the Building Conservation Directory 2000, retrieved from www.buildingconservation.com/articles/time/time1.htm (accessed 7 June 2010).

8 In fact, this understates the number of individual buildings (as it can include a terrace of 50 individual houses), and English Heritage gives the approximate number of individual properties as 500,000.

9 D. Cruickshank, *Night Waves: Free Thinking Festival*, BBC Radio 3, 9.15pm, 4 January 2010.

10 English Heritage, *The Heritage Dividend: Measuring the Results of English Heritage Regeneration*, London: English Heritage, 1999.

11 www.an-architecture.com/2010/09/preservation-omaamo-at-venice-biennale.html; www.designboom.com/weblog/cat/9/view/11395/rem-koolhaas-cronocaos-preservation-tour.html; www.designboom.com/weblog/cat/9/view/11424/rem-koolhaas-oma-cronocaos-preservation-tour-part-three.html; www.designboom.com/weblog/

cat/9/view/11428/rem-koolhaas-oma-cronocaos-preservation-tour-part-four.html (all accessed 15 June 2011).

12 'Empty property: protect and survive – experts' practical advice on safeguarding your investments from squatters and damage', *Property Week* in association with Aviva, www.propertyweek.com/free-white-paper-empty-property-protect-and-survive/5011294.article (accessed 21 January 2011).

13 C. Ward, *The Hidden History of Housing*, Institute for Contemporary History, King's College, London, September 2004, retrieved from www.historyandpolicy.org/papers/policy-paper-25.html#squatters (accessed 21 May 2010).

14 P. Walker 'Largest postwar prefab estate to be demolished', the *Guardian*, 2 January 2011, retrieved from www.guardian.co.uk/society/2011/jan/02/postwar-prefab-houses-demolition-london (accessed 10 February 2011).

15 See for example: K. Cochrane, 'Overnight success', the *Guardian G2,* 12 October 2010, pp. 6–9; S. Manzoor, 'Pop-up culture', the *Guardian*, 5 January 2011, p. 3.

16 A. Beckett, 'In the gaps developers left, another world is being built', the *Guardian*, 21 August 2010, p. 30.

17 A. Lukowski, 'Pop in on some pop-up theatre', *Time Out*, 23–9 September 2010, p. 18.

18 O. Wainwright (ed.), *Legacy Plus: Interim Uses and East London's Olympic Legacy*, London: The Architecture Foundation, 2010.

19 *Pop-Up City* exhibition from 24 March to 6 May 2010: www.newlondonarchitecture.org/exhibition.php?id=153&name=Pop%20Up%20City (accessed 11 June 2010).

20 http://network.propertyweek.com/group/sitelife (accessed 3 November 2010).

3: Temporary urbanism: drivers and conditions

1 Z. Bauman, *Liquid Modernity*, ANSE Conference, 2004, retrieved from http://anse.eu/html/history/2004%20Leiden/bauman%20englisch.pdf (accessed 14 June 2011); Z. Bauman, *Liquid Modernity*, Oxford: Blackwell, 2000; Z. Bauman*, Liquid Times: Living in an Age of Uncertainty*, Cambridge: Polity Press, 2007. See also: http://sociology.leeds.ac.uk/bauman/ (accessed 29 November 2010).

2 European Commission, *State of European Cities Report*, Study contracted by the European Commission, 2007.

3 J. Herron, 'Borderland/borderama/Detroit', in G. Wilkins (ed.), *Distributed Urbanism: Cities After Google Earth*, London: Routledge, 2010, pp. 63–86.

4 Herron, 'Borderland/borderama/Detroit', p. 72.

5 E. Villagomez, 'Claiming residual spaces in the heterogeneous city', in J. Hou (ed.), *Insurgent Public Space: Guerrilla Urbanism and the Remaking of Contemporary Cities*, London: Routledge, 2010, p. 82.

6 R. Beauregard, 'Shrinking cities in the United States in historical perspective', in *The Future of Shrinking Cities: Problems, Patterns and Strategies of Urban Transformation in a Global Context*, University of Carolina, May 2009, Monograph 2009-01, p. 68.

7 Shrinking Cities International Research Network (SCiRN), launched in 2004 by the Institute of Urban and Regional Development at the University of California, Berkeley, is coordinating global comparative research into the phenomenon.

8 R. Kohoutek and C. Kamleithner, 'Temporary uses, deregulation and urbanity', in F. Haydn and R. Temel (eds), *Temporary Urban Spaces: Concepts for the Use of City Space*, Basel: Birkhäuser, 2006, p. 37.

9 P. Arlt, 'Urban planning and interim use', in Haydn and Temel (eds), *Temporary Urban Spaces*, p. 39.

10 R. Temel, 'The temporary in the city', in Haydn and Temel (eds), *Temporary Urban Spaces*, p. 56.

11 Local Data Company, 17 September 2010, retrieved from www.localdatacompany.com/news-and-media/2010/9/17/hsbc-one-in-eight-town-centre-shops-empty-report-finds.html (accessed 26 October 2010).

12 A. Morton and R. Ehrman, *More Homes: Fewer Empty Buildings*, Policy Exchange, Research Note, March 2011, retrieved from www.policyexchange.org.uk/assets/More_Homes.pdf (accessed 30 March 2011).

13 Chartered Management Institute, *Management Futures: The World in 2018*, London, March 2008, retrieved from www.managers.org.uk/print/research-analysis/research/current-research/management-futures-world-2018-march-2008 (accessed 11 February 2011).

14 www.flexibility.co.uk/flexwork/index.htm (accessed 11 February 2011).

15 www.flexibility.co.uk/flexwork/offices/office-shrinking.htm (accessed 11 February 2011).

16 www.flexibility.co.uk/flexwork/general/commuters-leave-jobs.htm (accessed 11 February 2011).

17 K. Joyce, R. Pabayo, J. Critchley and C. Bambra, *Flexible Working Conditions and Their Effects on Employee Health and Wellbeing*, Cochrane Database of Systematic Reviews 2010, Issue 2.

18 T. Dwelly, A. Lake and L. Thompson, *Workhubs: Smart Workspaces for the Low Carbon Economy*, Workhubs Network, supported by the UK Department of Communities and Local Government, the Homes & Communities Agency, Commission for Rural Communities, Advantage West Midlands and South East of England Development Agency, June 2010, www.ruralsussex.org.uk/assets/assets/HBB-Workhubsfinalreport2010%20part1.pdf (accessed 14 June 2011); www.flexibility.co.uk/flexwork/location/homeworking-statistics-2009.htm (accessed 11 February 2011).

19 This includes self-employed, directors of limited companies with no employees, plus freelancers working under a PAYE umbrella company.

20 J. Kitching and D. Smallbone, *Defining and Estimating the Size of the UK Freelance Workforce*, Project Report, UK: Professional Contractors Group, 2008; Professional Contractors Group, *Fairness, Clarity, Recognition: Manifesto for Freelancing*, November 2009, retrieved from www.pcg.co.uk/cms/documents/POLICY_AND_CAMPAIGNS/PCG%20MANIFESTO%20FOR%20FREELANCING.pdf (accessed 8 October 2011).

21 M. Dixon, 'The flexible worker: the unstoppable trend of working anywhere', retrieved from www.flexibility. co.uk/flexwork/general/mark-dixon-regus.htm (accessed 11 February 2011).

22 Enterprise Nation, *Home Business Report 2009*, Enterprise Nation with support from BT, November 2009, retrieved from www.btplc.com/Thegroup/BTUKandWorldwide/BTRegions/England/Factsandfigures/EnterpriseNationHomeBusinessReport2009-Nov09.pdf; www.flexibility. co.uk/flexwork/location/home-enterprise.htm (both accessed 11 February 2011).

23 C. Anderson, 'The new new economy: more startups, fewer giants, infinite opportunity', *Wired*, 17 June 2010, retrieved from www.wired.com/culture/culturereviews/ magazine/17-06/nep_essay (accessed 24 November 2010).

24 C. Anderson, 'In the next Industrial Revolution, atoms are the new bits', *Wired*, February 2010, retrieved from www.wired.com/magazine/2010/01/ff_newrevolution/ (accessed 26 October 2010); P. MacInnes, 'Forget *Avatar*, the real 3D revolution is coming to your front room', the *Observer*, 4 April 2010, retrieved from www. guardian.co.uk/technology/2010/apr/04/3d-printing-design (accessed 25 October 2010).

25 A. Hitoshi and M. Masahige, 'Megahouse', in Wilkins (ed.), *Distributed Urbanism*, pp. 57–62.

26 J.L. Chase, M. Crawford and J. Kaliski (eds), *Everyday Urbanism*, New York: The Monacelli Press, 2nd edition, 2008.

27 Kohoutek and Kamleithner, 'Temporary uses, deregulation and urbanity', pp. 29–30.

28 B. Merker, 'Taking place: Rebar's absurd tactics in generous urbanism', in Hou (ed.), *Insurgent Public Space*, pp. 45–58.

29 H. Bey, *T.A.Z.: The Temporary Autonomous Zone, Ontological Anarchy, Poetic Terrorism*, New York: Autonomedia, 2nd edition, 2003.

30 A. Petti, 'Temporary Zones: alternative spaces or territories of socio-spatial control?', in *Post-It City: Occasional Urbanities* December, 2005, p. 245, retrieved from www. seacex.es/Spanish/Publicaciones/POST_IT_CITY_CIUDADES_OCASIONALES/Post-It%20City.%20Occasional%20 Urbanities.pdf (accessed 11 November 2010).

31 Rebecca Hopkinson, '*T.A.Z.: The Temporary Autonomous Zone* by Hakim Bey', retrieved from http://think-magazine.com/index.php?option=com_ content&view=article&id=429:taz-the-temporary-autonomous-zone-by-hakim-bey&catid=1:non-fiction&Itemid=39 (accessed 22 February 2011).

32 Hopkinson, '*T.A.Z.: The Temporary Autonomous Zone* by Hakim Bey'.

33 http://madebymany.com/blog/temporary-autonomous-zone-revisited (accessed 15 June 2011).

34 Urban Unlimited, *The Shadow City: Freezones in Brussels and Rotterdam*, Urban Unlimited Rotterdam with o2-consult Antwerp, MUST Amsterdam, ds+V /OBR Rotterdam and VUB Brussels, 2004, retrieved from www.

urbanunlimited.nl/uu/downloads.nsf/10/255417E9A E33AE26C1256F0B003710D8/$file/Shadowcity.pdf (accessed 23 November 2010).

35 Urban Unlimited, *The Shadow City*, p. 12.

36 Urban Unlimited, *The Shadow City*, p. 12.

37 Urban Unlimited, *The Shadow City*, p. 15.

38 A. Bieber, 'Desires will break out of homes and put an end to the domination of boredom and the administration of misery', in R. Klanten and M. Hübner (eds), *Urban Interventions: Personal Projects in Public Spaces*, Berlin: Gestalten, 2010. p. 4.

39 Urban Catalyst, *Urban Pioneers: Temporary Use and Urban Development in Berlin*, Berlin: Jovis, 2007, p. 22.

40 J. Twentyman, 'Productivity on the move', in *Flexible Working Supplement*, Lyonsdown Media Group, 2010, retrieved from www.esf6cia.eu/usuaris/noticies/ arxius/30_1_flexible_lowres1.pdf (accessed 15 June 2011).

41 See for example: www.sundayadventureclub.nl; www.experimentadesign.nl/2008/en/0204.html (both accessed 31 January 2011).

42 P. Abhinav and Y. Shetty, *CitySpinning: Frameworks for a Collective Reinterpretation of the Ambient Possibilities of Public Space,* 2007, retrieved from http://cityspinning.org/wp-content/uploads/2008/01/draft-6-jan.pdf (accessed 24 February 2011).

4: The private sector response

1 T. Macalister, 'The dire state of real estate: credit crunch marks end of boom', the *Guardian*, 3 January 2008, retrieved from www.guardian.co.uk/ business/2008/jan/03/creditcrunch.realestate (accessed 11 October 2010).

2 Measured on an equally weighted basis and including the first break where applicable.

3 British Property Federation/IPD, *BPF IPD Annual Lease Review 2010*, London: BPF/IPD, August 2010, pp. 3–4, retrieved from www.bpf.org.uk/en/files/bpf_documents/BPF_Annual_Lease_Review_2010_13082010.pdf (accessed 6 April 2011).

4 N. Blumner, *Planning for the Unplanned: Tools and Techniques for Interim Use in Germany and the United States.* Occasional Papers, Berlin: Deutsches Institut für Urbanistik, 2006, retrieved from www.difu.de/dokument/ planning-for-the-unplanned-tools-and-techniques-for-interim. html (accessed 14 June 2011).

5 See: the Meanwhile Project's Meanwhile Lease, www. meanwhile.org.uk/useful-info/view/legal (accessed 1 April 2011).

6 P. Misselwitz, P. Oswalt and K. Overmeyer, 'Urban development without urban planning: a planner's nightmare or the promised land?' in Urban Catalyst, *Urban Pioneers: Temporary Use and Urban Development in Berlin*, Berlin: Jovis, 2007, pp. 102–9.

7 Quotation from interview with Dan Simon, Oubliette Arthouse.

8 Cousins Business Law, *Empty Property Business Rates Relief Cut from April 2011*, 2 February 2011, retrieved from www.business-lawfirm.co.uk/Blog/2011/02/Empty-Property-Business-Rates-Relief-Cut-from-April-2011/ (accessed 3 February 2011).

9 www.coinstreet.org/developments/gabrielswharf.html (accessed 21 April 2011).

10 Quotation from Ken Dytor, Urban Catalyst.

11 Set-aside was a policy introduced by the EU in the 1990s whereby potentially productive agricultural land was taken out of productive use as a means of reducing the 'grain mountain' and providing environmental benefits. E. Reynolds, 'Interwhile uses', article submitted for publication in *Journal of Urban Regeneration and Renewal*, 2011, 4, copy provided by the author.

12 Reynolds, 'Interwhile uses', p. 4.

13 Reynolds, 'Interwhile uses', p. 5.

14 Reynolds, 'Interwhile uses', p. 4.

15 J. Garrett, 'Cameron backs *Property Week*'s Site Life campaign', *Property Week*, 11 March 2011, retrieved from www.propertyweek.com/news/cameron-backs-property-weeks-site-life-campaign/5014763.article (accessed 21 April 2011).

16 See for example: N. Popper, 'From eyesores to eye-catchers', *Los Angeles Times*, 16 December 2010, retrieved from http://articles.latimes.com/print/2010/dec/16/business/la-fi-stalled-construction-20101216 (accessed 30 March 2011).

17 *Property Week*, 'How the West was won over by temporary uses', 4 June 2010; www.washington-apa.org/documents/HoldingPatternsCallForIdeas.pdf; www.seattle.gov/dpd/Planning/Design_Commission/Overview/DPDS017625.asp (accessed 16 June 2011).

18 C. Lang Ho, 'Hold this site', *Architect Magazine*, June 2010, retrieved from www.architectmagazine.com/development/hold-this-site.aspx (accessed 16 June 2011).

19 W.L. Hawke, 'Case study research exploring interim use brownfield projects and their feasibility in the United States', Urban and Environmental Program, Occidental College, http://departments.oxy.edu/uepi/uep/studentwork/09comps/Hawke%20uep%20comps.pdf (accessed 11 March 2011).

20 LocusLab, *No Vacancy! Exploring Temporary Use of Empty Spaces in the Central Eastside Industrial District*, Portland State University, June 2009, retrieved from www.planning.org/awards/2010/pdf/novacancy.pdf (accessed 21 April 2011).

21 J. King, 'High rises on hold: what to do with empty sites?', *San Francisco Chronicle*, 6 July 2009, retrieved from www.sfgate.com/cgi-bin/article.cgi?f=/c/a/2009/07/06/MNAP189P39.DTL (accessed 21 April 2011).

22 http://planning.dc.gov/DC/Planning/Across+the+City/Other+Citywide+Initiatives/Temporary+Urbanism+Initiative/Temporium+Report (accessed 21 April 2011).

23 J. O'Connell, 'Filling the void: when construction stalls, D.C. encourages temporary uses', *Washington Business Journal*, 16 November 2009, retrieved from www.bizjournals.com/washington/stories/2009/11/16/story6.html (accessed 21 April 2011).

24 J. Rigby, 'How meanwhile can be worthwhile', *Property Week*, 7 May 2010; www.space2online.com/ (accessed 16 June 2011).

25 www.extraverte.com/default.html (accessed 11 March 2011).

5: Temporary arenas for consumption

1 D. Ackerman and B. Gross, 'So many choices, so little time: measuring the effects of free choice and enjoyment on perception of free time, time pressure and time deprivation', in P. Keller and D. Rook (eds), *Advances in Consumer Research*, Vol. 30, 2003, pp. 290–4, Valdosta, GA: Association for Consumer Research, retrieved from www.acrwebsite.org/volumes/display.asp?id=8794 (accessed 14 June 2011).

2 D. Loy, 'Saving time: a Buddhist perspective on the end', in J. May and N. Thrift (eds), *Timespace: Geographies of Temporality* London: Routledge, 2001, pp. 264–6.

3 http://trendwatching.com/trends/nowism/ (accessed 2 December 2010).

4 http://trendwatching.com/trends/transumers.htm (accessed 29 November 2010).

5 http://trendwatching.com/trends/transumers.htm.

6 http://trendwatching.com/trends/transumers.htm.

7 J. de Boer, 'Trend 6: everything is a coffee bar', pop-upcity.net, 5 January 2011, retrieved from http://pop-upcity.net/2011/01/trend-6-everything-is-a-coffee-bar/ (accessed 1 March 2011).

8 www.drinkshopdo.com/Drink,_Shop_%26_Do/Drink,_Shop_%26_Do_%E2%80%94_Home.html (accessed 18 March 2011).

9 'Tracey Emin discusses "The Shop"', retrieved from www.tate.org.uk/modern/eventseducation/talksdiscussions/20637.htm; 'Tracey Emin on her previous life as a shop girl', *The Times*, 26 September 2009, retrieved from http://entertainment.timesonline.co.uk/tol/arts_and_entertainment/visual_arts/article6842723.ece (both accessed 1 November 2010).

10 Z. Williams, 'Outspoken', S*tylist Magazine,* Issue 52, 3 November 2010, p. 21, retrieved from www.stylist.co.uk (accessed 11 January 2011).

11 www.dialoguecollective.co.uk/home/exhibitions/pop-up-shop (accessed 24 March 2011).

12 K. Cochrane, 'Overnight success', the *Guardian* G2, 12 October 2010, pp. 6–9.

13 http://trendwatching.com/trends/transumers.htm.

14 *Property Week*, 'Brands catch on to "pop-up" craze"', 5 February 2010, retrieved from www.propertyweek.com/news/brands-catch-on-to-'pop-up'-craze/3157678.article (accessed 11 March 2011)

15 www.trendwatching.com/trends/POPUP_RETAIL.htm (accessed 29 November 2010).

225

16 Cochrane, 'Overnight success', p. 8.

17 Local Data Company, 17 September 2010, retrieved from www.localdatacompany.com/news-and-media/2010/9/17/hsbc-one-in-eight-town-centre-shops-empty-report-finds.html (accessed 26 October 2010).

18 In total there were over 9,000 charity shops in the UK and Ireland in 2010. http://en.wikipedia.org/wiki/Charity_shop (accessed 17 March 2011).

19 East of England Development Agency (EEDA), *Empty Shops and Premises: Researching the Baseline*, EEDA, March 2010, retrieved from www.eeda.org.uk/files/meanwhile_Space_EEDA_Report_Final_vfinal_external.pdf (accessed 26 October 2010).

20 R. Booth, 'Artists' creative use of vacant shops brings life to desolate high streets', the *Guardian*, 18 February 2009, retrieved from www.guardian.co.uk/artanddesign/2009/feb/18/slack-space-vacant-shops (accessed 26 October 2010).

21 Communities and Local Government, *Looking After Our Town Centres*. DCMS, April, London: HMSO, 2009, p. 27.

22 On the former, see: N. Harrison, 'Vacant shops leading to North–South divide', *Retail Week*, 9 September 2010, retrieved from www.retail-week.com/property/vacant-shops-leading-to-north-south-divide/5017005.article (accessed 26 October 2010).

23 Led by the Development Trusts Association as part of its wider Advancing Assets for Communities programme supported by the CLG. Meanwhile Space, a non-profit Community Interest Company, is its delivery partner. www.meanwhilespace.com (accessed 14 June 2010).

24 Meanwhile Project, 'No time to waste …', May 2010, retrieved from www.meanwhile.org.uk/useful-info/misc/Meanwhile_Project_16pp_sml.pdf (accessed 11 March 2011).

25 'Meanwhile use: business case and learning points', SQW Consulting (for the Meanwhile Project), May 2010, retrieved from www.meanwhile.org.uk/useful-info/misc/SQW%20-%20Meanwhile%20Use%20Report%20May%2010.pdf (accessed 28 January 2011).

26 'Meanwhile use: business case and learning points', p.16.

27 EEDA, *Empty Shops and Premises*.

28 EEDA, *Empty Shops and Premises*.

29 EEDA, *Empty Shops and Premises*, p. 14.

30 H. Hanra, 'Art's great squatting revolution', *The Times*, 16 January 2010, retrieved from http://entertainment.timesonline.co.uk/tol/arts_and_entertainment/visual_arts/article6988391.ece (accessed 24 January 2011).

31 www.artscouncil.org.uk/funding/investment-in-arts/art-empty-spaces/art-empty-spaces-case-studies/; www.artscouncil.org.uk/news/art-empty-spaces/ (both accessed 26 October 2010).

32 L. Siegle, 'Dan Thompson's innovation: the Empty Shop Network', the *Observer*, 23 May 2010, retrieved from www.guardian.co.uk/environment/2010/may/23/lucy-siegle-the-innovator-dan-thompson-esn (accessed 27 October 2010).

33 www.popupartloop.com/about.php; www.chicagoloopalliance.com/events.php?id=317 (both accessed 16 June 2011).

34 'It will never last: pop-up restaurants', retrieved from www.squaremeal.co.uk/feature/will-never-last-pop-up-restauran (accessed 16 June 2011).

35 K. Spicer, 'Is this London's most fashionable restaurant?' *The Sunday Times*, 16 November 2008, retrieved from www.timesonline.co.uk/tol/life_and_style/food_and_drink/article5139964.ece (accessed 16 June 2011).

36 www.independent.co.uk/life-style/food-and-drink/reviews/pierre-koffmann-restaurant-on-the-roof-selfridges-400-oxford-street-w1-1824079.html (accessed 24 March 2011).

37 www.royalacademy.org.uk/ra-magazine/autumn-2008/cafe-culture,195,RAMA.html (accessed 24 March 2011).

38 www.guardian.co.uk/lifeandstyle/wordofmouth/2009/may/29/underground-restaurants-msmarmitelover-hardeep; Z. Williams, 'The secret feast', the *Guardian*, 10 February 2009, retrieved from www.guardian.co.uk/lifeandstyle/2009/feb/10/underground-restaurants-london; http://en.wikipedia.org/wiki/Underground_restaurant (all accessed 16 June 2011).

39 http://en.wikipedia.org/wiki/Car_boot_sale (accessed 17 March 2011).

40 http://en.wikipedia.org/wiki/Garage_sale (accessed 17 March 2011).

41 http://en.wikipedia.org/wiki/Farmers'_market; www.farmers-markets.co.uk/history-of-farmers-markets-c11.html (all accessed 17 March 2011).

6: The city as a stage

1 M. de Certeau, *The Practice of Everyday Life*, Berkeley: University of California Press, 1984; J.L. Chase, M. Crawford and J. Kaliski (eds), *Everyday Urbanism*, New York: The Monacelli Press, 2nd edition, 2008; M. Mean and C. Tims, *People Make Places*, London: Demos/JRF, 2005; M. Miessen and K. Cuypers, *Spaces of Uncertainty*, Wuppertal: Müller und Busmann, 2002.

2 E. Villagomez, 'Claiming residual spaces in the heterogeneous city', in J. Hou (ed.), *Insurgent Public Space: Guerrilla Urbanism and the Remaking of Contemporary Cities*, London: Routledge, 2010, p. 82.

3 M. Crawford, 'The current state of everyday urbanism', in Chase, Crawford and Kaliski (eds), *Everyday Urbanism*, p. 12.

4 G. la Varra, 'POST-IT CITY: the other European public spaces', 2003, retrieved from http://subsol.c3.hu/subsol_2/contributors0/lavarratext.html; 'Post it city: the final space in the contemporary city', in *Post-It City: Occasional Urbanities*, 2003, retrieved from www.seacex.es/Spanish/Publicaciones/POST_IT_CITY_CIUDADES_OCASIONALES/Post-It City. Occasional Urbanities.pdf, quotation from the latter at p. 237 (both accessed 11 November 2010).

5 The exhibition was first staged in 2008 at the Barcelona Contemporary Cultural Center (CCCB) with a Latin American tour in 2009–10. See: C. Gomez Moya, '*Post-It City: Occasional City*', review, 2009, retrieved from www.latinart.com/exview.cfm?id=320 (accessed 11 November 2010). The case studies are written up in *Post-It City: Occasional Urbanities*, pp. 255–71.

6 La Varra, 'POST-IT CITY'.

7 La Varra, 'POST-IT CITY'.

8 La Varra, 'POST-IT CITY'.

9 K. Franck and Q. Stevens (eds), *Loose Space*, London: Routledge, 2007.

10 Franck and Stevens, *Loose Space*, p. 26.

11 Franck and Stevens, *Loose Space*, p. 3.

12 Franck and Stevens, *Loose Space*, p. 7.

13 Franck and Stevens, *Loose Space*, p. 4.

14 Franck and Stevens, *Loose Space*, p. 17.

15 H. Armstrong, 'Time, dereliction and beauty: an argument for "landscapes of contemplation"', *The Landscape Architect,* IFLA Conference Papers, May 2006, pp. 116–27, retrieved from www.aila.org.au (accessed 3 November 2010); I. de Sola-Morales, 'Terrain vagues', in *Quardens 212 Tierra-Agua,* Barcelona: Collegio de Arquitecos de Catalunya, pp. 34–44.

16 Armstrong, 'Time, dereliction and beauty', p. 119.

17 www.osservatorionomade.net/ (accessed 16 June 2011).

18 H. Lownsbrough and J. Deunderman, *Equally Spaced?*, London: Demos, 2007.

19 Crawford, 'The current state of everyday urbanism', p. 14.

20 M. Crawford, 'Blurring the boundaries: public space and private life', in Chase, Crawford and Kaliski (eds), *Everyday Urbanism*, p. 25.

21 J. de Boer, 'Flying Grass Carpet: a landscaping fairytale', popupcity.net, 16 December 2008, retrieved from http://popupcity.net/2008/12/flying-grass-carpet-a-landscaping-fairytale (accessed 1 March 2011).

22 J. Rojas, 'Latino urbanism in Los Angeles', in Hou (ed.), *Insurgent Public Space*, p. 36.

23 P. Wu, 'How outsiders find home in the city', in Hou (ed.), *Insurgent Public Space*, pp. 135–46.

24 F. Benítez, *Garde l'Est*, retrieved from www.ciutatsocasionals.net/englishEXPOCOWEB/proyectos/21benitezgarde/index.htm (accessed 3 March 2011).

25 J. Rigby, 'Top of the pop-ups', *Property Week*, 16 April 2010.

26 http://en.wikipedia.org/wiki/Ghost_bike (accessed 23 February 2011).

27 J. Stein, 'Ghost riders', 15 June 2008, retrieved from http://nymag.com/news/features/47819/ (accessed 23 February 2011).

28 M. Davies, 'Fortress Los Angeles: the militarization of urban space', in M. Sorkin (ed.), *Variations on a Theme Park*, New York: Hill and Wang, 1992.

29 B. Barber, 'Malled, mauled and overhauled: arresting suburban sprawl by transforming suburban malls into usable civic space', in M. Henaff and T.B. Strong (eds), *Public Space and Democracy*, Minneapolis: University of Minnesota Press, 2001.

30 G. Doron, *Transgressive Architecture: Testing the Boundaries of Inclusiveness*, Paper 00177, The Bartlett School of Architecture, University College, London, retrieved from www.openspace.eca.ac.uk/conference/proceedings/PDF/Doron.pdf (accessed 18 October 2010).

31 P. Abhinav and Y. Shetty, *CitySpinning: Frameworks for a Collective Reinterpretation of the Ambient Possibilities of Public Space*, 2007, retrieved from http://cityspinning.org/wp-content/uploads/2008/01/draft-6-jan.pdf (accessed 24 February 2011).

32 J. Hou, '(Not) your everyday public spaces', in Hou (ed.), *Insurgent Public Space*, p. 1.

33 B. Merker, 'Taking place: Rebar's absurd tactics in generous urbanism', in Hou (ed.), *Insurgent Public Space*, pp. 45–58.

7: Culture and counterculture

1 M. Stern and S. Seifert, *Cultivating 'Natural' Cultural Districts*, Creativity and Change: A collaboration between the Social Impact of the Arts project and the Reinvestment Fund funded by the Rockefeller Foundation, 2007, retrieved from http://trfund.com/resource/downloads/creativity/NaturalCulturalDistricts.pdf (accessed 17 November 2010).

2 F. Jameson, *Postmodernism, or the Cultural Logic of Late Capitalism*, New York: Verso, 1999, retrieved from www.marxists.org/reference/subject/philosophy/works/us/jameson.htm (accessed 22 November 2010).

3 S. Hall, 'The centrality of culture: notes on the cultural revolutions of our time', in K. Thompson (ed.), *Media and Cultural Regulation*, London: Sage, 1997, p. 209, retrieved from www.henryagiroux.com/links/centrality%20of%20culture.pdf (accessed 22 November 2010).

4 L. MacRitchie, 'The sincerity of events', in N. Childs and J. Walwin (eds), *A Split Second of Paradise: Live Art, Installation and Performance*, London: Rivers Oram Press, 1998, p. 21; See also: L. Alkemade, 'Temporality: the strength of being uncertain', retrieved from www.lobkealkemade.nl/projecten/under construction/TP_essay_2009.pdf (accessed 31 January 2011).

5 MacRitchie, 'The sincerity of events', pp. 27–8.

6 MacRitchie, 'The sincerity of events', p. 22.

7 MacRitchie, 'The sincerity of events', p. 35.

8 R. Klanten and M. Hübner (eds), *Urban Interventions: Personal Projects in Public Spaces*, Berlin: Gestalten, 2010.

9 L. Feireiss, 'Livin' in the city: the urban space as creative challenge', in Klanten and Hübner (eds), *Urban Interventions*, pp. 2–3.

10 A. Bieber, 'Desires will break out of homes and put an end to the domination of boredom and the administration of misery', in Klanten and Hübner (eds), *Urban Interventions*, p. 4.

11 Bieber, 'Desires will break out of homes and put an end to the domination of boredom and the administration of misery', p. 4.

12 Bieber, 'Desires will break out of homes and put an end to the domination of boredom and the administration of misery', p. 4.

13 Feireiss, 'Livin' in the city', p. 2.

14 Feireiss, 'Livin' in the city', p. 2.

15 Bieber, 'Desires will break out of homes and put an end to the domination of boredom and the administration of misery', p. 5.

16 R. Dixon, 'Quick on the draw', the *Guardian*, 29 January 2011, p. 7.

17 www.cronolisboa.org (accessed 16 June 2011).

18 J. Malloy, 'What is left of planning?! Residual planning', in T. Schwarz and S. Rugare (eds), *Pop-Up City*, Urban Infill No.2, Cleveland Urban Design Collaborative, Kent State University, 2009, p. 21.

19 Malloy, 'What is left of planning?!', p. 22.

20 Malloy, 'What is left of planning?!', p. 25.

21 Malloy, 'What is left of planning?!', p. 34.

22 M.A. LaFond, 'eXperimentcity', in J. Hou (ed.), *Insurgent Public Space: Guerrilla Urbanism and the Remaking of Contemporary Cities*, London: Routledge, 2010, p. 63.

23 M. Kennedy, 'Fourth plinth shortlist announced for London Olympics contenders', the *Guardian*, 19 July 2010, retrieved from www.guardian.co.uk/artanddesign/fourth-plinth (accessed 5 October 10).

24 V. Thorpe, 'Blink and miss the show', the *Guardian Weekly*, 9 July 10, p. 34.

25 See: www.raumlabor.net/ (accessed 1 March 2011).

8: Activism and community use

1 Urban Catalyst, *Urban Pioneers: Temporary Use and Urban Development in Berlin*, Berlin: Jovis, 2007, p. 22.

2 Urban Catalyst, *Urban Pioneers*, p. 22.

3 J. Vasagar, 'Clearing 2010: universities offer lifeline to top students', the *Guardian*, 19 August 2010, retrieved from www.guardian.co.uk/education/2010/aug/18/clearing-2010-universities-offer-lifeline (accessed 13 October 2010).

4 Association of Graduate Recruiters, *Class of 2010 Faces Uphill Struggle for Jobs*, Warwick: AGR, 6 July 2010, retrieved from www.agr.org.uk/content/Class-of-2010-Faces-Uphill-Struggle-for-Jobs (accessed 13 October 2010).

5 Trades Union Congress, *Youth Unemployment Increasing in Two Thirds of Local Authorities across UK*, London: TUC, 11 August 2010, retrieved from www.tuc.org.uk/social/tuc-18322-f0.cfm (accessed 15 October 2010).

6 International Labour Organisation, *Global Employment Trends for Youth*, Geneva: ILO, August 2010, retrieved from www.ilo.org/wcmsp5/groups/public/---ed_emp/---emp_elm/---trends/documents/publication/wcms_143349.pdf (accessed 15 October 2010).

7 Urban Catalyst, *Urban Pioneers*, p. 39.

8 Carnegie UK Trust, *The Shape of Civil Society to Come: Report from the Inquiry into the Future of Civil Society in the UK and Ireland*, London: Carnegie UK Trust, retrieved from www.carnegieuktrust.org.uk/files/main/Shape%20of%20civil%20society%20to%20come_2.pdf (accessed 13 January 2011).

9 E. Evans and J. Saxton, *The 21st Century Volunteer: A Report on the Changing Face of Volunteering in the 21st Century*. London: nfpSynergy, 2005.

10 R. Brooks, 'Young people and political participation: an analysis of European Union policies', *Sociological Research Online*, 2009, 14(1), retrieved from www.socresonline.org.uk/14/1/7.html (accessed 21 January 2011).

11 A. Dunn, J. Foot, J. Gaventa and T. Zipfel, *Champions of Participation: Engaging Citizens in Local Governance*, International learning Event Report, 2007, retrieved from www2.ids.ac.uk/logolink/resources/downloads/Championsper cent20Report.pdf (accessed 15 October 2010).

12 Power Inquiry, *Power to the People: The Report of Power: An Independent Inquiry into Britain's Democracy*, York: Joseph Rowntree Foundation, 2006; D. Kane, J. Clarke, S. Lesniewski, J. Wilton, B. Pratten and K. Wilding, *The UK Civil Society Almanac*, London: NCVO, 2009.

13 E. Brodie, E. Cowling and N. Nissen, *Understanding Participation: A Literature Review*, London: Involve, December 2009, retrieved from http://pathwaysthrough-participation.org.uk/wp-content/uploads/2009/09/Pathways-literature-review-final-version.pdf (accessed 14 June 2011).

14 Communities and Local Government, *Strong and Prosperous Communities: The Local Government White Paper* (Cm6939), London: HMSO, 2006.

15 Communities and Local Government, *Communities in Control: The Local Government White Paper* (Cm7427), London: HMSO, 2008.

16 J. Kitching and D. Smallbone, *Defining and Estimating the Size of the UK Freelance Workforce*, Project Report, UK: Professional Contractors Group, 2008; Professional Contractors Group, *Fairness, Clarity, Recognition: Manifesto for Freelancing*, November 2009, retrieved from www.pcg.co.uk/cms/documents/POLICY_AND_CAMPAIGNS/PCG%20MANIFESTO%20FOR%20FREELANCING.pdf (accessed 8 October 2011).

17 C. Feiss, 'Social enterprise: the fledgling fourth sector', the *Financial Times*, 15 June 2009, retrieved from www.ft.com/cms/s/0/6e8285f2-5944-11de-80b3-00144feabdc0.html#axzz1FG9nS8yZ (accessed 28 February 2011).

18 www.socialenterpriselive.com/se100/aims (accessed 17 June 2011).

19 Feiss, 'Social enterprise'.

20 Social Investment Task Force, *Social Investment Ten Years On*, Final Report of the Social Investment Task Force, April 2010, retrieved from www.socialinvestment-taskforce.org/downloads/SITF_10_year_review.pdf (accessed 17 June 2011).

21 C. Giotis, 'Charity bank announces record loans', *Social Enterprise*, 12 May 2010, retrieved from www.social-enterpriselive.com/section/news/money/20100512/charity-bank-announces-record-loans (accessed 11 January 2011).

22 Cabinet Office, *Building the Big Society*, 2010, retrieved from www.cabinetoffice.gov.uk/media/407789/building-big-society.pdf (accessed 13 October 2010).

23 HM Treasury, *Spending Review 2010*, 20 October 2010, retrieved from www.hm-treasury.gov.uk/spend_sr2010_easyread.htm (accessed 22 March 2011).

24 R. Moore, 'Let's put on the chow right here ...', the *Observer*, The New Review, 20 June 2010, p. 35; R. Moore, 'Meet Britain's most promising young architects', the *Observer,* The New Review, 9 January 2011, pp. 12–15.

25 J. de Boer, 'Trend 4: pop-up everywhere', popupcity.net, 6 January 2011, retrieved from http://popupcity.net/2011/01/trend-4-pop-up-everywhere/ (accessed 1 March 2011).

26 Goethe-Institut, 'Urban laboratory: temporary architecture', retrieved from www.goethe.de/kue/arc/dos/dos/sls/sdz/en3802817.htm (accessed 11 March 2011)

27 J. de Boer, 'Built overnight: Gecekondu in Sausalito Almere', popupcity.net, 22 June 2009, retrieved from http://popupcity.net/2009/06/built-overnight-gecekondu-in-sausalito-almere/ (accessed 1 March 2011).

28 J. de Boer, 'Temporary bar made from IKEA storage boxes', popupcity.net, 3 March 2010, retrieved from http://popupcity.net/2010/03/temporary-bar-made-from-ikea-storage-boxes/ (accessed 1 March 2011).

29 www.raumlabor.net/?p=2944 (accessed 1 March 2011).

30 C. Kuang, '145-foot inflatable dome to rise in nation's hot air capital, D.C.', retrieved from www.fastcompany.com/blog/cliff-kuang/design-innovation/145-foot-inflatable-dome-will-rise-dc (accessed 17 June 2011).

31 www.worldarchitecturenews.com/index.php?fuseaction=wanappln.projectview&upload_id=1979 (accessed 11 March 2011).

32 www.artdaily.com/index.asp?int_sec=11&int_new=42326&int_modo=1; www.raumlabor.net/?p=2848 (both accessed 1 March 2011).

33 www.coronasavethebeach.org/en/home/ (accessed 17 June 2011).

34 J. Beekmans, 'A trashy hotel', popupcity.net, 25 January 2011, retrieved from http://popupcity.net/2011/01/a-trashy-hotel/ (accessed 14 June 2011).

35 CABE Space, *Public Space Lessons: Land in Limbo: Making the Best Use of Vacant Urban Spaces*, London: CABE Space, May 2008.

36 www.spatialagency.net/database/guerrilla.gardening; http://en.wikipedia.org/wiki/Guerrilla_gardening (both accessed 31 January 2011).

37 N. Hope and V. Ellis, *Can You Dig It? Meeting Community Demand for Allotments*, New Local Government Network, 2009, retrieved from www.nlgn.org.uk/public/

wp-content/uploads/can-you-dig-it.pdf (accessed 6 October 2010).

38 See for example: www.landshare.net/index/ (accessed 6 October 2010).

39 A. Correy, 'Ephemeral landscapes: a case for temporary landscape design in a changing society', talk given on 28 May 1978 at the Utopian Technology Fair, University of Sydney, retrieved from www.aila.org.au/profiles/correy/pdf/ephemeral.pdf (accessed 6 October 2010).

40 atelier d'architecture autogérée (aaa), www.urbantactics.org/ (accessed 26 January 2011).

41 www.what-if.info/20_vacant_lots.html; A. Shepard, 'Can city dwellers be more self-sufficient?', *The Times*, 28 June 2008, retrieved from www.timesonline.co.uk/tol/news/environment/article4225138.ece (both accessed 25 January 2011).

42 www.what-if.info/Vacant_Lot_no1.html (accessed 25 January 2011).

43 www.sundayadventureclub.nl; www.experimentadesign.nl/2008/en/0204.html (both accessed 31 January 2011).

44 http://experimentadesign.nl/2008/en/0204.html.

45 E. Krasny, 'Spaces for action and for laughing too: on the public effect of participation in urban spaces', in F. Haydn and R. Temel (eds), *Temporary Urban Spaces: Concepts for the Use of City Space*, Basel: Birkhäuser, 2006, pp. 86–7.

46 N. Blumner, *Planning for the Unplanned: Tools and Techniques for Interim Use in Germany and the United States*, Occasional Papers, Deutsches Institut für Urbanistik, Berlin, 2006, retrieved from www.difu.de/dokument/planning-for-the-unplanned-tools-and-techniques-for-interim.html (accessed 14 June 2011).

47 Raumpioniere, in Urban Catalyst, *Urban Pioneers*, pp. 36–47.

9: Creative cities and the gentrification dilemma

1 C. Landry, *The Art of City Making*. London: Earthscan, 2006.

2 J. O'Connor, *The Cultural and Creative Industries: A Review of the Literature*, Creative Partnerships, Arts Council, London, November 2007, pp. 38–9.

3 For a summary of the definitional issues see: O'Connor, *The Cultural and Creative Industries*, pp. 41–51.

4 DCMS, *Creative Industries Mapping Document*, UK Department of Culture, Media and Sport, 1998, revised 2001.

5 J. Nowak, *Creativity and Neighbourhood Development: Strategies for Community Investment*, The Reinvestment Fund, in collaboration with the Social Impact of the Arts project at the University of Pennsylvania, 2007, p. 1, retrieved from www.trfund.com/resource/downloads/creativity/creativity_neighborhood_dev.pdf (accessed 17 November 2010).

6 Nowak, *Creativity and Neighbourhood Development*, p. 13.

7 S. Breuer, *Harbouring Creative Industries: Creative Milieus as a Catalyst for Harbour Regeneration*, Tilburg University, MA Thesis, European Urban Cultures, 2006.

8 Urban Unlimited, *The Shadow City: Freezones in Brussels and Rotterdam*, Urban Unlimited Rotterdam with o2-consult Antwerp, MUST Amsterdam, ds+V /OBR Rotterdam and VUB Brussels, 2004, p. 5, retrieved from www.urbanunlimited.nl/uu/downloads.nsf/10/255417E9AE33AE26C1256F0B003710D8/$file/Shadowcity.pdf (accessed 23 November 2010).

9 G.J. Hospers and R. van Dalm, 'How to create a creative city? The viewpoints of Richard Florida and Jane Jacobs', *Foresight: The Journal of Future Studies, Strategic Thinking and Policy*, 2005, 7 (4), pp. 8–12.

10 J. Gerend, 'Temps welcome: how temporary uses can revitalize neighborhoods', *Planning: The Magazine of the American Planning Association*, December 2007, 73 (11), pp. 24–7.

11 E. Knob and W. Grillitsch, 'Dolmusch X-press', in T. Schwarz and S. Rugare (eds), *Pop-Up City*, Urban Infill No.2, Cleveland Urban Design Collaborative, Kent State University, 2009, pp. 65–7.

12 M.A. LaFond, 'eXperimentcity', in J. Hou (ed.), *Insurgent Public Space: Guerrilla Urbanism and the Remaking of Contemporary Cities,* London: Routledge, 2010, p. 61.

13 'Berliner Raumressourcen', in Urban Catalyst, *Urban Pioneers: Temporary Use and Urban Development in Berlin*, Berlin: Jovis, 2007, pp. 28–30.

14 P. Oswalt, K. Overmeyer and P. Misselwitz, 'Patterns of the unplanned', in Schwarz and Rugare (eds), *Pop-Up City*, p. 14.

15 K. Pallagst, 'Shrinking cities: planning challenges from an international perspective', in T. Schwarz and S. Rugare (eds), *Cities Growing Smaller,* Urban Infill No.1, Cleveland Urban Design Collaborative, Kent State University, 2008, p. 12.

16 Urban Catalyst, *Urban Pioneers*, p. 24.

17 P. Arlt, 'Urban planning and interim use', in F. Haydn and R. Temel (eds), *Temporary Urban Spaces: Concepts for the Use of City Space*, Basel: Birkhäuser, 2006.

18 B. Lange, 'Entrepreneurial temporary use: an incubator for the creative economy', in Urban Catalyst, *Urban Pioneers*, pp. 135–42.

19 Breuer, *Harbouring Creative Industries*, p. 19.

20 Lange, 'Entrepreneurial temporary use', p. 141.

21 'Conversation with Tanja Mühlhans, Creative Milieus', in Urban Catalyst, *Urban Pioneers*, p. 130; Arlt, 'Urban planning and interim use', p. 41.

22 Urban Catalyst, *Urban Pioneers*, p. 131.

23 LaFond, 'eXperimentcity', p. 63.

24 www.lonelyplanet.com/germany/berlin (accessed 22 January 2011).

25 P. Beaumont, 'A city's soul is swept aside by money', the *Observer,* 16 January 2011, p. 2.

26 B. Bulick, C. Coletta, C. Jackson, A. Taylor and S. Wolff, *Cultural Development in Creative Communities*, Americans for the Arts, Monograph, November 2003;

R. Florida, *The Rise of the Creative Class: And How It's Transforming Work, Leisure, Community and Everyday Life*, New York: Basic Books, 2002, retrieved from www.americansforhearts.org/NAPD/files/10731/Cultural%20Development%20in%20Creative%20Communities%20(November%202003).pdf (accessed 8 October 2011).

27 J. Peck, 'Struggling with the creative class', *International Journal of Urban and Regional Planning Research*, December 2005, 29 (4), pp. 740–70; B. Douglas and D. Morrow, *Competing for Talent: Implications for Social and Cultural Policy in Canadian City Regions*, SRA, Department of Canadian Heritage, Ottawa, 2003; N. Bradford, 'Creative cities structured policy dialogue backgrounder', Background Paper F46, Family Network, Canadian Policy Research Networks, Ottawa, 2004; M. Nathan, 'The wrong stuff: creative class theory, diversity and city performance', IPPR Centre for Cities. Discussion Paper No.1, 2005, retrieved from www.ippr.org/centreforcities; A. Pratt 'Creative cities: the cultural industries and the creative class', *Geografiska B*, 2008, 90 (2), pp. 107–17.

28 A. Pratt, 'Urban regeneration: from the arts "feel good" factor to the cultural economy – a case study of Hoxton, London', *Urban Studies*, May 2009, 46 (5–6), pp. 1041–61, retrieved from http://usj.sagepub.com/content/46/5-6/1041.short (accessed 8 October 2011).

29 Florida, *The Rise of the Creative Class*.

30 T. Meisel and W. Wieczorek, 'Travelling through the inner city: form follows fiction', June 2003, retrieved from www.republicart.net/disc/empire/meiselwieczorek01_en.htm (accessed 11 January 2011).

31 www.spatialagency.net/database/park.fiction (accessed 11 January 2011).

32 Meisel and Wieczorek, 'Travelling through the inner city'.

33 C. Twickel, 'Activists bring flashmob style tactics to war on gentrification', *Spiegel Online*, 9 July 2010, retrieved from www.spiegel.de/international/zeitgeist/0,1518,716179,00.html (accessed 17 June 2011).

34 P. Oehmke, 'Squatters take on the creative class: who has the right to shape the city?', *Spiegel Online*, 1 July 2010, retrieved from www.spiegel.de/international/germany/0,1518,670600,00.html (accessed 11 January 2011).

35 Urban Unlimited, *The Shadow City*, p. 47.

36 J. Modder and J. Saris, *Creative Spaces in the Netherlands*, 41st IsoCaRP Congress, 2005, retrieved from www.isocarp.net/Data/case_studies/625.pdf (accessed 8 April 2011).

37 City of Amsterdam, Bureau Broedplaatsen, *Building the Basis for a Creative Amsterdam Metropolitan Area: Art Factories Programme 2008–2012*, Amsterdam, October 2008, p. 7, retrieved from http://bureaubroedplaatsen.amsterdam.nl/images/Art_Factories_Programme_Engels.pdf (accessed 8 April 2011).

38 City of Amsterdam, *Building the Basis for a Creative Amsterdam Metropolitan Area*, p. 11.

39 City of Amsterdam, *Building the Basis for a Creative Amsterdam Metropolitan Area*, p. 17.

230

40 M. Stern and S. Seifert, *Cultivating 'Natural' Cultural Districts*, Creativity and Change: A collaboration between the Social Impact of the Arts project and the Reinvestment Fund funded by the Rockefeller Foundation, 2007, p.1, retrieved from http://trfund.com/resource/downloads/creativity/NaturalCulturalDistricts.pdf (accessed 17 November 2010).

41 J. Nowak, *Creativity and Neighbourhood Development: Strategies for Community Investment*, The Reinvestment Fund, in collaboration with the Social Impact of the Arts project at the University of Pennsylvania, 2007, p. 2, retrieved from www.trfund.com/resource/downloads/creativity/creativity_neighborhood_dev.pdf (accessed 17 November 2010).

42 City of Amsterdam, *Building the Basis for a Creative Amsterdam Metropolitan Area*, p. 11.

43 Stern and Seifert, *Cultivating 'Natural' Cultural Districts*, p. 1.

44 J. Malloy, 'What is left of planning?! Residual planning', in Schwarz and Rugare (eds), *Pop-Up City*, p. 21.

45 A. Freeman, 'London's creative workforce (2009 update)', Working Paper 40, GLA Economics, February 2010, retrieved from http://legacy.london.gov.uk/mayor/economic_unit/docs/wp40.pdf (accessed 6 April 2011).

46 Skillset, 'Strategic skills assessment for the creative media industries, London, June 2010', retrieved from www.skillset.org/uploads/pdf/asset_15384.pdf?1 (accessed 6 April 2011).

47 Skillset, 'Strategic skills assessment for the creative media industries, London, June 2010'.

48 London and Partners, *London Creative Industries*, March 2011, retrieved from www.thinklondon.com/downloads/Think_London_reports/Think_London_reports/London_Creative_Industries_-_the_essential_next_step_for_your_business.pdf (accessed 6 April 2011).

49 Pratt, 'Urban regeneration', p. 6.

50 Pratt, 'Urban regeneration', p. 10.

51 www.shoreditchtrust.org.uk/Affordable-Workspace (accessed 8 April 2011).

52 www.villageunderground.co.uk/about (accessed 8 April 2011).

53 Urban Unlimited, *The Shadow City*, pp. 14–15.

10: Re-imagining the city: planning for temporary activity

1 J. & L. Gibbons LLP, *muf* architecture/art, *Making Space in Dalston*, prepared for London Borough of Hackney and Design for London/LDA, July 2009.

2 See for example: CABE, *Creating Successful Masterplans: A Guide for Clients*, London: CABE, April, 2008, retrieved from www.cabe.org.uk/publications/creating-successful-masterplans (accessed 11 November 2010).

3 See for example: M. Provoost, 'The Wimby! method', in J.L. Chase, M. Crawford and J. Kaliski (eds), *Everyday Urbanism*, New York: The Monacelli Press, 2nd edition, 2008, p. 207.

4 J. & L. Gibbons LLP, *muf* architecture/art, *Making Space in Dalston*, p. 16.

5 M. de Certeau, *The Practice of Everyday Life*, Berkeley: University of California Press, 1988.

6 B. Kirshenblatt-Gimblett, 'Performing the city: reflections on the urban vernacular', in Chase, Crawford and Kaliski (eds), *Everyday Urbanism*, p. 19.

7 B. Merker, 'Taking place: Rebar's absurd tactics in generous urbanism', in J. Hou (ed.), *Insurgent Public Space: Guerrilla Urbanism and the Remaking of Contemporary Cities*, London: Routledge, 2010, p. 49.

8 R. Temel, 'The temporary in the city', in F. Haydn and R. Temel (eds), *Temporary Urban Spaces: Concepts for the Use of City Space*, Basel: Birkhäuser, 2006, p. 57.

9 J. Kaliski, 'The present city and the practice of city design', in Chase, Crawford and Kaliski (eds), *Everyday Urbanism*, p. 108.

10 M. Crawford, 'The current state of everyday urbanism', in Chase, Crawford and Kaliski (eds), *Everyday Urbanism*, p. 14.

11 M. Crawford, 'Blurring the boundaries: public space and private life', in Chase, Crawford and Kaliski (eds), *Everyday Urbanism*, p. 25.

12 Crawford, 'The current state of everyday urbanism', p. 12.

13 Kaliski, 'The present city and the practice of city design', p. 90.

14 Kaliski, 'The present city and the practice of city design', p. 103.

15 Kaliski, 'The present city and the practice of city design', p. 102.

16 Kaliski, 'The present city and the practice of city design', p. 104.

17 Kaliski, 'The present city and the practice of city design', p. 106.

18 Kaliski, 'The present city and the practice of city design', p. 108.

19 M. Speaks, 'Rotterdam 1979–2007: from ideology to market communism and beyond', in G. Wilkins (ed.), *Distributed Urbanism: Cities After Google Earth*, London: Routledge, 2010, p. 51.

20 F. Haydn, 'A material that never comes to rest: concepts and potentials of temporary space', in Haydn and Temel (eds), *Temporary Urban Spaces*, p. 73.

21 S. Marshall, *Cities, Design and Evolution*, Oxford: Routledge, 2008, p. 279.

22 Marshall, *Cities, Design and Evolution*, pp. 276–7.

23 P. Misselwitz, P. Oswalt and K. Overmeyer, 'Urban development without urban planning: a planner's nightmare or the promised land?', in Urban Catalyst, *Urban Pioneers: Temporary Use and Urban Development in Berlin*, Berlin: Jovis, 2007, p. 106.

24 K. Kelly, 'The new socialism: global collectivist society is coming online', *Wired Magazine*, 17 June 2010, retrieved from www.wired.com/culture/culturereviews/magazine/17-06/nep_newsocialism?currentPage=all (accessed 24 November 2010).

25 Kelly, 'The new socialism'.

26 D. Barrie, '"Open source" place-making', article commissioned by Architecture + Design, Scotland, September 2010, p. 3, retrieved from www.scribd.com/doc/41008414/Open-Source-Place-making (accessed 25 February 2011).

27 Barrie, '"Open source" place-making', p. 1.

28 Conservative Party, *Open Source Planning*, Policy Green Paper No.14, retrieved from www.conservatives.com/~/media/Files/Green%20Papers/planning-green-paper.ashx (accessed 2 March 2011).

29 Barrie, '"Open source" place-making'.

11: The four-dimensional city

1 M. Pogoreutz, 'Urban intelligence', in F. Haydn and R. Temel (eds), *Temporary Urban Spaces: Concepts for the Use of City Space*, Basel: Birkhäuser, 2006, pp. 79–80.

2 A. Spiegl and C. Teckert, 'Tom Waits 4'33"', in Haydn and Temel (eds), *Temporary Urban Spaces*, pp. 102–3.

3 Urban Catalyst, *Strategies for Temporary Uses: Potential for Development of Urban Residual Areas in European Metropolises*, September 2003, retrieved from http://templace.com/think-pool/attach/download/1_UC_finalR_synthesis007b.pdf?object_ id=4272&attachment_id=4276 (accessed 22 November 2010).

4 Conservative Party, *Open Source Planning*, Policy Green Paper No.14, retrieved from www.conservatives.com/~/media/Files/Green%20Papers/planning-green-paper.ashx (accessed 2 March 2011).

5 www.communities.gov.uk/publications/localgovernment/decentralisationguide (accessed 2 March 2011).

6 'Westfield and Land Securities back campaign to let communities use mothballed development sites', Press Release, 15 March 2010, retrieved from www.bpf.propertymall.com/newsroom/pressreleases/document/23863/westfield-and-land-securities-back-campaign-to-let-communities-use-mothballed-development-sites (accessed 16 October 2010).

7 N. Blumner, *Planning for the Unplanned: Tools and Techniques for Interim Use in Germany and the United States*. Occasional Papers, Deutsches Institut für Urbanistik, Berlin, 2006, retrieved from www.difu.de/dokument/planning-for-the-unplanned-tools-and-techniques-for-interim.html (accessed 14 June 2011).

8 DCLG, *Review of the Use Classes Order and Part 4 of the GPDO (Temporary Uses)*, DCLG, September 2001.

9 Planning Advisory Service, *Local Development Orders: Stage 1 Research Report on Stakeholder Views and Practice Issues*, March 2009, www.pas.gov.uk/pas/aio/106047 (accessed 27 October 10); Communities and Local Government, *Looking After Our Town Centres*, DCMS, April 2009, p. 27; M. Donnelly, 'Easing planning rules', *Planning*, 11 March 2011, p. 24.

10 K. Larkin and Z. Wilcox, *What Would Maggie Do?*, Centre for Cities, February 2011, retrieved from www.centreforcities.org/assets/files/2011%20Research/11-02-25%20Enterprise%20Zones.pdf (accessed 21 March 2011).

11 A. Sissons and C. Brown, *Do Enterprise Zones Work?*, Ideopolis Policy Paper, The Work Foundation, February 2011, p. 3, retrieved from www.theworkfoundation.com/assets/docs/publications/283_Enterprise%20Zones_24%20Feb_FINAL.PDF (accessed 21 March 2011).

12 K. Campbell, *Massive Small: The Operating Programme for Smart Urbanism*, retrieved from http://smarturbanism.org.uk/ (accessed 12 March 2011).

13 Campbell, *Massive Small*, p. 116.

14 C. Ward, *The Hidden History of Housing*, Institute for Contemporary History, King's College, London, September 2004, retrieved from www.historyandpolicy.org/papers/policy-paper-25.html#squatters (accessed 21 May 2010).

15 R. McCrum, 'How E.F. Schumacher, author of the global bestseller *Small is Beautiful*, came back into fashion', the *Observer*, The New Review, 27 March 2011, pp. 8–11; E.F. Schumacher, *Small is Beautiful: A Study of Economics as if People Mattered*, London: Blond and Briggs, 1973.

16 Pogoreutz, 'Urban intelligence'; J. Malloy, 'What is left of planning?! Residual planning', in T. Schwarz and S. Rugare (eds), *Pop-Up City*, Urban Infill No.2, Cleveland Urban Design Collaborative, Kent State University, 2009, p. 34.

17 J. Jacobs, *The Death and Life of Great American Cities*, New York: Random House, 1961, p. 6, quoted in I. Gendelman, T. Dobrowolsky and G. Aiello, 'Urban archives: public memories of everyday places', in J. Hou (ed.) *Insurgent Public Space: Guerrilla Urbanism and the Remaking of Contemporary Cities*, London: Routledge, 2010, p. 188.

232

Selected bibliography

P. Abhinav and Y. Shetty, *CitySpinning: Frameworks for a Collective Reinterpretation of the Ambient Possibilities of Public Space,* 2007, retrieved from http://cityspinning.org/wp-content/uploads/2008/01/draft-6-jan.pdf (accessed 24 February 2011).

D. Ackerman and B. Gross, 'So many choices, so little time: measuring the effects of free choice and enjoyment on perception of free time, time pressure and time deprivation', in P. Keller and D. Rook (eds), *Advances in Consumer Research*, Vol. 30, 2003, pp. 290–4, Valdosta, GA: Association for Consumer Research, retrieved from www.acrwebsite.org/volumes/display.asp?id=8794 (accessed 14 June 2011).

S. Aiba and O. Nishida, 'Re-City, Tokyo', in J. Hou (ed.), *Insurgent Public Space: Guerrilla Urbanism and the Remaking of Contemporary Cities*, London: Routledge, 2010.

L. Alkemade, 'Temporality: the strength of being uncertain', retrieved from www.lobkealkemade.nl/projecten/under construction/TP_essay_2009.pdf (accessed 31 January 2011).

D. Alpert and K. Boese, 'Bruce-Monroe to get "temporary urbanism" over parking lot', *Washington Post*, 11 March 2010, retrieved from http://greatergreaterwashington.org/kent/page/3 (accessed 21 April 2011).

C. Anderson, 'In the next Industrial Revolution, atoms are the new bits', *Wired,* February 2010, retrieved from www.wired.com/magazine/2010/01/ff_newrevolution/ (accessed 26 October 2010).

C. Anderson, 'The new new economy: more startups, fewer giants, infinite opportunity', *Wired*, 17 June 2010, retrieved from www.wired.com/culture/culturereviews/magazine/17-06/nep_essay (accessed 24 November 2010).

Architecture+Design Scotland, 'Speirs Locks', 2010, retrieved from www.ads.org.uk/urbanism/features/speirs-locks (accessed 20 March 2011).

P. Arlt, 'Urban planning and interim use', in F. Haydn and R. Temel (eds), *Temporary Urban Spaces: Concepts for the Use of City Space*, Basel: Birkhäuser, 2006.

H. Armstrong, 'Time, dereliction and beauty: an argument for "landscapes of contemplation"', *The Landscape Architect*, IFLA Conference Papers, May 2006, pp. 116–27, retrieved from www.aila.org.au (accessed 3 November 2010).

Arts Council, 'Art in Empty Spaces: turning vacant spaces into creative places', 13 August 2009, retrieved from http://press.artscouncil.org.uk/content/detail.aspx?releaseid=800&newsareaid=2 (accessed 14 June 2011).

Arts Council, 'Theatre Absolute opens the doors to its Shop Front Theatre', 3 December 2009, retrieved from www.artscouncil.org.uk/news/theatre-absolute-opens-doors-its-shop-front-theatr (accessed 14 June 2011).

Association of British Theatre Technicians, the District Surveyors Association and the Institute of Licensing, *Technical Standards for Places of Entertainment*, February 2009.

Association of Graduate Recruiters, *Class of 2010 Faces Uphill Struggle for Jobs*, Warwick: AGR, 6 July 2010, retrieved from www.agr.org.uk/content/Class-of-2010-Faces-Uphill-Struggle-for-Jobs (accessed 13 October 2010).

B. Barber, 'Malled, mauled and overhauled: arresting suburban sprawl by transforming suburban malls into usable civic space', in M. Henaff and T.B. Strong (eds), *Public Space and Democracy*, Minneapolis: University of Minnesota Press, 2001.

D. Barrie, '"Open source" place-making', article commissioned by Architecture+Design Scotland, September, 2010, retrieved from www.scribd.com/doc/41008414/Open-Source-Place-making (accessed 25 February 2011).

Z. Bauman, *Liquid Modernity*, Oxford: Blackwell Publishers, 2000.

Z. Bauman, *Liquid Modernity*, ANSE Conference, 2004, retrieved from http://anse.eu/html/history/2004%20Leiden/bauman%20englisch.pdf (accessed 14 June 2011).

Z. Bauman, *Liquid Times: Living in an Age of Uncertainty*, Cambridge: Polity Press, 2007.

BBSR, *The Impact of Temporary Use of Land on Sustainable Urban Development*, German Federal Ministry of Transport, Building and Urban Affairs (BMVBS), 2008, retrieved from www.bbr.bund.de/nn_25904/BBSR/EN/RP/ExWoSt/Studies/TemporaryUse/02__Concept.html (accessed 14 June 2011).

P. Beaumont, 'A city's soul is swept aside by money', the *Observer*, 16 January 2011, p. 2.

R. Beauregard, 'Shrinking cities in the United States in historical perspective', in *The Future of Shrinking Cities: Problems, Patterns and Strategies of Urban Transformation in a Global Context*, University of Carolina, May 2009, Monograph 2009-01.

A. Beckett, 'In the gaps developers left, another world is being built', the *Guardian*, 21 August 2010, p. 30.

J. Beekmans, 'Guerrilla bicycle lanes', popupcity.net, 11 February 2009, retrieved from http://popupcity. net/2009/02/guerrilla-bicycle-lanes/ (accessed 14 June 2011).

J. Beekmans, 'Run Mokum, run!', popupcity.net, 9 September 2010, retrieved from http://popupcity.net/2010/09/run-mokum-run/ (accessed 10 January 2011).

J. Beekmans, 'A trashy hotel', popupcity.net, 25 January 2011, retrieved from http://popupcity.net/2011/01/a-trashy-hotel/ (accessed 14 June 2011).

F. Benítez, *Gare L'Est, retrieved from* www.ciutatsocasionals.net/englishEXPOCOWEB/proyectos/21benitezgarde/index.htm (accessed 3 March 2011).

H. Bey, *T.A.Z.: The Temporary Autonomous Zone, Ontological Anarchy, Poetic Terrorism*, New York: Autonomedia, 2nd edition, 2003.

H. Bey, *The Temporary Autonomous Zone,* retrieved from: http://hermetic.com/bey/taz3.html#labelPirateUtopias (accessed 22 February 2011).

A. Bieber, 'Desires will break out of homes and put an end to the domination of boredom and the administration of misery', in R. Klanten and M. Hübner (eds), *Urban Interventions: Personal Projects in Public Spaces*, Berlin: Gestalten, 2010.

N. Blumner, *Planning for the Unplanned: Tools and Techniques for Interim Use in Germany and the United States.* Occasional Papers, Berlin: Deutshes Institut für Urbanistik, 2006, retrieved from www.difu.de/dokument/planning-for-the-unplanned-tools-and-techniques-for-interim.html (accessed 14 June 2011).

C. Bogman, 'Pop-up', retrieved from www.carmelabogman.nl/?module=Basis%20Hoofdmenu&actie=&subactie=39 (accessed 2 March 2011).

R. Booth, 'Artists' creative use of vacant shops brings life to desolate high streets', the *Guardian*, 18 February 2009, retrieved from www.guardian.co.uk/artanddesign/2009/feb/18/slack-space-vacant-shops (accessed 26 October 2010).

N. Bradford, 'Creative cities structured policy dialogue backgrounder', *Background paper F46, Family Network*, Canadian Policy Research Networks, Ottawa, 2004.

S. Breuer, *Harbouring Creative Industries: Creative Milieus as a Catalyst for Harbour Regeneration*, Tilburg University, MA Thesis European Urban Cultures, 2006.

British Property Federation / IPD, *BPF IPD Annual Lease Review 2010*, London: BPF/IPD, August 2010, retrieved from www.bpf.org.uk/en/files/bpf_documents/BPF_Annual_Lease_Review_2010_13082010.pdf (accessed 6 April 2011).

E. Brodie, E. Cowling and N. Nissen, *Understanding Participation: A Literature Review*, London: Involve, December 2009, retrieved from http://pathwaysthroughparticipation.org.uk/wp-content/uploads/2009/09/Pathways-literature-review-final-version.pdf (accessed 14 June 2011).

R. Brooks, 'Young people and political participation: an analysis of European Union policies', *Sociological Research Online*, 2009, 14 (1), retrieved from www.socresonline.org.uk/14/1/7.html (accessed 21 January 2011).

B. Bulick, C. Coletta, C. Jackson, A. Taylor and S. Wolff, *Cultural Development in Creative Communities,* Americans for the Arts, Monograph, November 2003.

CABE, *Creating Successful Masterplans: A Guide for Clients*, London: CABE, April, 2008, retrieved from www.cabe.org.uk/publications/creating-successful-masterplans (accessed 11 November 2010).

CABE Space, *Public Space Lessons: Land in Limbo: Making the Best Use of Vacant Urban Spaces*, London: CABE Space, May 2008.

Cabinet Office, *Building the Big Society*, 2010, retrieved from www.cabinetoffice.gov.uk/media/407789/building-big-society.pdf (accessed 13 October 2010).

K. Campbell, *Massive Small: The Operating Programme for Smart Urbanism*, retrieved from http://smarturbanism.org.uk/ (accessed 12 March 2011).

Carnegie UK Trust, *The Shape of Civil Society to Come: Report from the Inquiry into the Future of Civil Society in the UK and Ireland*, London: Carnegie UK Trust, retrieved from www.carnegieuktrust.org.uk/files/main/Shape%20of%20civil%20society%20to%20come_2.pdf (accessed 13 January 2011).

Chartered Management Institute, *Management Futures: The World in 2018*, London, March 2008, retrieved from www.managers.org.uk/print/research-analysis/research/current-research/management-futures-world-2018-march-2008 (accessed 11 February 2011).

J.L. Chase, M. Crawford and J. Kaliski (eds), *Everyday Urbanism*, New York: The Monacelli Press, 2nd edition, 2008.

City of Amsterdam, Bureau Broedplaatsen, *Building the Basis for a Creative Amsterdam Metropolitan Area, Art Factories Programme 2008–2012*, Amsterdam, October 2008, retrieved from http://bureaubroedplaatsen.amsterdam.nl/images/Art_Factories_Programme_Engels.pdf (accessed 8 April 2011).

K. Cochrane, 'Overnight success', the *Guardian G2*, 12 October 2010, pp. 6–9.

Communities and Local Government, *Strong and Prosperous Communities: The Local Government White Paper* (Cm6939), London: HMSO, 2006.

234

Communities and Local Government, *Communities in Control: The Local Government White Paper* (Cm7427), London: HMSO, 2008.

Communities and Local Government, *Looking After Our Town Centres,* DCMS, April, London: HMSO, 2009.

The Community Design Collaborative, 'Designing for temporary use', Infill Philadelphia, 2 November 2009, retrieved from http://blog.cdesignc.org/designing-for-temporary-use/ (accessed 14 June 2011).

Conservative Party, *Open Source Planning*, Policy Green Paper No.14, retrieved from www.conservatives.com/~/media/Files/Green%20Papers/planning-green-paper.ashx (accessed 2 March 2011).

A. Correy, 'Ephemeral landscapes: a case for temporary landscape design in a changing society', talk given on 28 May 1978 at the Utopian Technology Fair, University of Sydney, retrieved from www.aila.org.au/profiles/correy/pdf/ephemeral.pdf (accessed 6 October 2010).

Cousins Business Law, *Empty Property Business Rates Relief Cut from April 2011*, 2 February 2011, retrieved from www.business-lawfirm.co.uk/Blog/2011/02/Empty-Property-Business-Rates-Relief-Cut-from-April-2011/ (accessed 3 February 2011).

Coventry University, 'ICE tenant Theatre Absolute open their doors for the Shop Front Theatre', Institute of Applied Entrepreneurship, retrieved from www.coventry.ac.uk/researchnet/ice/News/Pages/NewsDetail.aspx?ItemQuery1=20 (accessed 14 June 2011).

M. Crawford, 'Blurring the boundaries: public space and private life', in J.L. Chase, M. Crawford and J. Kaliski (eds) *Everyday Urbanism,* New York: The Monacelli Press, 2nd edition, 2008.

M. Crawford, 'The current state of everyday urbanism', in J.L. Chase, M. Crawford and J. Kaliski (eds), *Everyday Urbanism,* New York: The Monacelli Press, 2nd edition, 2008.

D. Cruickshank, *Night Waves: Free Thinking Festival*, BBC Radio 3, 9.15 pm, 4 January 2010.

L. Davies, 'Farmers bring rural reality to Champs Elysées', the *Guardian*, 24 May 2010, p. 15, retrieved from www.guardian.co.uk/world/2010/may/23/french-farmers-champs-elysees (accessed 16 June 2011).

M. Davies, 'Fortress Los Angeles: the militarization of urban space', in M. Sorkin (ed.), *Variations on a Theme Park*, New York: Hill and Wang, 1992.

J. Davis, 'Interim use: a designation or towards a way of life?', in O. Wainwright (ed.), *Legacy Plus: Interim Uses and East London's Olympic Legacy*, London: The Architecture Foundation, 2010.

DCLG, *Review of the Use Classes Order and Part 4 of the GPDO (Temporary Uses)*, DCLG, September 2001.

DCMS, *Creative Industries Mapping Document*, UK Department of Culture, Media and Sport, 1998, revised 2001.

J. de Boer, 'Flying Grass Carpet: a landscaping fairytale', popupcity.net, 16 December 2008, retrieved from http://popupcity.net/2008/12/flying-grass-carpet-a-landscaping-fairytale/ (accessed 1 March 2011).

J. de Boer, 'Built overnight: Gecekondu in Sausalito Almere', popupcity.net, 22 June 2009, retrieved from http://popupcity.net/2009/06/built-overnight-gecekondu-in-sausalito-almere/ (accessed 1 March 2011).

J. de Boer, 'Temporary bar made from IKEA storage boxes', popupcity.net, 3 March 2010, retrieved from http://popupcity.net/2010/03/temporary-bar-made-from-ikea-storage-boxes/ (accessed 1 March 2011).

J. de Boer, 'The pop-up lunch bag', popupcity.net, 16 August 2010, retrieved from http://popupcity.net/2010/08/the-pop-up-lunch-bag/ (accessed 1 March 2011).

J. de Boer, 'Street Dinner: a secret pop-up restaurant', popupcity.net, 10 December 2010, retrieved from http://popupcity.net/2010/12/street-dinner-a-secret-pop-up-restaurant/ (accessed 1 March 2011).

J. de Boer, 'Trend 6: everything is a coffee bar', popupcity.net, 5 January 2011, retrieved from http://popupcity.net/2011/01/trend-6-everything-is-a-coffee-bar/ (accessed 1 March 2011).

J. de Boer, 'Trend 4: pop-up everywhere', popupcity.net, 6 January 2011, retrieved from http://popupcity.net/2011/01/trend-4-pop-up-everywhere/ (accessed 1 March 2011).

M. de Certeau, *The Practice of Everyday Life*, Berkeley: University of California Press, 1984.

I. de Sola-Morales, 'Terrain vagues', in *Quardens 212 Tierra-Agua*, Barcelona: Collegio de Arquitecos de Catalunya, pp. 34–44.

M. Dixon, 'The flexible worker: the unstoppable trend of working anywhere', retrieved from www.flexibility.co.uk/flexwork/general/mark-dixon-regus.htm (accessed 11 February 2011).

R. Dixon, 'Quick on the draw', the *Guardian,* 29 January 2011, p. 7.

M. Donnelly, 'Easing planning rules', *Planning*, 11 March 2011, p. 24.

G. Doron, *Transgressive Architecture: Testing the Boundaries of Inclusiveness*, Paper 00177, The Bartlett School of Architecture, University College, London, retrieved from www.openspace.eca.ac.uk/conference/proceedings/PDF/Doron.pdf (accessed 18 October 2010).

B. Douglas and D. Morrow, *Competing for Talent: Implications for Social and Cultural Policy in Canadian City Regions*, SRA, Department of Canadian Heritage, Ottawa, 2003.

235

A. Dunn, J. Foot, J. Gaventa and T. Zipfel, *Champions of Participation: Engaging Citizens in Local Governance*, International learning Event Report, 2007, retrieved from www2.ids.ac.uk/logolink/resources/downloads/Championspercent20Report.pdf (accessed 15 October 2010).

T. Dwelly, A. Lake and L. Thompson, *Workhubs: Smart Workspaces for the Low Carbon Economy*, Workhubs Network, June 2010, retrieved from www.ruralsussex.org.uk/assets/assets/HBBWorkhubsfinalreport2010%20part1.pdf (accessed 14 June 2011).

East of England Development Agency (EEDA), *Empty Shops and Premises: Researching the Baseline*, EEDA, March 2010, retrieved from www.eeda.org.uk/files/meanwhile_Space_EEDA_Report_Final_vfinal_external.pdf (accessed 26 October 2010).

English Heritage, *The Heritage Dividend: Measuring the Results of English Heritage Regeneration*, London: English Heritage, 1999.

Enterprise Nation, *Home Business Report 2009*, Enterprise Nation with support from BT, November 2009, retrieved from www.btplc.com/Thegroup/BTUKandWorldwide/BTRegions/England/Factsandfigures/EnterpriseNation-HomeBusinessReport2009-Nov09.pdf (accessed 11 February 2011).

European Commission, *State of European Cities Report*, Study contracted by the European Commission, 2007.

E. Evans and J. Saxton, *The 21st Century Volunteer: A Report on the Changing Face of Volunteering in the 21st Century*, London: nfpSynergy, 2005.

L. Feireiss, 'Livin' in the city: the urban space as creative challenge', in R. Klanten and M. Hübner (eds), *Urban Interventions: Personal Projects in Public Spaces*, Berlin: Gestalten, 2010.

C. Feiss, 'Social enterprise: the fledgling fourth sector', the *Financial Times*, 15 June 2009, retrieved from www.ft.com/cms/s/0/6e8285f2-5944-11de-80b3-00144feabdc0.html#axzz1FG9nS8yZ (accessed 28 February 2011).

R. Florida, *The Rise of the Creative Class: And How It's Transforming Work, Leisure, Community and Everyday Life*, New York: Basic Books, 2002.

K. Franck and Q. Stevens (eds), *Loose Space*, London: Routledge, 2007.

A. Freeman, 'London's creative workforce (2009 update)', Working Paper 40, GLA Economics, February 2010, retrieved from http://legacy.london.gov.uk/mayor/economic_unit/docs/wp40.pdf (accessed 6 April 2011).

J. Gallagher, *Reimagining Detroit: Opportunities for Redefining an American City*, Detroit, MI: Wayne State University Press, 2010.

J. Garrett, 'Cameron backs *Property Week*'s Site Life campaign', *Property Week*, 11 March 2011, retrieved from www.propertyweek.com/news/cameron-backs-property-weeks-site-life-campaign/5014763.article (accessed 21 April 2011).

J. Gerend, 'Temps welcome: how temporary uses can revitalize neighborhoods', *Planning: The Magazine of the American Planning Association*, December 2007, 73 (11), pp. 24–7.

J&L Gibbons LLP, *muf* architecture/art, *Making Space in Dalston*, prepared for London Borough of Hackney and Design for London/LDA, July 2009.

C. Giotis, 'Charity Bank announces record loans', *Social Enterprise*, 12 May 2010, retrieved from www.socialenterpriselive.com/section/news/money/20100512/charity-bank-announces-record-loans (accessed 11 January 2011).

Goethe-Institut, 'Urban laboratory: temporary architecture', retrieved from www.goethe.de/kue/arc/dos/dos/sls/sdz/en3802817.htm (accessed 11 March 2011).

C. Gomez Moya, '*Post-It City: Occasional City*', review, 2009, retrieved from www.latinart.com/exview.cfm?id=320 (accessed 11 November 2010).

S. Hall, 'The centrality of culture: notes on the cultural revolutions of our time', in K. Thompson (ed.), *Media and Cultural Regulation*, London: Sage, 1997.

R. Halliburton, 'Pop-up goes extreme', *Time Out*, 10–16 February 2011, pp. 26–7.

H. Hanra, 'Art's great squatting revolution', *The Times*, 16 January 2010, retrieved from http://entertainment.timesonline.co.uk/tol/arts_and_entertainment/visual_arts/article6988391.ece (accessed 24 January 2011).

N. Harrison, 'Vacant shops leading to North–South divide', *Retail Week*, 9 September 2010, retrieved from www.retail-week.com/property/vacant-shops-leading-to-north-south-divide/5017005.article (accessed 26 October 2010).

R. Hattan, 'Competition: new land of opportunity', *Property Week*, 2 July 2010, retrieved from www.propertyweek.com/comment/competition-new-land-of-opportunity/5002071.article (accessed 16 October 10).

W.L. Hawke, 'Case study research exploring interim use brownfield projects and their feasibility in the United States', Urban and Environmental Program, Occidental College, retrieved from http://departments.oxy.edu/uepi/uep/studentwork/09comps/Hawke%20uep%20comps.pdf (accessed 11 March 2011).

F. Haydn, 'A material that never comes to rest: concepts and potentials of temporary space', in F. Haydn and R. Temel (eds), *Temporary Urban Spaces: Concepts for the Use of City Space*, Basel: Birkhäuser, 2006.

F. Haydn and R. Temel (eds), *Temporary Urban Spaces: Concepts for the Use of City Spaces*, Basel: Birkhäuser, 2006.

236

H-L. Hentila and T. Lindborg, *Temporary Uses of Central Residual Spaces as Urban Development Catalysts*. Paper presented in ERSA Congress, Jyvaskyla, 27–30 August 2003, retrieved from www-sre.wu-wien.ac.at/ersa/ersa-confs/ersa03/cdrom/papers/242.pdf (accessed 28 September 2010).

J. Herron, 'Borderland/borderama/Detroit', in G. Wilkins (ed.), *Distributed Urbanism: Cities After Google Earth*, London: Routledge, 2010.

A. Hitoshi and M. Masahige, 'Megahouse', in G. Wilkins (ed.), *Distributed Urbanism: Cities After Google Earth*, London: Routledge, 2010.

HM Treasury, *Spending Review 2010*, 20 October 2010, retrieved from www.hm-treasury.gov.uk/spend_sr2010_easyread.htm (accessed 22 March 2011).

H. Hoby 'Peckham raises the roof', the *Observer*, 5 July 2009, retrieved from www.guardian.co.uk/artanddesign/2009/jul/05/art-goldsmiths (accessed 25 January 2011).

N. Hope and V. Ellis, *Can You Dig it? Meeting Community Demand for Allotments*, New Local Government Network, 2009, retrieved from www.nlgn.org.uk/public/wp-content/uploads/can-you-dig-it.pdf (accessed 6 October 2010).

G.J. Hospers and R. van Dalm, 'How to create a creative city? The viewpoints of Richard Florida and Jane Jacobs', *Foresight: The Journal of Future Studies, Strategic Thinking and Policy*, 2005, 7 (4), pp. 8–12.

J. Hou (ed.), *Insurgent Public Space: Guerrilla Urbanism and the Remaking of Contemporary Cities*, London: Routledge, 2010.

S. Ignatidou, 'Popping up along the East London Line: the new way to dine' 26 January 2011, retrieved from www.eastlondonlines.co.uk/2011/01/popping-up-along-the-east-london-line-the-new-way-to-dine/ (accessed 14 June 2011).

International Labour Organisation, *Global Employment Trends for Youth*, Geneva: ILO, August 2010, retrieved from www.ilo.org/wcmsp5/groups/public/---ed_emp/---emp_elm/---trends/documents/publication/wcms_143349.pdf (accessed 15 October 2010).

J. Jacobs, *The Death and Life of Great American Cities*, New York: Random House, 1961.

F. Jameson, *Postmodernism, or The Cultural Logic of Late Capitalism*, New York: Verso, 1999, retrieved from www.marxists.org/reference/subject/philosophy/works/us/jameson.htm (accessed 22 November 2010).

K. Joyce, R. Pabayo, J. Critchley and C. Bambra, *Flexible Working Conditions and Their Effects on Employee Health and Wellbeing*, Cochrane Database of Systematic Reviews 2010, Issue 2.

D. Kane, J. Clarke, S. Lesniewski, J. Wilton, B. Pratten and K. Wilding, *The UK Civil Society Almanac*, London: NCVO, 2009.

R. Kapuściński, *Another Day of Life*, London: Penguin Classics, 2001.

K. Kelly, 'The new socialism: global collectivist society is coming online', *Wired Magazine*, 17 June 2010, retrieved from www.wired.com/culture/culturereviews/magazine/17-06/nep_newsocialism?currentPage=all (accessed 24 November 2010).

M. Kennedy, 'Fourth plinth shortlist announced for London Olympics contenders', the *Guardian,* 19 July 2010, retrieved from www.guardian.co.uk/artanddesign/fourth-plinth (accessed 5 October 2010).

J. King, 'High rises on hold: what to do with empty sites?', *San Francisco Chronicle*, 6 July 2009, retrieved from www.sfgate.com/cgi-bin/article.cgi?f=/c/a/2009/07/06/MNAP189P39.DTL (accessed 21 April 2011).

J. King, 'Myriad ideas to fill void of empty lots', *San Francisco Chronicle,* 26 January 2010, retrieved from http://articles.sfgate.com/2010-01-26/news/17835710_1_public-art-green-development-empty-lots (accessed 11 March 2011).

B. Kirshenblatt-Gimblett, 'Performing the city: reflections on the urban vernacular', in J.L. Chase, M. Crawford and J. Kaliski (eds), *Everyday Urbanism,* New York: The Monacelli Press, 2nd edition, 2008.

J. Kitching and D. Smallbone, *Defining and Estimating the Size of the UK Freelance Workforce*, Project Report, UK, Professional Contractors Group, 2008.

R. Klanten and M. Hübner (eds), *Urban Interventions: Personal Projects in Public Spaces*, Berlin: Gestalten, 2010.

E. Knob and W. Grillitsch, 'Dolmusch X-press', in T. Schwarz and S. Rugare (eds), *Pop-Up City*, Urban Infill No.2, Cleveland Urban Design Collaborative, Kent State University, 2009.

R. Kohoutek and C. Kamleithner, 'Temporary uses, deregulation and urbanity', in F. Haydn and R. Temel (eds), *Temporary Urban Spaces: Concepts for the Use of City Space*, Basel: Birkhäuser, 2006.

E. Krasny, 'Spaces for action and for laughing too: on the public effect of participation in urban spaces', in F. Haydn and R. Temel (eds), *Temporary Urban Spaces: Concepts for the Use of City Space*, Basel: Birkhäuser, 2006.

C. Kuang, '145-foot inflatable dome to rise in nation's hot air capital, D.C.', retrieved from www.fastcompany.com/blog/cliff-kuang/design-innovation/145-foot-inflatable-dome-will-rise-dc (accessed 17 June 2011).

237

C. Kuang, 'MacroSea turns dumpster diving into family fun', 10 July 2009, retrieved from www.fastcompany.com/blog/cliff-kuang/design-innovation/dumpster-diving-becomes-fun-family-outing (accessed 16 June 2011).

N. Kulish, 'In East Germany, a decline as stark as a wall', the *New York Times*, 18 June 2009, retrieved from www.nytimes.com/2009/06/19/world/europe/19germany.html (accessed 2 December 2010).

M.A. LaFond, 'eXperimentcity', in J. Hou (ed.), *Insurgent Public Space: Guerrilla Urbanism and the Remaking of Contemporary Cities*, London: Routledge, 2010.

C. Landry, *The Art of City Making*. London: Earthscan, 2006.

B. Lange, 'Entrepreneurial temporary use: an incubator for the creative economy', in Urban Catalyst, *Urban Pioneers: Temporary Use and Urban Development in Berlin*, Berlin: Jovis, 2007.

C. Lang Ho, 'Hold this site', *Architect Magazine*, June 2010, retrieved from www.architectmagazine.com/development/hold-this-site.aspx (accessed 16 June 2011).

K. Larkin and Z. Wilcox, *What Would Maggie Do?* Centre for Cities, February 2011, retrieved from www.centreforcities.org/assets/files/2011%20Research/11-02-25%20Enterprise%20Zones.pdf (accessed 21 March 2011).

G. la Varra, 'POST-IT CITY: the other European public spaces', 2003, retrieved from http://subsol.c3.hu/subsol_2/contributors0/lavarratext.html (accessed 11 November 2010).

G. la Varra, 'Post-it city: the final space in the contemporary city', in *Post-It City: Occasional Urbanities*, 2003, retrieved from www.seacex.es/Spanish/Publicaciones/POST_IT_CITY_CIUDADES_OCASIONALES/Post-It City. Occasional Urbanities.pdf (accessed 11 November 2010).

Local Data Company, 17 September 2010, retrieved from www.localdatacompany.com/news-and-media/2010/9/17/hsbc-one-in-eight-town-centre-shops-empty-report-finds.html (accessed 26 October 2010).

LocusLab, *No Vacancy! Exploring Temporary Use of Empty Spaces in the Central Eastside Industrial District*, Portland State University, June 2009, retrieved from www.planning.org/awards/2010/pdf/novacancy.pdf (accessed 21 April 2011).

London and Partners, *London Creative Industries*, March 2011, retrieved from www.thinklondon.com/downloads/Think_London_reports/Think_London_reports/London_Creative_Industries_-_the_essential_next_step_for_your_business.pdf (accessed 6 April 2011).

K. Long, 'The Big Society begins in Dalston', the *Evening Standard*, 30 June 2010, p. 31.

K. Long, 'Shopping and shipping', the *Evening Standard*, 2 March 2011, retrieved from http://goliath.ecnext.com/coms2/gi_0199-14468686/SHOPPING-AND-SHIPPING-Boxpark-is-html (accessed 16 April 2011).

H. Lownsbrough and J. Deunderman, *Equally Spaced?*, London: Demos, 2007.

D. Loy, 'Saving time: a Buddhist perspective on the end', in J. May and N. Thrift (eds), *Timespace: Geographies of Temporality*, London: Routledge, 2001.

A. Lukowski, 'Pop in on some pop-up theatre', *Time Out*, 23–9 September 2010, p. 18.

T. Macalister, 'The dire state of real estate: credit crunch marks end of boom', the *Guardian*, 3 January 2008, retrieved from www.guardian.co.uk/business/2008/jan/03/creditcrunch.realestate (accessed 11 October 2010).

R. McCrum, 'How E.F. Schumacher, author of the global bestseller *Small is Beautiful*, came back into fashion', the *Observer*, The New Review, 27 March 2011, pp. 8–11.

P. McGuigan, 'GINGERLINE', retrieved from www.spectator.co.uk/scoff/6657798/gingerline.thtml (accessed 16 June 2011).

P. MacInnes, 'Forget *Avatar*, the real 3D revolution is coming to your front room', the *Observer*, 4 April 2010, retrieved from www.guardian.co.uk/technology/2010/apr/04/3d-printing-design (accessed 25 October 2010).

L. MacRitchie, 'The sincerity of events', in N. Childs and J. Walwin (eds), *A Split Second of Paradise: Live Art, Installation and Performance*, London: Rivers Oram Press, 1998.

A. McSpadden, 'Instant cities: a memo to our times', retrieved from www.ciutatsocasionals.net/englishEXPO-COWEB/archivocastellano/centrodocumentacion/textosdocumentacion/DAMn%B016_p90_Post-It_Cities.pdf (accessed 3 March 2011).

J. Malloy, 'What is left of planning?! Residual planning', in T. Schwarz and S. Rugare (eds), *Pop-Up City*, Urban Infill No.2, Cleveland Urban Design Collaborative, Kent State University, 2009.

S. Manzoor, 'Pop-up culture', the *Guardian*, 5 January 2011, p. 3.

S. Marshall, *Cities, Design and Evolution*, Oxford: Routledge, 2008.

B. Masi, 'Defining urban-agrarian space' in S. Rugare and T. Schwarz, (eds) *Cities Growing Smaller*, Urban Infill No.1, Cleveland Urban Design Collaborative, Kent State University, 2008.

M. Mean and C. Tims, *People Make Places*, London: Demos/JRF, 2005.

238

The Meanwhile Project, *Meanwhile Use: Benefits to Stakeholders and the Future of Meanwhile Use*, The Meanwhile Project and SQW Consulting, April 2010, retrieved from www.meanwhile.org.uk/useful-info/manuals/Benefits_StakeholdersMeanwhile_Future.pdf (accessed 3 February 2011).

The Meanwhile Project, 'Meanwhile use: business case and learning points', SQW Consulting (for the Meanwhile Project), May 2010, retrieved from www.meanwhile.org.uk/useful-info/misc/SQW%20-%20Meanwhile%20Use%20Report%20May%2010.pdf (accessed 28 January 2011).

Meanwhile Project, 'No time to waste …', May 2010, retrieved from www.meanwhile.org.uk/useful-info/misc/Meanwhile_Project_16pp_sml.pdf (accessed 11 March 2011).

B. Meinhold, '*Cool Water, Hot Island* winning design for Times Square makeover', *Inhabitat*, 25 May 2010, retrieved from http://inhabitat.com/cool-water-hot-island-winning-design-for-times-square-makeover/ (accessed 31 January 2011).

T. Meisel and W. Wieczorek, 'Travelling through the inner city: form follows fiction', June 2003, retrieved from www.republicart.net/disc/empire/meiselwieczorek01_en.htm (accessed 11 January 2011).

B. Merker, 'Taking place: Rebar's absurd tactics in generous urbanism', in J. Hou (ed.), *Insurgent Public Space: Guerrilla Urbanism and the Remaking of Contemporary Cities*, London: Routledge, 2010.

M. Miessen and K. Cuypers, *Spaces of Uncertainty*, Wuppertal: Müller und Busmann, 2002.

P. Misselwitz, P. Oswalt and K. Overmeyer, 'Urban development without urban planning: a planner's nightmare or the promised land?' in Urban Catalyst, *Urban Pioneers: Temporary Use and Urban Development in Berlin*, Berlin: Jovis, 2007.

J. Modder and J. Saris, *Creative Spaces in the Netherlands*, 41st IsoCaRP Congress, 2005, retrieved from www.isocarp.net/Data/case_studies/625.pdf (accessed 8 April 2011).

R. Moore, 'Let's put on the chow right here …', the *Observer,* The New Review, 20 June 2010, p. 35.

R. Moore, 'Meet Britain's most promising young architects', the *Observer,* The New Review, 9 January 2011, pp. 12–15.

A. Morton and R. Ehrman, *More Homes: Fewer Empty Buildings*, Policy Exchange, Research Note, March 2011, retrieved from www.policyexchange.org.uk/assets/More_Homes.pdf (accessed 30 March 2011).

M. Nathan, 'The wrong stuff: creative class theory, diversity and city performance', IPPR Centre for Cities, Discussion Paper No.1, 2005, retrieved from www.ippr.org/centreforcities (accessed 17 November 2010).

J. Nowak, *Creativity and Neighbourhood Development: Strategies for Community Investment*, The Reinvestment Fund, in collaboration with the Social Impact of the Arts project at the University of Pennsylvania, 2007, p. 2, retrieved from www.trfund.com/resource/downloads/creativity/creativity_neighborhood_dev.pdf (accessed 17 November 2010).

J. O'Connell, 'Filling the void: when construction stalls, D.C. encourages temporary uses', *Washington Business Journal*, 16 November 2009, retrieved from www.bizjournals.com/washington/stories/2009/11/16/story6.html (accessed 21 April 2011).

J. O'Connor, *The Cultural and Creative Industries: A Review of the Literature*, Creative Partnerships, London: Arts Council, November 2007.

P. Oehmke, 'Squatters take on the creative class: who has the right to shape the city?' *Spiegel Online*, 1 July 2010, retrieved from www.spiegel.de/international/germany/0,1518,670600,00.html (accessed 11 January 2011).

P. Oswalt, K. Overmeyer and P. Misselwitz, 'Patterns of the unplanned' in T. Schwarz and S. Rugare (eds), *Pop-Up City*, Urban Infill No.2, Cleveland Urban Design Collaborative, Kent State University, 2009.

K. Pallagst, 'Shrinking cities: planning challenges from an international perspective', in S. Rugare and T. Schwarz (eds), *Cities Growing Smaller,* Urban Infill No.1, Cleveland Urban Design Collaborative, Kent State University, 2008.

M. Pearce, *Saving Time: A Review of the Conservation Movement in Britain in the 20th Century*, reproduced from the Building Conservation Directory 2000, retrieved from www.buildingconservation.com/articles/time/time1.htm (accessed 7 June 2010).

J. Peck, 'Struggling with the creative class', *International Journal of Urban and Regional Planning Research*, December 2005, 29 (4), pp. 740–70.

A. Petti, 'Temporary Zones: alternative spaces or territories of socio-spatial control?', in *Post-It City: Occasional Urbanities* December 2005, p. 245, retrieved from www.seacex.es/Spanish/Publicaciones/POST_IT_CITY_CIUDADES_OCASIONALES/Post-It%20City.%20Occasional%20Urbanities.pdf (accessed 11 November 2010).

T. Phillips, 'Urbanism for the masses', the *Guardian Weekly*, 31 December 2010, p. 28.

Planning Advisory Service, *Local Development Orders*, Stage 1 Research Report on Stakeholder Views and Practice Issues, March 2009, retrieved from www.pas.gov.uk/pas/aio/106047 (accessed 27 October 2010).

M. Pogoreutz, 'Urban intelligence', in F. Haydn and R. Temel (eds), *Temporary Urban Spaces: Concepts for the Use of City Space*, Basel: Birkhäuser, 2006.

239

N. Popper, 'From eyesores to eye-catchers', *Los Angeles Times*, 16 December 2010, retrieved from http://articles. latimes.com/print/2010/dec/16/business/la-fi-stalled-construction-20101216 (accessed 30 March 2011).

Power Inquiry, *Power to the People: The Report of Power: An Independent Inquiry into Britain's Democracy*, York: Joseph Rowntree Foundation, 2006.

A. Pratt, 'Creative cities: the cultural industries and the creative class', *Geografiska B*, 2008, 90 (2), pp. 107–17.

A. Pratt, 'Urban regeneration: from the arts "feel good" factor to the cultural economy. A case study of Hoxton, London', *Urban Studies*, May 2009, 46 (5–6), pp. 1041–61.

Professional Contractors Group, *Fairness, Clarity, Recognition: Manifesto for Freelancing*, November 2009, retrieved from www.pcg.co.uk/cms/documents/POLICY_AND_CAMPAIGNS/PCG%20MANIFESTO%20FOR%20FREELANCING. pdf (accessed 8 October 2011).

Property Week, 'Brands catch on to "pop-up" craze', 5 February 2010, retrieved from www.propertyweek.com/news/brands-catch-on-to-'pop-up'-craze/3157678.article (accessed 11 March 2011).

Property Week, 'How the West was won over by temporary uses', 4 June 2010, retrieved from www.property-week.com/news/how-the-west-was-won-over-by-temporary-uses/3164222.article (accessed 14 June 2011).

Property Week, 'Empty property: protect and survive', 10 January 2011, retrieved from www.propertyweek.com/free-white-paper-empty-property-protect-and-survive/5011294.article (accessed 21 January 2011).

M. Provoost, 'The Wimby! method', in J.L. Chase, M. Crawford and J. Kaliski (eds), *Everyday Urbanism*, New York: The Monacelli Press, 2nd edition, 2008.

E. Randolph, 'The best seats in Times Square', the *New York Times*, 7 June 2009, retrieved from www.nytimes. com/2009/06/08/opinion/08mon4.html (accessed 20 January 2011).

E. Reynolds, 'Interwhile uses', article submitted for publication in *Journal of Urban Regeneration and Renewal*, 2011, 4, copy provided by the author.

J. Rigby, 'Top of the pop-ups', *Property Week*, 16 April 2010.

J. Rigby, 'How meanwhile can be worthwhile', *Property Week*, 7 May 2010.

J. Rojas, 'Latino urbanism in Los Angeles', in J. Hou (ed.), *Insurgent Public Space: Guerrilla Urbanism and the Remaking of Contemporary Cities*, London: Routledge, 2010.

M. Roth, 'SF's proposal to reduce blight will create a tenuous balance', SFStreetsBlog.org, 22 February 2010, retrieved from http://sf.streetsblog.org/2010/02/22/sfs-proposal-to-reduce-blight-will-create-a-tenuous-balance/ (accessed 17 June 2011).

S. Rugare and T. Schwarz (eds), *Cities Growing Smaller*, Urban Infill No.1, Cleveland Urban Design Collaborative, Kent State University, 2008.

S. Ruoppila, 'Eastern European cities in the making: temporary land use as a tool for cultural projects', *Journal for Northeast Issues*, 2004, 3, retrieved from www.kaupunkikettu.fi/temporary2004.html (accessed 22 November 2010).

M. Ryzik, 'Forget the trash bag, bring a towel', the *New York Times*, 19 July 2009, retrieved from www.nytimes. com/2009/07/20/arts/design/20pool.html?_r=1 (accessed 2 March 2011).

SallyB2, 'Art preview: rooftop sculpture park in Peckham', 30 June 2009, retrieved from http://londonist. com/2009/06/art_preview_rooftop_sculpture_park. php?gallery0Pic=2 (accessed 25 January 2011).

E.F. Schumacher, *Small is Beautiful: A Study of Economics as if People Mattered*, London: Blond and Briggs, 1973.

T. Schwarz, 'Ad hoc urbanism: adventures in temporary use' in T. Schwarz and S. Rugare (eds), *Pop-Up City*, Urban Infill No.2, Cleveland Urban Design Collaborative, Kent State University, 2009.

T. Schwarz and S. Rugare (eds), *Pop-Up City*, Urban Infill No.2, Cleveland Urban Design Collaborative, Kent State University, 2009.

P.B. Shelley, *Miscellaneous and Posthumous Poems of Percy Bysshe Shelley*, London: W. Benbow, 1826.

A. Shepard, 'Can city dwellers be more self-sufficient?', *The Times*, 28 June 2008, retrieved from www.timeson-line.co.uk/tol/news/environment/article4225138.ece (accessed 25 January 2011).

M. Shepherd, 'Great Portland makes its development Marcol', *Property Week*, 12 February 2010, retrieved from www.propertyweek.com/great-portland-makes-its-development-marcol/3158109.article

L. Siegle, 'Dan Thompson's innovation: the Empty Shop Network', the *Observer*, 23 May 2010, retrieved from www.guardian.co.uk/environment/2010/may/23/lucy-siegle-the-innovator-dan-thompson-esn (accessed 27 October 2010).

A. Sissons and C. Brown, *Do Enterprise Zones Work?* Ideopolis Policy Paper, The Work Foundation, February 2011, retrieved from www.theworkfoundation. com/assets/docs/publications/283_Enterprise%20 Zones_24%20Feb_FINAL.PDF (accessed 21 March 2011).

240

Site Life Debate, 2010, retrieved from www.mean-while.org.uk/useful-info/misc/PW_roundtable_Meanwhile_06aaproved.pdf (accessed 28 January 2011).

Skillset, 'Strategic skills assessment for the creative media industries, London, June, 2010', retrieved from www.skillset.org/uploads/pdf/asset_15384.pdf?1 (accessed 6 April 2011).

Social Investment Task Force, *Social Investment Ten Years On*, Final Report of the Social Investment Task Force, April 2010, retrieved from www.socialinvestmenttask-force.org/downloads/SITF_10_year_review.pdf (accessed 17 June 2011).

Space Hijackers, 'ANARCHITECTURE', retrieved from http://subsol.c3.hu/subsol_2/contributors0/spacehijack-erstext.html (accessed 11 November 2010).

M. Speaks, 'Rotterdam 1979–2007: from ideology to market communism and beyond', in G. Wilkins (ed.), *Distributed Urbanism: Cities After Google Earth*, London: Routledge, 2010.

K. Spicer, 'Is this London's most fashionable restaurant?', *The Sunday Times,* 16 November 2008, retrieved from www.timesonline.co.uk/tol/life_and_style/food_and_drink/article5139964.ece (accessed 16 June 2011).

A. Spiegl, and C. Teckert, 'Tom Waits 4'33"', in F. Haydn and R. Temel (eds), *Temporary Urban Spaces: Concepts for the Use of City Space*, Basel: Birkhäuser, 2006.

SPUR, *Secrets of San Francisco: Our City's Privately Owned Public Open Spaces*, San Francisco Planning and Urban Research Association, 19 November 2008, retrieved from www.spur.org/publications/library/report/secretsofsanfrancisco_010109 (accessed 16 June 2011).

STEALTH.unlimited (A. Dzokic and M. Neelen) and I. de Kiev-ith, 'Constituting the interim' in *Vacant NL: Where Archi-tecture Meets Ideas*, retrieved from http://en.nai.nl/.../Booklet_Vacant_NL,_where_architecture_meets_ideas (accessed 8 October 2011).

J. Stein, 'Ghost riders', 15 June 2008, retrieved from http://nymag.com/news/features/47819/ (accessed 23 February 2011).

M. Stern and S. Seifert, *Cultivating 'Natural' Cultural Dis-tricts*, Creativity and Change: A collaboration between the Social Impact of the Arts Project and the Reinvest-ment Fund funded by the Rockefeller Foundation, 2007, retrieved from http://trfund.com/resource/downloads/creativity/NaturalCulturalDistricts.pdf (accessed 17 November 2010).

R. Temel, 'The temporary in the city', in F. Haydn and R. Temel (eds), *Temporary Urban Spaces: Concepts for the Use of City Space*, Basel: Birkhäuser, 2006.

L. Tennyson, 'Will urban beaches become the norm?', retrieved from www.rudi.net/node/16422 (accessed 25 January 2011).

J.W. Thomas, *Infill Philadelphia: Boldness Redefines 'Com-munity Center'*, PlanPhilly, 4 November 2009, retrieved from http://planphilly.com/boldness-can-redefine-commu-nity-center-infill-philadelphias-design-charrette (accessed 17 June 2011).

A. Thorpe, 'Pop-up hotels set to provide cheap temporary rooms', the *Observer*, 22 November 2009, retrieved from www.guardian.co.uk/travel/2009/nov/22/pop-up-hotels-travel (accessed 14 June 2011).

V. Thorpe, 'Blink and miss the show', the *Guardian Weekly*, 9 July 2010, p. 34.

Tokyo Metropolitan University Research Project, *21st Cen-tury COE Program*, retrieved from www.tmu-arch.sakura.ne.jp/pdf/35_recity_e.pdf (accessed 29 March 2011).

M. Townsend, 'Return of underground rave culture is fuelled by the recession and Facebook', the *Observer,* 7 November 2010, p. 36.

Trades Union Congress, 'Youth unemployment increasing in two thirds of local authorities across UK', London: TUC, 11 August 2010, retrieved from www.tuc.org.uk/social/tuc-18322-f0.cfm (accessed 15 October 2010).

J. Twentyman, 'Productivity on the move' in *Flexible Work-ing Supplement*, Lyonsdown Media Group, 2010, retrieved from www.esf6cia.eu/usuaris/noticies/arxius/30_1_flex-ible_lowres1.pdf (accessed 15 June 2011).

C. Twickel, 'Activists bring flashmob style tactics to war on gentrification'*,* Spiegel Online, 9 July 2010, retrieved from www.spiegel.de/international/zeit-geist/0,1518,716179,00.html (accessed 17 June 2011).

UN Habitat, *Urban Trends Fact Sheet*, 5 October 2009, retrieved from www.unhabitat.org/documents/GRHS09/FS1.pdf (accessed 16 March 2011).

Urban Catalyst, *Strategies for Temporary Uses: Potential for Development of Urban Residual Areas in European Metropolises*, September 2003, retrieved from http://template.com/think-pool/attach/download/1_UC_finalR_synthesis007b.pdf?object_id=4272&attachment_id=4276 (accessed 22 November 2010).

Urban Catalyst, *Urban Pioneers: Temporary Use and Urban Development in Berlin*, Berlin: Jovis, 2007.

Urban Unlimited, *The Shadow City: Freezones in Brussels and Rotterdam*, Urban Unlimited Rotterdam with o2-con-sult Antwerp, MUST Amsterdam, ds+V /OBR Rotterdam and VUB Brussels, 2004, retrieved from www.urbanun-limited.nl/uu/downloads.nsf/10/255417E9AE33AE26C1256F0B003710D8/$file/Shadowcity.pdf (accessed 23 November 2010).

241

J. Vasagar, 'Clearing 2010: universities offer lifeline to top students', the *Guardian*, 19 August 2010, retrieved from www.guardian.co.uk/education/2010/aug/18/clearing-2010-universities-offer-lifeline (accessed 13 October 2010).

E. Villagomez, 'Claiming residual spaces in the heterogeneous city', in J. Hou (ed.), *Insurgent Public Space: Guerrilla Urbanism and the Remaking of Contemporary Cities*, London: Routledge, 2010.

O. Wainwright (ed.), *Legacy Plus: Interim Uses and East London's Olympic Legacy*, London: The Architecture Foundation, 2010.

P. Walker 'Largest postwar prefab estate to be demolished', the *Guardian*, 2 January 2011, retrieved from www.guardian.co.uk/society/2011/jan/02/postwar-prefab-houses-demolition-london (accessed 10 February 2011).

C. Ward, *The Hidden History of Housing*, Institute for Contemporary History, King's College, London, September, 2004, retrieved from www.historyandpolicy.org/papers/policy-paper-25.html#squatters (accessed 21 May 2010).

G. Wilkins (ed.), *Distributed Urbanism: Cities After Google Earth*, London: Routledge, 2010.

Z. Williams, 'The secret feast', the *Guardian*, 10 February 2009, retrieved from www.guardian.co.uk/lifeandstyle/2009/feb/10/underground-restaurants-london (accessed 11 January 2011).

Z. Williams, 'Outspoken', *Stylist Magazine*, Issue 52, 3 November 2010, p. 21, retrieved from www.stylist.co.uk (accessed 11 January 2011).

Useful websites

ABC No Rio, www.abcnorio.org/

Architecture Foundation, www.architecturefoundation.org.uk/

Arts Council, www.artscouncil.org.uk/

atelier d'architecture autogérée (aaa), www.urbantactics.org/

Building History, www.buildinghistory.org/

Cable Factory, www.kaapelitehdas.fi/en/factory/

Chicago Loop Alliance, www.chicagoloopalliance.com/

Cineroleum, www.cineroleum.co.uk/info/

Dialogue Collective, www.dialoguecollective.co.uk/

Electric Hotel, www.sadlerswells.com/show/Electric-Hotel/

Experiment City, http://experimentcity.net/en/

Flexibility, www.flexibility.co.uk/

Flying Grass Carpet, http://flyinggrasscarpet.org/

GreenThumb, http://greenthumbnyc.org/

London Festival of Architecture, www.lfa2010.org/

Meanwhile Project, www.meanwhile.org.uk/

Meanwhile Space, www.meanwhilespace.com/

Oubliette Arthouse, http://theoubliette.co.uk/

People's Supermarket, www.thepeoplessupermarket.org/

Permanent Breakfast, www.p-breakfast.net/

Planning Help, www.planninghelp.org.uk/

Pop-Up City, http://popupcity.net/

Raumlabor, www.raumlabor.net/

Rebar, www.rebargroup.org/portfolio/

Shopjacket, www.shopjacket.co.uk/

Site Life, http://network.propertyweek.com/group/sitelife/

Shoreditch Trust, www.shoreditchtrust.org.uk/

Skip Garden, www.kingscrosscentral.com/skip_garden/

Social Enterprise, www.socialenterpriselive.com/

Space Hijackers, www.spacehijackers.co.uk/

Spatial Agency, www.spatialagency.net/

Street Dinner, www.streetdinner.it/home.html/

STEALTH, www.stealth.ultd.net/stealth/

Sunday Adventure Club, www.sundayadventureclub.nl/

Templace, www.templace.com/

Theatre Absolute, www.theatreabsolute.co.uk/

Theatre Delicatessen, www.theatredelicatessen.co.uk/

Trendwatching, http://trendwatching.com/

Urban Tactics, www.urbantactics.org/home.html/

Village Underground, www.villageunderground.co.uk/

What Happens When, www.whathappenswhennyc.com/

Illustration credits

All images by the authors unless otherwise stated below. Every effort has been made to contact and acknowledge copyright owners, but the authors and publisher would be pleased to have any errors or omissions brought to their attention so that corrections may be published at a later printing. Page number(s) followed by credit.

2 © Guardian News and Media Ltd, 2010
13 © Google Earth 2011, Tele Atlas, Data SO, NOAA, US Navy NGA, GEBCO
16 Photograph: Clara Bacou
20 Photograph: Paul Storrie. Courtesy: Victoria Lee
28 Photograph: John Sturrock
30 Photograph: Colin Hampden-White. Courtesy: The Oubliette Arthouse
36 © Architecture Foundation. Photograph: David Grandorge
39 Photograph: John Sturrock
49 London Festival of Architecture. Courtesy: Peter Murray
54 Photograph: John Sturrock
56 Courtesy: Dinosaurs Unleashed Ltd and Land Securities
59 Courtesy: Camden Town Unlimited/Shaw Corporation
63 Courtesy: *Property Week*
75 Photograph: John Sturrock
76 Courtesy: LDA/Design for London
80 Courtesy: Camden Town Unlimited/Shaw Corporation
81 Photograph: Urban Realm. Courtesy: Shopjacket
83 Photograph: Emli Bendixen. Courtesy: GINGERLINE
85 Photograph: Nina Gryf. Courtesy: GINGERLINE
91 Courtesy: *muf* architecture/art
92 Photograph: Oliver Bishop-Young
93 (top) Courtesy: *muf* architecture/art
99 Photographs: Osamu Nishida. Courtesy: Shin Aiba
100 Photographs: Carmela Bogman and Rogier Martens
101 Photographs: Steph Mantis. Courtesy: Alexandra Pulver
102 Photograph: The Flying Grass Carpet, Studio ID Eddy and HUNK-design

105 Photographs: Antonia Wagner. Courtesy: Macro Sea
106 © Rebar Group, used with permission
111 (top left) London Festival of Architecture. Courtesy: Peter Murray
111 (bottom left) Photograph: Luke Hayes. London Festival of Architecture. Courtesy: Peter Murray
111 (right) Photograph: Agnese Sanvito. London Festival of Architecture. Courtesy: Peter Murray
113 Photograph: Katie Standke. © Rebar Group, used with permission
114 © Rebar Group, used with permission
115 © Rebar Group, used with permission
128–9 Photographs: John Sturrock
135 Colin Hampden-White. Courtesy: The Oubliette Arthouse
139 Courtesy: Steve McAdam, Fluid Architects
151 Photograph: Morley von Sternberg. Courtesy: Paloma Strelitz
153 Courtesy: Alex de Rijke, dRMM Architects
155 Photograph: John Sturrock
159 Courtesy: John Gallagher, *Reimagining Detroit: Opportunities for Redefining an American City*
178 Courtesy: *muf* architecture/art
180–1 Courtesy: LDA/Design for London
189 Courtesy: LDA/Design for London
190 Courtesy: Allies and Morrison/Argent
191–3 Courtesy: Witherford Watson Mann Architects
194–6 Courtesy: *muf* architecture/art
201 Courtesy: Steve McAdam, Fluid Architects
203–5 Courtesy: LDA/Design for London
206–8 Courtesy: *Property Week*
210 Courtesy: Studio Egret West

Index

Page numbers in italic denote an
illustration